D1605824

Keeping left?
Ceres and the French Socialist Party

For Monique

DAVID HANLEY

Keeping left?

Ceres and the French Socialist Party

A contribution to the study of
fractionalism in political parties

MANCHESTER
UNIVERSITY PRESS

Published by MANCHESTER UNIVERSITY PRESS
Oxford Road, Manchester, M13 9PL, UK
and 51 Washington Street, Dover, NH 03820, USA

British Library cataloguing in publication data
Hanley, David
  Keeping left? : Ceres and the French Socialist
  Party : a contribution to the study of fractionalism
  in political parties.
  1. Ceres—History   2. Parti socialiste (France)—History
  I. Title
  324.244'074   JN3007.86

Library of Congress cataloging in publication data
applied for
ISBN 0-7190-1764-5 cased

Typeset by Pen to Print, Colne

Printed in Great Britain
by The Alden Press, Oxford

CONTENTS

FIGURES AND TABLES

LIST OF FIGURES

LIST OF TABLES

ACKNOWLEDGEMENTS

A great many people have helped with the writing of this book. First I must thank, in strict alphabetical order, those French people who were kind enough to spend hours answering my questions. I have put party activists, commentators and academic specialists together in the confidence that they will know which hat they were wearing when we spoke; F. Autain, R. Barailla, A. Bartoli, A. Bergounioux, F. Borella, F. Borie, J.-M. Boucheron, P. Braud, P. Buffotot, J.-B. Castilla, J.-P. Chagnollaud, M. Charzat, J.-P. Chevènement, L. Chopier, M. Coffineau, M. Debout, J. and J. Durupt, R. Fajardie, J.-C. Fayard, P. Faye, G. Fisson, J.-C. Grandbastien, D. Groscolas, Y. Guillou, J. Guyard, J.-J. Guyot, P. Hardouin, E. Hervé, P. Heurtin, J.-C. Hourcade, J. Ion, G. Jacot, D. Lecourriard, G. Martinet, R. Massard, D. Mathieu, A. Melliet, J. Meyer, J.-P. Michel, G. Mingotaud, J. Morel, D. Motchane, J. Natiez, M. Navas, J.-F. Neel, P. Noë, G. Parentin, B. Parmentier, J.-L. Parodi, C. Payen, P. Perrineau, T. Pfister, C. Pierret, M. Plomb, J. Puech, B. Py, A. Queval, W. Roux-Marchand, G. Sarre, M. Souvignet, G. Toutain, A. Traca, B. Vennin, J. Vincent, P. Warnier, M. Wolf, C. Ysmal.

I owe a particular debt to our many friends in France who offered hospitality and encouragement, in particular to Hugues and Marie-Ange Portelli. Friends and colleagues in Britain have also been generous with their help and I would like to thank Eric Dàrier, Vladimir Fisera and Tom Lyne. Sophie Bowlby and John Silk were helpful beyond the call of duty with the survey work, and it has been encouraging to work for so long with Pat Kerr and Neville Waites. Finally I am grateful to Ann Bedford, Sally Hayter and Lorraine Standing for their efforts at the keyboard.

This work could never have been undertaken without the generosity of the Nuffield Foundation, whose award of a Research Fellowship in 1980–81 enabled me to do much fieldwork. Reading University Research Board, Reading Graduate School of European and International Studies and the British Academy have helped with travel expenses. Needless to say none of the above bears any responsibility for what follows.

David Hanley

INTRODUCTION

Given up for dead in 1969 but twelve years later the winner of the presidency and the biggest parliamentary majority in French republican history, the Parti socialiste (PS) is an alluring subject for historian and political scientist. Such indeed is the plethora of work by partisans and academics alike that it seems hard to justify another work. But the PS is in one way a special party. Unlike most of its colleagues in the Socialist International (the PSI is a notable exception) it operates an open, institutionalised system of fractionalism. Les tendances, as the subunits are known, have been vigorous in the new PS since its inception and hardly surprisingly, for in truth they have usually been present ever since the modern socialist party was set up in 1905. They have coexisted in relationships ranging from intelligent and productive competition to civil war. Little serious attention has been paid to this phenomenon in our view. The literature certainly refers to the fractions. But they are either taken for granted, in the case of outside observers or, in the case of partisan approaches, the aim is usually to promote one fraction at the expense of others.

All this takes place at a very ideological level and there is thus little attempt to assess the real nature and functioning of subparty groups. Yet surely these have much to do with the party's success. When it began its rise as a potential party of government, it was widely seen as a focus of debate, a forcing-ground for forward-looking ideas and policies which were bold but somehow plausible. It also appeared as a breeding ground for teams of young, articulate and technically competent leaders. Thirdly, the PS exerted a wide social appeal; if its activist élites were increasingly educated white-collars, as is usually the case nowadays in such parties, then its discourse clearly appealed, judging by its electoral performances, to a much wider public in which manual workers, farmers, white-collars of all grades, businessmen and professionals could fuse into what the party called a class-front. Now all these aspects of the party's appeal are arguably mediated through its system of fractions; these help give it the elasticity necessary to achieve so wide an appeal. For that reason alone the fractional phenomenon would repay closer study.

But there is another aspect also. Among the fractions the most self-assertive and confident was always Ceres (Centre d'études, de recherches et d'éducation socialiste). It understood why subparty groups were important, how they could be used, what gains they could bring. As a rule it was frank about this. At all key points in the party's development, to 1981 and beyond, Ceres had a key role. It was a constant catalyst or *primus movens*. At its peak Ceres had an aura of youth and daring, but also of being very much in tune with the spirit of its era; this was of course an image which it sought. If other groups were forced to organise, it was because Ceres had done so. The history of Ceres is thus that of a fraction; but the history of PS fractions is very much that of Ceres. Hence our account will constantly juxtapose Ceres and its rivals.

Ceres is of course a left fraction and proud of it. Every socialist party has such a group, usually much less organised than Ceres. These groups are little known. Yet when a social-democratic party with moderate leaders and an impeccably reformist programme takes several million votes in an election somewhere in the developed world, how many of those voters are voting positively for that programme and how many reluctantly, accepting it as a *pis-aller*, while desiring much more fundamental change in the direction of socialism? Possibly not as many as the eight million which Tony Benn claimed to discern after Labour's catastrophe in 1983; but we may safely conclude that the numbers of such people do not run into millions. Yet the groups which articulate, however incoherently, their desires, that is the lefts in socialist parties, have received scant mention on the whole.

This study is a small attempt to rectify the omission, and it has been encouraged by the fact that as left fractions go, Ceres is undoubtedly one of the more successful. Not that it has been totally successful, for as we shall see, the tasks which await socialist lefts are probably the most difficult ones in politics. Ceres has done better than many such groups and may yet do even better; and if on investigation some of its facets have proved less appealing than they did from a distance, this still does not diminish its worth as an object of study.

After first considering generally the problem of sub-party groups, we deal with this phenomenon in the context of reformist socialist parties, isolating the specificity of left fractions. We shall then (Chapter 2) concentrate on the French PS, looking at it historically and analytically from the standpoint of fractionalism. Having thus set the context for Ceres, we then examine its ideology and structures (Chapters 3 and 4). An important part of this latter is Ceres' subnational operations (Chapter 5). We then appraise the fraction's performance in government (Chapter 6), before passing on to our conclusion which attempts to generalise from Ceres experience and set it very tentatively into a comparative framework. Although we have had to discuss ideology – more than we should have liked – we have been constantly concerned to relate it to the key factor of organisation. For in so far as Ceres has succeeded it has been through an alliance of the two. If this seems at times to have led to an obsession with l'appareil at the expense of global theory, then we can only plead for forgiveness, citing in our defence the massively ideological slant of most existing literature. If there is one conclusion that has come repeatedly to our minds while working on this project it is that however sophisticated the ideological product it still has to be sold to the consumer. And for the time being the only way to achieve that is organisation and hard work.

CHAPTER 1

Party and fraction

*If the statute of a party says 'factions are prohibited', the provision will
remain a flatus voci – words with no consequence.*   G . Sartori

1.1   SUBPARTY GROUPS – GENERAL CONSIDERATIONS

'A part is an aggregate of individuals forming constellations of
rival groups.'[1] Thus speaks one of the most lucid and original
analysts of subparty groups in recent times. Any party is likely to
contain a host of such groups, large or small, formal or informal,
one-dimensional or multi-dimensional. This study deals only with
groups of a certain size or at least a certain salience, and having a
clear identity and distinct objectives. We might in an attempt to
define such groups begin with Beller and Belloni's definition of a
faction, namely 'any relatively organised group that exists within
the context of some other group and which (as a *political faction*)
competes with other rivals for power advantages within the larger
group of which it is part'.[2]

Political science knows such groups as factions, and so they are
invariably described by party rivals (a compliment returned with
interest). Yet as Sartori shows, this term has pejorative connotations.
Originally it referred to the gentlemen's cliques which preceded
modern parties as they emerged during the last century. The word has
a clear condemnatory ring; factionalists are people who put their own
selfish interest before that of the whole to which they belong.
Ultimately they would prefer to split the party rather than renounce
the pursuit of these private goals. Thus while party leaders and rivals,
and even academic observers might be quite happy to call the
subgroups factions – and while in many cases the word would be

justified in exactly the sense used above – this is not always true. It would be appropriate, then, to find a less loaded term.

As this is a work mainly about a French party, we might examine a French concept sometimes used to describe our phenomenon, namely *tendance*. We had in fact thought of using its translation, tendency. But this involves problems. Since Richard Rose's article,[3] the word has come to designate less an organisation or subgroup than a set of political attitudes, to some extent divorced from those who may express them at any time. 'Tendency' thus refers to something almost disincarnate: we could say that there was a pro-hanging tendency in the British Conservative party or an anti-EEC one in Labour, which find expression through different people at different times. Tendency supporters are mortal, the tendency itself immortal. However, even if we disagreed with Rose's formulation, there remains the fact that in French *tendance* has, especially on the left where it is most frequently found, most of the pejorative associations of the English 'faction'. Thus the rules of the socialist party (PS) say specifically:[4] 'there is total freedom of discussion within the party but no organised tendency (*tendance*) will be tolerated'. Roland Cayrol has in his study of subparty groupings devised a scale of relative badness in which *tendance* comes below *courant*. It is just about the limit of the tolerable (so far as the leadership is concerned), whereas the next step down, *la fraction*, goes beyond the bounds of acceptable dissent.[5] The discussion between leaders of PS groups in *Nouvelle Revue socialiste* bemoaned the fact that *courants* had now degenerated into *tendances* and were demobilising and weakening the party.[6]

The most neutral word in French is probably *courant*, itself copied from the Italian *correnti*. But there are snags here also. 'Currents' in English has ready associations with water or electricity, but not with politics. In French indeed one often feels that it is used as a kind of exorcism, to avoid saying *tendance* or worse. In the same way, superstitious people in past ages would avoid pronouncing the name of the devil. In both cases the reaction is symptomatic: the hope is that the problem, if named differently or more flatteringly, will not return to haunt the living. Alas, both the devil and political activists are tenacious, and we still need to find a name for the phenomenon at hand.

The French speak of *sensibilité* or *mouvance*. Thus the PS is said to contain a 'sensibilité autogestionnaire'. So it does, but this corresponds closely to what Rose means by a tendency, and as such can be found within a wide range of groups across the party. Both Ceres and its Rocardian rivals can be said to belong to this sensibility. Similarly, *mouvance* (literally 'wake') is too loose, for it covers a broad swathe of people many of whom will be outside the group one wishes to pin down. Not everyone in the wake of J.-P. Chevènement belongs to Ceres; and possibly not all Ceres is in the wake of Chevènement.

We are left then with Sartori's suggestion of fraction. Although for French analysts it has a pejorative ring (cf. Cayrol above), this is less evident in English; after all in mathematics, a fraction is merely part of a whole – a purely descriptive term. We shall henceforth use 'fraction' to describe significant subparty units with a recognisable identity and project. If at any time they are labelled in a less neutral way (e.g. called 'factional') then this will be intended as a deliberate value-judgement. To those who object that current usage is well on the way to consecrating 'faction' as the all-purpose term, we can only reply that this is a regrettable development. For the term clearly harbours overtones of conspiracy and illegitimacy when used to describe subparty groups. We hold such groups to be nothing of the kind, but simply a normal, healthy phenomenon and arguably essential to the survival of certain parties. Hence our attempt to rehabilitate the less loaded 'fraction'. We are aware of the weight of orthodoxy, but feel that it is time that this orthodoxy of prejudice was challenged. We thus sollicit readers' forbearance as we attempt to right what seems to us a terminological wrong.

Recent debate has isolated many of the general features of fraction-alism and we will summarise these findings before embarking on a discussion of the PS in particular.

To begin with a subjective point, a fraction must have a sense of distinct identity. Members must be aware that they belong not just to a party but to a lesser unit as well. Whether they identify more with this than with the party can be a very tricky point, and we shall return to it. We see two factors as necessary for this identity to cohere. Firstly it must be distinct enough to be recognised by rival fractions; much of the internal life and dynamics of fractions only makes sense when set against the behaviour of similar but competing groups. Secondly the party apparatus (local or national as the case may be) must be able to recognise the fraction as something to be reckoned with, if not actually a threat; this is logical, as the apparatus is usually that which the fraction is trying to influence or supplant. Once the apparatus recognises and joins battle with the fraction then its existence is really confirmed.

This is not to say that existence is synonymous with salience or even visibility. Fractionalists can know that their group exists and has a project, even if the fact is not advertised or even if it is concealed. So of course can their rivals. To take two distinct examples, everyone knows that there exists a Poperenite fraction in the PS, even though it has no official existence (i.e. it does not present motions or candidates' slates to congress), having years ago dissolved into the Mitterrand majority. But there is a broadsheet which gives a distinct Poperenite view of current affairs, and in some federations the machinery is known to be run by Poperenites, even though they appear in official literature as Mitterrandists. Why this should be so is not our immediate concern; we simply wish to show that existence is not necessarily conterminous with visibility. Similarly the Militant tendency (the English word being used for once in its French sense!) denies its existence with increasing difficulty in the face of evidence.[7] But anyone with experience of Labour party branches or general management committees can recognise with ease these 'supporters of the newspaper'.

Nor is size an absolute criterion. With quite few members a fraction can have all the necessary self-awareness and elaborate its project within the party, even if that project is never destined to progress far. The mini-fractions of Italian parties, well analysed by Sartori, are a case in point.[8] In the French context, we could cite supporters of Motion F (people who split from Ceres in 1979) and who potentially could have formed a viable fraction inside the PS. Their failure to do so proves another point made by Sartori and which we shall take up below, namely that the number of fractions (and their size) is crucially determined by certain institutional features of the party, particularly its internal electoral system and whether or not this has an entry threshold.

But if absolute size is not crucial, what Hine calls coverage is.[9] This wide-ranging term refers to the breadth of areas of activity which a fraction undertakes. A fraction with good coverage will thus be active across the party and not just at one level (say members of parliament or youth movement); it will try to be active across the whole territory and not just in one zone (though many fractions do in fact have a mainly regional base). In policy terms it will have views on most areas; indeed it must, if it wants to present itself as a serious leadership candidate for party or eventually country. Groups with limited coverage do not really qualify as fractions. If they are one-issue groups (attached practically exclusively to one issue or groups of related issues such as, say, gay rights or anti-pollution questions) then it would be better to call them issue-groups. Variants of this can be found in what Sartori terms 'witness-groups'.[10] These espouse a very unrealistic set of goals or values which they know have little chance of being implemented, but which they feel they must publicise. There are also veto-groups, which are *ad hoc* coalitions of people whose interests and organisations might normally be different but who come together to stop movement on certain questions. Sartori gives no examples of these but we might cite as models from the Labour party that group of union leaders who band together regularly to oppose the adoption of an incomes policy, or perhaps the coalition which for many years prevented the party from changing its policy on Northern Ireland. Normally such groups would be divided or divergent on other issues, but they know how to come together when vital interests are menaced.

The problematic of coverage suggests another key factor, durability. There would seem to be a break-point for fractions. Either they fail to get off the ground at all (e.g. the attempt to found a women's fraction in the PS in the seventies or maybe, guessing at the future, the movement that seeks separate representation for black people in the Labour party); or, once established, it becomes hard to eradicate them (though obviously their strength varies up and down). In our view this has to do with the almost Sartrean way in which fractions often define themselves, that is primarily negatively in relation to the others. To a large extent, this study will claim, they are what the other is not. If Rocard's supporters are the 'American left', then Ceres has to be the French left. One's own legitimacy is defined by the illegitimacy of the other. But if fractions are to keep reminding self and others of their identity – and this we will see to be a feature of their behaviour – then the other needs always to be there as well. Fraction leaders and members will feel better, then, the longer the comrade/enemy is there. Every church needs its devil and it seems that the durability and reproductive capacity of fractions is to some extent a function of the degree of antagonism they enjoy. Perhaps the existence of successful parties, in terms of their internal life at least, depends to some extent on the vigour and combativeness of their fractions.

Coverage also raises the key variable of organisation. PS literature frequently and piously protests that *courants* should by all means debate, but not form their own organisation for seeking to consolidate their influence. One presumes that the authors of such nonsense are far too disingenuous to believe it. At the very least a serious fraction must be able to formulate and publicise its ideas, get out its vote at local or national level and place its people in those areas (inside and outside the party) where it may gain a foothold. None of this will happen spontaneously, and we may expect to find that the greater the success achieved in these fields by a fraction, the better its organisation. Most literature on French fractionalism concentrates heavily on its ideology, ignoring the material underpinnings of this. Thus what is often presented as a Homeric battle of principle needs also to be seen as a struggle for power and influence between organised groups.

Probably the most interesting debates on fractions focus on their origins and motivations. One obvious cause is the previous existence of fractions as separate parties before they joined up in some new bigger organisation. This was the case with the Japanese Liberals, and we shall see that it was an important factor with the PS.[11]

In such mergers, members will often bring with them many of the habits developed in the past organisation – shared analyses, ways of working, loyalties based on common experience. They may also bring, as in the Japanese case, something more concrete, i.e. organisational structures which survive intact in the new party virtually emasculating the latter's official structures from the start.

One simplistic interpretation assimilates fractions to the designs of their leaders. Such views are frequently aired about the PS, which is seen as a loose collection of ambitious would-be presidents and their camp-followers. While the theory in some cases is undoubtedly true, and while the role of fraction leaders is of crucial importance, as will be shown, it is much too summary to be regarded as a global explanation. For one thing it glosses over real ideological or policy differences that can exist, and more crucially it presupposes a mass of uncritical members under the sway of a charismatic leader. Our experience suggests that this gravely underestimates the sort of motivation which brings people into fractional activity.

Once again Sartori is helpful here.[12] He revives Hume's distinction between fractions of principle and those of interest. The former are characterised by ideological motives above all. Members are attached to certain values and beliefs and we may expect them to be interested in policy and programmatic issues. Interest-based fractions are mainly interested in power for its own sake, or at least for the career opportunities it can bring. Presumably leader-based fractions fit more readily into this category than others, though not automatically so. The assumption would be that members perceive that only by being in fraction X or Y can one obtain access to such-and-such a reward (electoral candidacy, employment, post in apparatus, etc.).[13] While the distinction is attractive in theory the two types of interest are, in practice, likely to be blurred and it would probably be very hard to find pure samples of either. Sartori holds that many Italian fractions (in the PSI and DC) are purely interest-based and that such ideology as they might profess is a camouflage for their interests. Thus frequent shifts of position by a fraction might suggest that ideology is relatively unimportant and that it is interest-based; whereas a principled fraction should experience great difficulty in adjusting its ideology. But in fact it is very hard to find pure fractions (other than at their embryonic – or terminal – stage as witness-groups perhaps) for a simple reason. Supporters of principles want to see them carried out as policy; but this is impossible unless they have some power. Hence they are obliged, in order to obtain this power, to enter the struggle for posts, careers etc. whether they like it or not. They may even as the price of agreement over one principle be led to freeze or modify others. In other words, so far as the question of material gratifications is concerned, there will usually come a point when the fraction of principle comes to resemble strangely the fraction of interest.

We come here to the heart of the fractional question. There is no easy answer to the question as to why people join fractions, any more than there is to the question: why do they join parties? We shall argue in Chapter 2 our hypotheses about PS fractions, but let us enunciate them briefly here. In our view membership of PS fractions is seldom a matter of pure interest in the sense of career opportunities, etc. Cayrol says that fractions are set up from a permutation of five elements, the weight of which varies according to the context. These are: the adoption of a common political project; the existence of social diversification within the party; fidelity to leaders; and two categories which overlap, 'a shared political past' and subscribing to a 'shared political culture'.[14] (A shared culture is something one acquires largely as a result of shared experiences.) Cayrol's first category is indeed close to the last two in that all three privilege political culture and ideology. For many PS members this is the real base of fractional commitment. We should realise that for many of them, the chance to live out an ideology in the company of like-minded people from a similar milieu is in itself a strong gratification; others might seek more concrete forms of satisfaction (office-holding, financial rewards, etc.). Furthermore whatever members' initial motivation, they find that they have joined a structure which has laws of its own; it seems likely to us that with time their identification with it may well increase, irrespective of material rewards, and that this growing loyalty may come to figure more prominently as a motivation in their behaviour and thoughts. In short, fractions are as much about belonging as about succeeding.

We may now sum up our argument so far. The fractions which interest us must be of a certain salience and durability, and cover wide aspects of party activity. While their salience is not necessarily synonymous with visibility, they do to some extent depend on conflict with rivals and leadership for retaining their sense of identity and cohesion. While their performance may well depend on party structures, their origins and motivations are varied. Material consider- ations of office and careers may be important, but we should not forget that fidelity to an ideology can be an equally potent source of satisfaction and that such ideology, and the experiences of those who share in it, can create bonds of its own. With these considerations in mind we may turn from generalities to parties of a special type.

1.2 PARTIES OF THE SOCIALIST LEFT AND THEIR FRACTIONS

It is now necessary to define the category or genus to which our subject the PS belongs. Again we must hesitate over terminology; if the term 'social-democratic' seems *a priori* to cover parties like the PS which are to be found in the Socialist International, there are, we shall see, problems in its application to France and other Mediterranean countries. Equally, to call such parties simply 'socialist' is too loose;

communist, trotskyite and other parties which are quite distinct use
this term on occasions. The term 'non-communist left' is sometimes
used, but this is negative and in any case includes parties which are not
the same as the ones under discussion (e.g. the Italian Radicals or
Republicans or the French PSU are not by any means the same as the
PS). All in all, reformist is probably the best label, but even here there
are parties who describe themselves thus and which have specifically
distanced themselves from the socialist tradition. One example is the
réformateurs of the early seventies in France, which was a mixture of old-
fashioned Radical anti-clericals and christian democrats. It does not
seem impossible to us, either, to extend the term to parties which are
sometimes placed on the centre-right of the political spectrum, even if
those parties do not describe themselves as reformists: examples might
be Fine Gael in Ireland or even Gaullism in France. Latin American
populisms like APRA or MNR might also be demonstrated to fit into a
reformist tradition. We will then to reduce ambiguity use the term
'reformist socialist' to describe the PS and similar parties; for if they are
visibly reformist, they also aspire to a socialism which, however
maximally or minimally defined, is seen by them as being different
from the 'existing socialism' created by marxism-leninism. There is
much recent literature on such parties and we shall try to be brief.[15]

One can best comprehend the realities of such parties by saying
what they are not. To take an obvious point first, they are defined by a
break on their right. Although varying degrees of collaboration with
centre or populist parties are possible, there will come a point at which
these latter part company with them, either on doctrinal grounds or on
hard-and-fast policy choices. For reformist socialists believe that the
capitalist system of production secretes fundamental injustices; these
may be corrected either in an ad hoc ameliorative fashion or more
ambitiously in an incremental way, successive improvements gradually
making for a qualititative change in the nature of the socio-economic
system. There should thus occur a point where the changes will prove
too much for the non-socialist reformers, and the epistemological
break, as it were, occurs. The break may occur at any point along a
broad continuum of change and it may be difficult for theory to foresee
the point at which this split between progressive conservatives and
reformist socialists will occur, especially when one looks beyond the
rhetoric of both camps to their actual policies; it is probably more

likely to occur as a result of practice. But we assume there to be a spatial barrier of this sort.

Similarly the theoretical – and real – space which reformist socialism occupies in a political system is bounded on its left by leninism. Its whole approach to politics may be seen as a refusal of leninism and the organisational and political consequences thereof. Although some reformist socialists use marxist analysis of capitalism, although many believe that the history of mankind is the history of class-struggle and that socialism (whatever they understand by this) is inevitable, they none the less refuse the full consequences of leninist analysis. These are, briefly, that left to its own devices the working class will never develop more than a trade-union consciousness which is merely defensive and thus be unable to realise its historic task of overthrowing capitalism. To do this it needs a new instrument, the revolutionary party, which will raise its consciousness, and prepare it for the seizure of power, destruction of the capitalist state and building of socialism. The characteristics of such parties are well known and we discuss them in Section 3.3; they are evoked here simply to show what reformist socialism is not. Predicated as it is on a different logic, its parties have a different structure. If they are aware of the antagonism between capital and labour, then they do not foresee a revolutionary outcome to this struggle. On the contrary it is possible to create a compromise or situation of equilibrium that may last indefinitely. Some elements of the party will see this as a transitory situation on the road to socialism; others will see it as an end in itself and may even call it socialism. This does not matter overmuch; the important thing is that the compromise be sought and achieved.

The political expression of such compromise is electoral democracy with its inbuilt supposition of alternation in government. Unlike leninists, reformist socialists see electoral democracy as allowing the popular classes to make genuine choices, including the right of choosing pro-capitalist governments if such is their wish. The socio-economic content of such reformism is, first, the type of welfare-state protection afforded by the state to individuals (against the major risks of sickness, accident, ageing etc.), which has become familiar in developed states since 1945. Alongside it has usually come some attempt to redistribute wealth (via fiscal policy) and life-chances (through education, anti-discrimination legislation, etc.). In order to secure such redistribution most analysts see steady economic growth as a necessary condition. In practice reformist socialism has looked to a mixed economy to achieve this, where state intervention (role of public sector, demand management, credit policy) are used as much to bolster the private sector as to fulfil doctrinal commitments.

Most of this is quite banal, but what interests us here is its organisational consequences for parties of this type. For we believe such parties to be more prone than any other type to fractional pressures. It should be clear that in developed societies these parties are at the focal point of social change. If there is to be any significant modification in the allocation of economic and cultural resources, any widening of life-chances, then they are almost certain to be involved. If the finely balanced capitalist democracies are to avoid immobilism or the erosion of gains already made by the lower classes without passing through a revolution, then strong reformist parties are vital. But this key position has a number of factors making for instability which are always likely to split the parties. These issues may be divided into two heads: one concerns general views of ideology, policy and strategy, and the other is linked with organisation. Among the first category figures the question of the nature or extent of change. Is capitalism simply to be amended *ad hoc*, or are reforms part of an incremental move towards a new mode of production? If so, what are the characteristics of the latter?

A second problem is the speed at which change might occur, almost irrespective of what sort of change it is. Even if reformist socialists can agree on immediate or mid-term priorities, the question of making them acceptable to a wide electorate can pose problems. Labour's dilemmas in the 1983 General Election are a classic example. Can one better achieve a mid-term objective (e.g. nuclear disarmament) by making concessions to public apprehensions in the short term (keeping Polaris), or is it better to confront the electorate at once with a fundamental choice?

Redistribution of income is a problem which also highlights the speed and extent of change. Callaghan's 1979 government is believed to have lost the election because *inter alia* it had encouraged the erosion of pay differentials between the unskilled and the skilled, higher-earning layer of the working class, who were attracted by the Conservatives' more free-for-all approach. Would it have been better to defer such egalitarian measures until more propitious times? And in any case, what sort of differentials are desirable here? Can one know this other than by trial and error?

Another related problem is that of strategy. Even if members agree on objectives, the means to attain them are not always evident. Until very recently, no reformist socialist would turn his back on the chance of strong economic growth as measured in terms of GNP. Yet even here argument raged between statists and incentivisers. The former look to government to fuel the motor of the economy, by such devices as extension of the public sector, investment controls, planning agreements and the like: incentivisers are sceptical as to how far government can really influence growth directly and rely more on the (largely untouched) private sector for investment and increased output, appealing to it by confidence-building devices (such as fiscal policy and support grants).

Economic strategy raises questions not just of how to relate to the party's adversary (capital) but also to its social base or allies. There is more than one way of aggregating social demand. Of late 'corporatist' strategies have been useful to reformist socialists as a way of incorporating organised labour quasi-officially into macro-economic policy-making. But there are always likely to be limits to such processes.[16] Once reached they will provoke conflict within the party. And how does a party like the PS or the PSP in Portugal, with no organised base in the national labour movement, cope when in government with the demands of the class it is supposed by its rhetoric to represent? Clearly some other type of relationship to organised labour must be invented. This also neglects the class allies of such parties. If, as is usually the case, the hard core of their support is working class, then this is seldom enough to ensure a governing majority in the country. Alliance strategies must be devised for links with other groups, such as the salaried middle class or perhaps small farmers; but the terms of such an alliance will again give rise to controversy, with some saying that too many concessions have been made at workers' expense.

Foreign affairs are another minefield. If most reformist socialists desire peaceful cooperation between nations, the ways to achieve it are not obvious. In particular socialists have faced enormous difficulties on the whole question of national loyalties.[17] How are they to articulate loyalty to their own nation with loyalty to the principle of change and reform that may well have transnational implication? The tension caused in the ranks of Western European socialism by the issue of the EEC or more recently the Euromissiles testifies eloquently to the possibilities for disagreement.

If the above points have borne on policy, the organisation of such parties provides further opportunity for diversity. First, most of them prize debate and argument as ends in themselves: such features are seen as a reflection of their commitment to pluralism in society at large. This may lead to an ostrich-like preoccupation with inner party life at the risk of being cut off from the real movement of society; Labour since 1979 would again be a *locus classicus*. But usually such pluralism is written into party rules. Often policy is made by the conference, itself an elective, therefore competitive, forum. National and local committees are usually similarly elective, even if real competition may be attenuated somewhat. Often such parties have corporate types of representation for special categories, ranging from the trade-union members of the Labour party to its small cohort of socialist societies for doctors, teachers, etc. Such organisational factors may well produce not just a locus for argument but also the organisation needed to make sure that arguments are won and followed up – in other words, fractionalism.

At the same time all the other classic causes of fractionalism alluded to above can turn up in parties of this type. Leader-based fractions, whether spoils- or ideologically-motivated, are frequent. And many of the parties have absorbed previous groups, these latter often keep their identity in the new structures. We would conclude, then, by repeating that reformist socialist parties by virtue of their special position at the interstices of change are subject to political and ideological lines of fracture far greater than those which affect parties on either side of them. Small wonder that they have more than their share of fractions.

1.3 THE PARTIES OF REFORMIST SOCIALISM AND THEIR LEFT FRACTIONS

Bearing in mind the inherent fissiparity of reformist socialist parties we may turn more closely to their left wings. For such fractions invariably exist and despite differences of emphasis or of national context they present a certain number of common features which we may identify. It must be stated now that what follows is a generalised model which deliberately abstracts from national and local variants of all kinds in the interests of making a clear hypothesis. We are aware that there is often more than one left fraction in a party, but we believe that these can usually be subsumed into our general model.

Left fractions are first defined in terms of their own party. They must see it as *no more than* reformist. They see the party as dominated most of the time by people (let us call them the right or centre of the party, though it must be stressed that these terms are highly fluid) who can always muster a formal majority within the party, even though they may not represent what it really wants. Such people may be organised in one or more fractions or just coexist in some more amorphous form. Whatever the case, they are not fully committed to socialism.

Thus if ever elected to office, such people will inevitably fail to carry out significant changes, even if these have been put on the party's programme and even if (an unlikely event) the 'moderates' themselves believe in some of them. They will thus capitulate to two kinds of pressures, the first of which is that of private capital. Symptoms of the latter's disapproval such as lack of 'confidence', refusal to invest, and runs on the currency, show the moderates that the limits of acceptable change have been reached. At the same time they are under pressure from the institutions of the capitalist state. Left critiques of this may range from the blanket attacks on 'civil servants' or the 'capitalist media' beloved of the Labour left to more sophisticated attempts to theorise how the different parts of the state apparatus may combine to impede change. But either way the conclusion is the same; the amount of permissible change is finite and the moderate centre or right of the party is happy to accept this and 'manage capitalism'.

Irrespective of the party's self-description – which may be quite radical – lefts will feel that the party as it is will never take its challenge to capital beyond certain limits. This conviction may be based on analysis of performance when in office, or of the party's mode of functioning, or of its policies or leaders; but whatever its source, such a conviction is essential to the constitution of a left fraction. It will express itself characteristically in scepticism as to the results obtained thus far by reformist socialism, through its redistributive policies based on an expanding mixed economy. Either the extent of redistribution is disputed or denied or, if admitted (as perhaps for Austria or Sweden), it will be denounced for its precariousness or for not going far enough.[18] Lefts tend to disbelieve in any kind of spontaneous or unobstructed incrementalism, believing either that capitalism can absorb many reforms and even reproduce itself better thanks to them, or that if necessary it can obstruct change at will.

Left socialists thus believe that structural changes – socio-economic, political and cultural – are necessary and possible. They may or may not call these revolutionary; they may use either traditional marxist or more likely sophisticated neo-marxist analyses, or simply concepts from their own national tradition to illustrate their problematic. They will almost certainly not agree in any detail on the type of socialism they see emerging from these changes (hardly suprisingly, since no such model has yet existed). But at a minimum it would involve the following: removal of the major areas of the economy from the control of private capital, probably to be run in greater or lesser measure by the workforce: radical changes in income patterns, generally in a more equalitarian sense: much wider participation in economic and political decision making by a better educated, informed and more critical citizenry: and extensive restructuring of the state apparatus in order to permit the above. Left socialists would probably share anti-imperialist concern about underdevelopment and unequal exchange. They would probably also be characterised by enthusiasm for new social movements, particuarly feminist and anti-militarist. This still leaves wide room for variance, not least in the realm of foreign affairs (which will remain notoriously difficult for socialists for the foreseeable future); but these underlying general principles would be endorsed by most of what we call left socialists.

Crucially, however, left socialists believe such transformation to be possible by democratic means. They specifically eschew insurrection as a means for the workers and their allies to take power. At most, in the light of experiences such as the overthrow of Allende in 1973 or the crushing of the austro-marxists in Vienna in 1934 they might highlight the possibility of violent aggression by the ruling class to defend its position and discuss the possibility of workers' self-defence. But the very choice of a reformist socialist party, as opposed to a leninist one, is significant. Left socialists believe that electoral victory by their party, alone or with allies, is the precondition of any structural change, even if they devote great energy to imagining links between electoral success and various non-party mass movements in civil society ('the movement from above and the movement from below', as Ceres used to say).

Electoral victory alone is no guarantee of real change. Often it can be the reverse, as once in office and whatever their original goals, party leaders give way to pressure from domestic and international capital and begin to trim their policies. What is vital, then, is that the party be prepared for a real struggle to impose socialist choices and priorities before and after electoral victory, to secure reforms that will bring the goal of socialism nearer. But for this to happen it must be organised as the left would like to see it. The likelihood of new parties being formed where the old one had failed has been ruled out, as has leninism, and probably rightly. European history is littered with the corpses of would-be supplanters of the reformist parties and failed left-socialist splinters; from the USPD in Germany through the ILP to the PSU the list is long.

The left has then to win over its own party. But this has implications on several levels, which historically have probably never been fulfilled in any one case. Obviously the party would need to have a programme designed by its left and stating (explicitly?) the sort of socialist desiderata set out above. That is probably the easiest task for the left, in fact. If other fractions are inclined to compromise then it is possible, given the elasticity of political vocabulary, for a left fraction to get much of its demands on to a party manifesto in more or less recognisable form.

More difficult would be a second task, assuring control of party machinery. This means that the left would have a clear and durable majority on the national leadership plus an adequate relay of élites at lower levels to assure continuity.

If this continuity were fulfilled it might mean that a third one was also, namely that the left was hegemonic in the party. This means more than winning a one-off victory at conference. Rather it means that the general outlines of its long-term project for change had won wide acceptance in the hearts and minds of members. In other words the left would have achieved a sort of cultural or emotional breakthrough to the party. The fraction would become the whole.

If it did that, the left might be in a position to take the most difficult hurdle of all, namely to become hegemonic not just among its own party but among the wider party electorate and beyond this across society generally. For only thus would it have a realistic chance of achieving without grave conflict the ambitious sort of change it seeks. Historically we know of no instance where this latter condition has been met.

Left socialists face a daunting task, then, and in the sixty years or more that they have had to contend with a communist party on their left and an increasingly constrained majority in their own party, it has not become any easier. Most of them are frank about their beliefs and aims, usually because they see history as on their side.[19] Usually their programmes are public and their people visible. They seldom feel a conflict of loyalty between their beliefs and their loyalty to the party, for they usually think that their idea of what the party should be is the correct one. Either the party was like that in the past, has become diverted and must be restored to its real identity; or else through sheer historical necessity it must become what the left want it to be. If it has not yet realised this fact, then the efforts of the left are doubly justified.

As a rule then the left has to win the party over or back from a reformist right. If it is serious in its aims it must put in an organisational effort. (However, it is true that the main interest of some left fractions seems to lie mainly in protest or bearing witness; in these cases gratification is clearly obtained through martyrdom-complexes rather than trying to realise one's goals.) Such an effort must be made right across the party's coverage. What does this involve?

First the left must have an operative ideology, which will be readily transferable into some sort of progammatic statement. Such ideology must enable supporters, actual and potential, to recognise themselves in it; it must offer them thus a series of blocks on which to build an identity. This will mean as well as including mobilising themes excluding certain themes in practice: you cannot nowadays seriously argue inside a reformist socialist party in favour of proletarian dictatorship, for instance. The ideology must somehow have a flavour of radical change and yet do so plausibly, suggesting that such change is within reach. In the last analysis a successful left-socialist ideology must combine elements of the utopian and the operational in a finely judged mix. Left-socialist ideology is not spontaneous; it has to be worked at.

On this basis a left fraction may proceed to the task of recruiting members. Obviously support will come in differential degrees, from the most articulate defenders of left theses to those who follow them for all the 'wrong' reasons (deference to leaders, clientelism, dislike of party establishment, imitation, and so on); but from among the convinced will come the élites whom the left will have to place in positions of authority. It must aim at office inside and outside the party apparatus; mayors, councillors and parliamentarians are just as important as branch chairmen or national executive members. Above all a serious fraction must invest in those delicate areas contiguous to the party – labour unions, youth and other social movements (feminists, environmentalists perhaps). It may even be necessary to have relationships (of variable geometry) with other parties or with similar elements in the reformist socialist parties of other countries. All these areas are full of deontological pitfalls for the unwary; the opportunity to make mistakes and the chances of being accused of bungling or treason are high. But they are unavoidable, for the party at large cannot afford to ignore such areas, so neither can its left.

On these bases, then, a left fraction might try to win hegemony. Its success will depend not just on its own efforts but also on those of its (majority) opponents in the party, and also on a whole range of factors from the wider political environment in which the party operates. In general history suggests that left fractions can only make limited progress; they are able only to place some of their priorities on the party programme and some of their people on its leadership. It is possible even to detect policy outcomes when the party is in office which may well not have happened without the pressure of a determined and organised left. But the left never wins total hegemony in party or country, and it is as if there were structural limits to its progress; so much so that many believe that the left's real function in these parties cannot be the stated one, namely, conquest of hegemony.[20] Willingly or unconsciously it plays a different systemic role from its ostensible one, so the argument runs. It is time to consider such arguments in detail.

One theory, from the revolutionary left, holds that the main function of left-socialist fractions is to blight its own chances.[21] By holding out the (delusive) prospect that socialism can be brought nearer through the transformation of the existing party, they help it to attract activists and voters who would otherwise join the revolutionary party (trotskyist or leninist) which states its options clearly. A variant of this thesis has it that left elements, by their very presence in reformist ranks, give the impression that these are genuinely democratic and pluralistic; their arguments and actions would thus be the insurance against the development of monolithism. But this impression is false, for there are always limits to what the left can achieve. The democratic space in which it moves is a small one and probably not a valuable one; in moments of crisis the leadership will close down this space by one means or another (expulsion, cooptation etc.). One type of analysis even believes that the most such fractions can achieve is to raise the consciousness of members to the point where they will eventually be ready to leave for a revolutionary organisation; the 'raiding-party' type of entrism believes this.

From a slightly different but equally pessimistic angle, some would say that this does not matter because of the type of person drawn by left fractions. These are said to be people who do not really want responsibility, especially governmental; rather, leftists prefer the luxury of opposition in party and country alike. Thus they can pillory the right and wallow in their maximalist demands, knowing that these will never be put to the test. This theory, which combines the concept of the witness-group with some moral and psychological snap-judgements, pivots heavily on the motivation of fractionalists, but should not be entirely dismissed, for it is true that there are gratifications of an ideological type to be had in politics without ever getting involved in power. Whether such considerations apply to left fractions as a general rule must however in the absence of detailed evidence be open to doubt.

Less cynical views assign to left fractions some more limited objectives. They hold that the left knows at heart that its aims are unrealisable, at least in the foreseeable future. It thus seeks lesser, intermediate aims. One is to corner as much space in the party as possible, so as to put down markers for the future. These positions can be used to battle against the party right and its temptations to sell socialism short. They can also be used to gratify those leftists who are interested in office, for this kind of analysis believes them to be made of flesh and bones. This explanation gives satisfaction to the ideologist in that the left achieves something (without it the party would have drifted further into opportunism) as well as to the instrumentalist.

A final reading sees left fractions as a safety valve.[22] Assuming, like other theories, that the left runs up against structural limits, its real function is to reveal what these limits are. In other words, when left people and ideas assume too great a salience they are a kind of orange light. The leadership knows that the party is about to strike trouble with its electorate and must find a riposte (usually by the classic means of either coopting some of the left and defusing the impact of its ideas, or by a purge). The real function of the left is then to show what the electorally acceptable limits of socialist reformism are; it is a political thermostat.

We see then that left fractions are a special genus, attached to a socialism qualitatively different from what reformism can bring, at least in the foreseeable future. Such a proejct supposes a sustained ideological and organisational effort to take the party, and there are hurdles of increasing difficulty to be jumped before the fraction becomes the whole and party and national hegemony could be achieved. Most left fractions describe their aims and hopes in these terms but a number of interpretations suggest that they have other objective functions, which range from siphoning off potential support from revolution, to providing emotional gratification, to warning reformist leaderships that their policies are becoming unworkable. Few leftists would of course accept these theories, but they can in any case only be tested by examining their application to an actual party. To this we now turn.

NOTES TO CHAPTER 1

1   G. Sartori, *Parties and Party Systems*, Cambridge University Press, 1976, p. 72.

2   F. Belloni and D. Beller, *Faction Politics: political parties and factionalism in comparative perspective*, Santa Barbara (Calif.), ABC-Clio, 1978, p. 419. For a recent review of fractionalism within contemporary parties see the papers from the ECPR workshop of 1980 on *Factionalism in Political Parties in Western Europe*.

3   R. Rose, 'Parties, factions and tendencies in Britain', *Political Studies* XII, 1, 1964, pp. 33–46.

4   *Parti socialiste*, *Status*, Paris, 1979, p. 12.

5 R. Cayrol, 'Courants, fractions, tendances', in P. Birnbaum (ed.), *Critiques des pratiques politiques*, Paris, Galilée, 1978, pp. 165–75.

6 'Démocratie, courants et cohésion dans le parti', *Nouvelle Revue Socialiste* 33, September 1978, pp. 7–17.

7 M. Crick, *Militant*, London, Faber, 1984.

8 Sartori, op. cit., pp. 85 ff.

9 D. Hine, 'Factionalism in West European Parties: A Framework for Analysis', *West European Politics* 5, January 1982, pp. 36–51.

10 Sartori, op. cit., p. 80.

11 Ibid., p. 90.

12 Ibid., p. 88.

13 Cf. D. Gaxie, 'Economie des partis et rétribution du militantisme', *Revue française de science politique*, XXVII, April 1977, pp. 123–55.

14 Cayrol, op. cit., p. 167.

15 For general as opposed to specifically national studies see A. Bergounioux and B. Manin, *La Social-démocratie ou le compromis*, Paris, PUF, 1979; C. Buci-Glucksmann and G. Therborn, *Le défi social-démocrate*, Paris, Maspéro, 1981; A. Bihr and J.-M. Heinrich, *La néo-socialdémocratie ou le capitalisme autogéré*, Paris, Le Sycomore, 1979; W. Brandt, B. Kreisky and O. Palme, *La social-démocratie et l'avenir*, Paris, Gallimard, 1976; F. Fejto, *La Social-démocratie quand-même*, Paris, Laffont, 1980; ISER, *La Social-démocratie en questions*, Paris, Editions de la Revue Politique et Parlementaire, 1981; A. Przeworski, 'Social Democracy as an historical phenomenon', *New Left Review* 122, July–August 1980, pp. 27–58; J. Ross (ed.), *Profils de la Social-démocratie européenne*, Paris, La Brèche, 1982; 'Social-démocraties européennes', *Le Monde diplomatique*, September 1981.

16 G. Lehmbruch and P. Schmitter, *Patterns of Corporatist Policymaking*, London, Sage, 1982; P. Schmitter and G. Lehmbruch, *Trends towards Corporatist Intermediation*, London, Sage, 1979; L. Panitch, 'Trade Unions and the Capitalist State', *New Left Review* 125, January–February 1981, pp. 21–44.

17 E. Cahm and V.-C. Fisera (eds), *Socialism and Nationalism in Contemporary Europe* (3 vols), Nottingham, Spokesman, 1980; B. Anderson, *Imagined Communities*, London, NLB, 1983; G. Minnerup and B. Jenkins, *Socialism and Nationalism*, London, Pluto, 1984.

18 On this score most left socialists would share the scepticism of someone who is not one of their number, and who criticises the limits of social democracy with some percipience, F. Parkin, *Class Inequality and Political Order*, London, Granada, 1971. For a similar conclusion, albeit with a compensation on the issue of ideological hegemony, see the case study by R. Scase, *Social Democracy in Capitalist Society*, London, Croom Helm, 1977. A more optimistic view of the reality of social democratic conquests is F. Castles, *The Social Democratic Image of Society*, London, Routledge and Kegan Paul, 1978 (cf. especially pp. 146–99).

19 'Invisible' left fractions like Militant are an obvious exception, but they belong to a different genus, viz. leninist or more usually trotskyist groups practising entrism. Their incidence – and real influence – is probably much less than the publicity accorded to them would suggest.

20 For an attempt to theorise the influence of left fractions in the French PS see M. and N. Sadoun, *Les courants de gauche au PS*, Université de Paris I (DES), 1973.

21 Cf. the critiques of H. Weber, followed by a discussion with Motchane and Chevènement in *Critique communiste* I, 1975, pp. 20–40. For a similar view from an ex-socialist turned communist see E. Scharf 'Uber die linken Sozialisten in der SPO',

Weg und *Ziel* 12, 1974, pp. 510–21. A very articulate British view is D. Coates, *The Labour Party and the Struggle for Socialism*, Cambridge University Press, 1974, pp. 177–217; *Labour in Power?*, London, Longman, 1980, pp. 227–56; 'Space and agency in the transition to socialism', *New Left Review* 135, September–October 1982, pp. 49–63.

22   Bergounioux and Manin, op. cit., p. 186.

CHAPTER 2

The French Socialist Party – unity and diversity

On comprend que l'existence de courants organisés ne soit pas un problème séculaire, mais bien une condition *sine qua non* de la vie interne du PS, ces 'partis dans le parti' permettant de donner à la lutte pour le pouvoir un caractère permanent et 'naturel'.   H. Portelli

Comme si le parti pouvait vivre démocratiquement avec la disparition des 'tendances', expression des contradictions réelles.   Y. Roucaute

2.1   THE NATURE OF THE PS – AN OVERVIEW

Within the camp of reformist socialism the PS is held to occupy a special place. If most of the parties discussed above are often called 'social-democratic', then one of the most perceptive recent analysts of the PS does not hesitate to write that 'the PS of today – and of yesterday – is basically foreign to the social-democratic tradition'.[1] The reasons for this claim are above all structural; as Portelli remarks, to qualify for the social-democratic lable it is not enough to profess a social-democratic ideology or even to carry out reforms when in office. A social-democracy worthy of the name needs a mass base in the working class, which usually means strong links with the organised labour movement. If it has this it is likely to meet Portelli's second condition for eligibility, namely a serious party machine with proper financial support, communication facilities, full-time staff, and so on. Unless a party meets these conditions it is a misnomer to call it social-democratic. In other words, social democracy is not just a matter of will or aspiration; one must also have the means. For unless one does, one will be unable to bargain with capital on a strong enough basis to secure the kind of compromise which we have seen to be at the heart of reformist socialism; and even if one were able by some means to obtain this, one would then have difficulty in getting one's members to observe it. According to this view, the classic types of social-democracy are to be found in Northern Europe, and the pre-1914 SPD would be the founding exemplar. As Portelli suggests, a number of Latin parties in Europe do not have such a base in the labour movement and cannot be called social-democratic. It was with this reservation in mind that we adopted the wider tag of reformist socialist.

The history of the French party shows it to be a failed or aspirant social-democracy.[2] Before the SFIO party (section française de l'Internationale ouvrière) emerged in 1905 from a grouping of smaller parties (see below), the possibility of a fruitful link with organised labour had already been squandered. In the 1890s the Workers' Party (POF) of Jules Guesde, the first marxist and indeed the first modern party in France, had attempted to establish party hegemony over the growing trade union movement. Guesde's concepts prefigured the 'conveyor-belt' notions of Lenin and Stalin; he saw the union as the industrial wing of the party whose job was to implement party directives in the factories. The party was the only significant political actor (Guesde kept referring to unions as the 'primary school of socialism'). This concept, forged by the intellectuals dominant in the POF, was not well received by workers, often more concerned with more concrete, work-related issues. Soon the unions, influenced by the growth of anarchist activism, would move away from Guesde and adopt the ideology of revolutionary syndicalism as enshrined in the Amiens charter of the CGT trade union centre in 1906. Its main tenets are classic by now. Looking to the working class to perform its own emancipation, it sees the means of struggle to be not the party but the union or *syndicat*. This 'natural grouping of producers' is not just a defence mechanism against exploitation, but a focus where the class can organise and educate itself so as to go over on to the revolutionary offensive. Moreover the union is seen as the embryo of a future society of self-governing units of producers. Such dogma naturally rejects socialist *parties* as irrelevant, if not harmful. It is not our intention to argue the merits of such a theory nor its representativity (recent research has pinned it down increasingly as a minority phenomenon, very much the preserve of skilled workers menaced by proletarisation). Suffice it to say here that it ruled out from the start an organic link between labour movement and socialist party.

From SFIO's point of view the false start was never made good. By 1914 syndicalism was showing signs of terminal weakness and the success of the Bolshevik revolution arguably killed its remaining mass appeal. But the labour movement still never gravitated towards the political party as in Germany or the UK. The interwar CGT was split between communists and independents, and when reunification came it was very much to the advantage of the former. After the Resistance during the Nazi occupation, communist hegemony over the CGT would be so complete as to force its reformist elements to split off and form Force Ouvrière (FO), but on a strictly non-party basis. Meanwhile, as is frequent in countries with a catholic culture, another part of the working class was organised on confessional lines in the CFTC, later CFDT, which for different reasons remained equally distant from the SFIO.

From the start then the party was stripped of links with the organisations of the class it claimed to represent, and this was crucial for its own development.[3] Unable to secure monopoly representation of the working class (which was in 1905 still underdeveloped in comparison with neighbouring states), the party sought to diversify its support, appealing especially to fractions of the peasantry and lower white-collars, often in the public service, and especially numerous in education.[4] These latter categories, along with the intellectuals who had launched the party, would always be prominent on leadership bodies; to counterbalance them there were relatively few of the 'organic intellectuals' of the working class such as emerged from the mass labour movements of Britain and Germany, where party and union were so much closer. But organisational and sociological underdevelopment was compensated by ideological overdevelopment. Thus SFIO was never content simply to define itself as a reformist party. It saw itself as a workers' party, predicated on marxist analyses of class-struggle, and committed to a proletarian revolution in order to realise socialism. This intransigence meant that for many years the idea of participation in coalition governments which might pass reforms conducive to socialism was rejected. Between the wars it took all the theological skill of party leader Léon Blum (plus the threat of fascism) to justify heading the Popular Front government of 1936–7; and even the important reforming governments of 1944–7 where SFIO figured prominently were a source of bitterness to many members, who believed in a revolutionary outcome and not reformist coalitions.

There grew up thus a widespread ideology, often summarised as Guesdism, which, as Bruce Graham rightly remarks, was curiously timeless.[5] The party was revolutionary; revolution was inevitable, and so was proletarian dictatorship. While awaiting it, the party must build its strength in electoral and other spheres but avoid so far as possible getting caught in government and its inevitable compromises. Much of the old Republican ideology had also become imperceptibly part of the Guesdist tradition, notably the view that secularism was a *sine qua non* of social progress. By the 1930s this mentality was widely shared through the ranks, and the intellectuals, major and minor, who ran the party declaimed their workerist slogans without fear of ridicule. Yet such ideology coexisted happily enough with a political *practice* that was often very pragmatic. Well before 1914 SFIO's electorate was quite diverse and it was on the way to becoming what might nowadays be called a catch-all party; the rise of a communist party (PCF) which soon proved better able to attract working-class voters meant that SFIO's share of these votes would stagnate and that it had to seek support of a yet further diversified nature. None of this support was turned away in the name of revolutionary principle. As well as occupying a distinct corner of national politics, SFIO had a strong base in local government. Here, rhetoric notwithstanding, its mayors and councillors strove to improve services and benefits for their voters. In some cases the type of relationship between officials and voters could fairly be described as clientelistic, with votes sought – and won – on the basis of services provided.

Yet more crucially, at national level when the party was in power (always in coalition) its policies were very much what one would expect from social-democracy or reformism. In 1936 Blum pursued policies of a reflationary pre-keynesian type to fight unemployment, priming the pump with wage-rises and holiday benefits. He also sought to incorporate the unions to some extent by according them representative status. Nationalisations were limited to armaments and some services. The 1944–7 tripartite governments (SFIO, PCF and christian democrats) nationalised further services and most credit, began a framework of limited indicative planning and laid the basis of a welfare state. Even Guy Mollet's Republican Front government of 1956–7 strove to improve pensions and holidays despite its involvement in the Algerian war.

Obscured as they were by the presence of coalition partners, by the continuing use of maximalist rhetoric or even by those arguments which ascribe the major credit for such changes to enlightened civil servants and not party leaders, these policy operations provide us with a clue as the real identity of SFIO. Structurally underdeveloped it certainly was in terms of class-base and resources; and to some extent its ideological overdevelopment was a function of this. Yet in terms of policy outcome it achieved broadly the sort of results we expect from a mass social-democratic party. Without the infrastructure of such a party it seems none the less to have played a similar systemic role in the political economy of France. We might thus expect to find it plagued by the tensions inherent in such parties and indeed, given the gap between its maximalist ideology and moderate performance, we might suppose that its fractional cleavages are even greater than those of classical social-democracy. We shall now examine it historically from a fractional point of view in order to test this hypothesis.

2.2   THE PS AND ITS FRACTIONS IN HISTORICAL PERSPECTIVE

The new SFIO party was formed in 1905 at the behest of the Second International.[6] Given that it was basically a fusion of Guesde's POF and Jaurès' Independents, plus some smaller but very identity-conscious groups, the ideological differences between these virtually guaranteed the presence of fractionalism.

Institutional factors increased this likelihood, though, and in particular the party's inability to create centralised structures. Members in the federations were determined to prevent parliamentarians from taking control and thus ensured that the *conseil national* (CN) and its offshoot the CAP (*commission administrative permanente*) kept them in a majority over the latter. As deputies had to act on a day-to-day basis and the CAP met less frequently, conflict was guaranteed; and the leaders were able to do little to change this situation. Linked to this mistrust was a material factor, lack of resources. Party dues were low and members not that numerous; thus by 1914 there existed probably only seven or eight national full-time officials – hardly enough to run an efficient machine from the centre.[7] Congress itself, the sovereign body of the party, adopted measures to increase disunity, giving places on the CAP from 1907 to supporters of minority motions. These places were effectively carved up in the resolutions committee where the leading signatories of motions, mainly from Paris, ran what amounted to a system of fractional cooptation.[8] Most signatures of motions took place in any case on a follow-my-leader basis, with powerful men (usually deputies) able to deliver virtual block-votes, out of considerations in which ideology did not as a rule figure strongly.[9] In short, institutional and structural factors blended perfectly with the habits and loyalties of incomers to produce a fragmented new structure. But how did this work in terms of left and right fractions?

The clash is usually depicted in terms of a Guesde-Jaurès confrontation, with Guesde representing a reductionist marxism which read off political phenomena crudely from the economic 'substructure' and Jaurès standing for a looser type of reformism, influenced by Republican and even idealist inputs. A recent work sums these up usefully.[10]

Guesde looked towards a revolutionary outcome in the short term, led by the working class and its party. Jaurès was an incremental reformist, seeking the alliance of the class with other non-bourgeois groups and their representatives. Guesde thus despised 'ministerialism' (i.e. joining coalition governments), while Jaurès worked towards a centre-left coalition. On other issues, differences were strong, ranging from the unions to secularism (Jaurès espoused this essential part of the Republican heritage more strongly, if anything, than Guesde) to international relations (Jaurès put more faith in détente and international working-class solidarity than Guesde, who varied from enthusiasm for 'the nation in arms' to fatalistic claims that war was inevitable unless revolution intervened).

Thus are the differences usually catalogued, and historians have been able to build up and counterpose two doctrinal poles. A revolutionary class-based line, albeit simplistic, confronts a mere reformism which, for all its dialectical skill, poses no fundamental challenge to capitalism. Many commentators indeed represent the history of the party ever since in terms of this polarity.[11] Like all broad syntheses it has the advantage of clarity, but on examination poses some problems.

In the first place this is not an ideological clash between marxism and idealism. Few marxists nowadays would recognise Guesde's reductionism and even less his catastrophism (capitalism is bound to collapse, tomorrow). Jaurès had a much better knowledge of marxism than Guesde, understanding the relationships between economic structure, social class and political response in a dialectical and not a mechanical way. In particular he understood the need for the working class to build up, via a long haul, what would nowadays be called hegemony, developing its own institutions and culture. His occasional speculational about non-material ultimate causes certainly does not enable us to take from him the label of marxist and pin it on Guesde.

Neither was then more marxist than the other, and neither was arguably more left. Certainly if we take issues like international relations or colonialism it would be hard to say there was a left/right split. Thus on imperialism, neither explained it properly in terms of capitalist development nor drew the conclusion that the correct socialist response was to call for self-determination for the colonies. Both remained ultimately within an imperial framework.

A third point concerns the nature of reformism. Jaurès was an avowed incrementalist,[12] the revolutionary Guesde decried reform as illusory or at best short-lived. But this ideology did not prevent a highly reformist political practice. Rimbert underlines the early participation by Guesdists in municipal politics.[13] Mayors did not prepare their townspeople for revolution but took measures that can only be called reformist – building houses, improving services, helping strikers and unemployed. Even in parliament Guesdists did more than make ritual denunciations of capitalism. As early as 1895 they had voted for Radical governments which tried to introduce income-tax. And if they voted after 1905 maximalist amendments to reform proposals (e.g. pensions bills), they none the less supported such measures.[14] What they were doing was staking out a purist position while being quite content to let the rest of the party do the 'reformist' dirty work.

Organisationally, the party's fractions were more similar than might be supposed. Assuming congress motions to be the codification of fractional existence, Ziebura shows these to have been written by the intellectual leaderships, often Parisian (though Guesdism was strongest in the North).[15] Little is known in detail about party sociology and in the absence of more detailed studies of federations before 1914 we are unable to suggest that for instance Guesde's supporters were workers, and those of Jaurès small farmers or petty-bourgeois. If as Ziebura claims the texts of the motions were probably ill-understood anyway by the mass membership, it seems likely that the key variable in securing support at federal or branch level was probably the power of the local notable, especially if he were a parliamentarian. These organisational parameters would apply to left and right alike.

One analyst is so sceptical of the received idea of the left/right split that he postulates a more variable basis of fractionalism. This he does by concentrating on the deputies alone, thereby distinguishing different fractional cleavages in the course of each parliament (six on reformism from 1906–10 and six different ones on international relations from 1910–14).[16] This suggests great fluidity within the two major poles of the party.

By 1914, then, the development curve of French socialism was visible beneath its self-description. SFIO saw itself as a marxist party of class-struggle, aiming at the socialisation, by revolutionary means, of the means of production and exchange. It was a broad-based party in terms of voters and to a lesser extent members; its support came from Northern industrialised France but also, south of the Loire, from the traditional Republican clientele of small farmers, traders, artisans and small-town professionals. The party's political practice was similarly eclectic: its reformist wing, dominant in parliament, drew conclusions from the variegated nature of support and sought class alliances with advanced fractions of the Republican bloc, hoping thus to realise reforms that would bring socialism near. The logic of this was to make SFIO a system-party.

The party left resisted this. Professing a more rigid marxism, it was hostile to participation in coalition and sceptical about reform. It is true that both locally and nationally, Guesdist behaviour often belied this in a pragmatic way. But that was irrelevant in terms of party culture, for Guesdism undoubtedly shaped the major lines of this. Its simple certitudes found their way into members' minds more readily than the subtle, long-term strategy of the Jauresians. We have thus a situation where the right defines party practice and the left its orthodoxy. This contradictory situation could last a long time, not just because the party was not in office but also because of its very decentralised structure, itself largely a legacy of its recent past, when it was several separate organisations. As for *organised* fractions, the rather scant evidence suggests that they were not well-structured and were probably mainly based on local leaders. It remained to see whether this would still be the case if new pressures were put on the party.

The creation of a communist party (PCF) in 1920 was precisely such a pressure. What it meant was that SFIO's position in the party system had changed; its comfortable monopoly of the far left position and of the working-class vote was now increasingly challenged. As it was less likely than ever to achieve a majority unaided the question of alliances on its left and right (i.e. with PCF or Radicals) could not be avoided. This question of alliances came to dominate party life and had particular implications for fractional behaviour.

The most vocally revolutionary members of the party having gone with the communist split in 1920, Blum and his allies (mainly deputies with strong local power bases) found it easier to attempt the right alliance as had Jaurès before them.[17] Hence the support for the Radicals of Édouard Herriot in the 1924 elections (le cartel des gauches) on the understanding that SFIO would support a government committed to moderate reform, but not join it. The resultant fiasco is well known.[18] Herriot's zeal for fiscal reform collapsed under pressure from the Bank of France and finance capital ('le mur d'argent'); soon his government was replaced by conservative ones led by Poincaré, which the Radicals then supported. The effects on SFIO were traumatic.

The party right argued that SFIO should have shown greater commitment to the cartel, even to the extent of joining the government. This resentment would eventually crystallise into the *néo* fraction (see below). On the left, activists saw confirmation of what they already knew, namely that there was no mileage in the Radical alliance, and began to organise to prevent a repeat. By May 1926 a new fraction, Bataille socialiste, was active in Paris; a year later it would confirm its national status by presenting a motion to congress.[19] Baker has set out its major characteristics, which he rightly sees as constituting a new left, in ideological terms; for the old left, Guesdism, was by now in effect the mainstream party ideology, even if it was used to cover the politics of moderate class compromise and alliance just described.

Leftists insisted on 'proletarian autonomy', that is, the party should aim to win workers' votes first, concentrating less on peasant or petty-bourgeois support. The consequence of this was a readiness to seek closer relationships with the PCF, ranging from electoral alliance to 'organic unity' or merger. Baker also highlights a third element, obsession with the fostering of a district working-class culture; this 'workerism' which tends to admire manual workers *qua* workers is highly typical of the guilt-complex which intellectuals often feel towards the class which they claim to support while knowing they are fortunate enough not to belong to it.

Much of this continues the trajectory of the old Guesdism, and often differences might be more of style or fervour than of substance. But Baker shows some differences. Geographically the older Guesdism tended to be more in the North, with its mining and textiles, whereas the newer variety did better among the more variegated categories of support south of the Loire. Baker suggests a rather instrumental explanation for this, namely that in areas of new left support many looked to the party to fulfil the corporate functions normally expected from trade unions, which were usually weak in such areas. The evidence for this is, he admits, somewhat speculative. More interesting in our view is another variable, that of national defence. For it seems that the newer more Southern Guesdism tended more to pacifist or anti-militarist sympathies; whereas the North, remembering the German occupation of 1914–18, was much more in favour of national defence. Paul Faure, general secretary who ran the party in alliance with Blum, is usually seen as typical of this Southern Guesdism.[20]

Until 1935 this new left functioned as a national fraction, with its intellectual and political leadership mainly Parisian. Although it published a broadsheet under the title which gave it its name, it was not much more organised than its pre-1914 equivalents. This would change as of 1935, however, with the creation of Pivert's Gauche révolutionnaire (GR).

Although springing from the same neo-Guesdist matrix as Bataille socialiste the GR would split from it and its leader Zyromski over crucial questions of foreign policy and defence. International relations would thus combine with pressure already existing in the domestic political system to drive a further fractional wedge through the party's left. Zyromski's increasing concern about fascism since the Nazi seizure of power in 1933 led him to enthusiastic support for the Popular Front over and above his normal desire for rapprochement with the PCF. His hope was that the Front would strengthen the recent Franco-Soviet defensive alliance and thus counter the spread of fascism. Bataille socialiste was ready for actual military intervention in Spain on the Republican side for similar reasons. The Pivertists had inherited their leader's horror of war and believed it to be a capitalist device, unjustifiable to socialists in any circumstances. The working classes should head off the threat of war and fascism by making the revolution first (this ignored the fact that in Germany and Italy the class was by now hardly in a state to do so). Hence the fraction opposed Blum's increased defence spending and supported his refusal to intervene in Spain. Clearly there was a real policy issue here which split the 'new left' asunder.

The fraction would gain increased autonomy, with its own structures of authority, parallel to those of the official party, its own press and subscriptions and even its own self-defence force, modelled on the unfortunate precedents of German and Austrian social-democracy.[21] Its impatience with Blum's 1937 'pause' in the reform programme led to increasing criticism of the government and Pivert's eventual resignation as government spokesman. Increasingly it would show all the symptoms of a party within the party, and in due course Faure would trap it into an illegal act (refusing to accept the dissolution of its power base, the Seine federation) and have it expelled from the party at the Royan congress of 1938. The Pivertists set up a short-lived party, the PSOP, which would proclaim itself trotskyite; the Zyromski faction stayed happily in SFIO.

If the thirties thus showed the growth of an increasingly organised left fractionalism (at their peak the new lefts controlled thirty-nine out of ninety federations and were the biggest single fraction in sixteen more), then the right of the party was not exempt from fissiparity, as the néo split of 1933 showed. Most néos were deputies with local power bases, often in the old Radical South. Enjoying an often clientelistic relationship with a basically moderate electorate, they tended naturally to favour alliance with Radicalism or even governmental participation.[22] It was SFIO reluctance to join such a government after the elections of 1932 that drove them out.

Their position was also complicated by institutional factors, mainly the relationship between the deputies who had to work on a day-to-day basis and the party committees, namely the Conseil national (CN) and CAP. Not only did these meet too infrequently to be able to advise the deputies, not only were they overweighted with Parisians who knew little of the political realities of say, the Mediterranean littoral, but the party itself constantly vacillated as to which of them should do what.[23] All this made for growing exasperation.

Another key factor was that of generations. Most of the leading néos were youngish men such as Déat and Marquet. These had not been socialised into the anti-ministerial culture of the old Guesdism to the same extent. This is probably much more important than a feature which has been more stressed, namely the attraction towards fascism professed by some néos. Blum made much of this when he criticised Marquet's slogan 'order, authority, nation'. This is not to deny that some were potential proto-fascists (Déat and Marquet did finish as Vichy ministers) but it is hard to believe this of men like Renaudel, who basically was a reformist and wanted to be in the place where reforms are set in motion, government. It is hard too to imagine that the regular voters in favour of participationist motions at congress were fascists (just as it is to claim that the majority of Pivertists were secret trotskyites). The fascist elements in the néo split came to fill a vacuum of frustration caused by the contradictory situation into which the party's Guesdist ideology and antiquated institutions had placed this group of deputies.[24]

These two fractionalisms of very different kinds tell us much about how SFIO worked. On the one hand was a deputy-centred revolt, with support on a personal or clientelistic basis but without much organisational infrastructure, created out of an institutional inadequacy itself dependent on an ideological view of politics (hatred of ministerialism and mistrust of representatives). On the other hand was a left mass movement, of increasingly sophisticated structure which was more of an ideological community; it could inspire the kind of commitment we expect towards a party in its own right, as the Pivertist split on a key matter of principle illustrated.

In their different ways both show the importance of the party system for fractionalism. For ever since the PCF pushed SFIO more into the centre of the system, its line on participation was bound to be tested more and more. This led to the néo split but it also marked the beginnings of a new, progressively more organised left. A second pressure from the international system then sent shock waves through this left, dividing it over the issue of war and hardening the Pivert group in its attitudes and organisation. A third factor created the conditions for marginalisation of the Pivertists, and this was actual participation in government. Now battles were not just about ideas at congress but they had real consequences in terms of policy outcomes. It was fundamentally because they could not stomach these that the far left quit. The prewar decade then provided some real lessons about how the party was affected by domestic and international contradictions. But there was little time to ponder them and in particular the key question they raised: was it not time to grasp the nettle of the permanent contradiction between the Guesdist revolutionary language and a practice which if Blum's stewardship was a guide, seemed honestly reformist? The outbreak of war suspended the question, but it remained entire at the Liberation.

SFIO's situation in the Fourth Republic was fundamentally different from before the war in one key respect. Far from being in permanent opposition it was, to use Harold Wilson's phrase, more a 'natural party of government'. It served with christian democrats (MRP) and PCF in the tripartite governments till 1947, then as the Cold War forced the PCF into opposition and Gaullism arose on the right of the political spectrum, the party found itself pinioned by the force of political gravity into a series of 'third force' governments. Opposed to communism and Gaullism alike, these strove mainly to preserve an increasingly fragile parliamentary democracy.[25] In 1956 Guy Mollet headed a centre–left government when the non-communist left emerged as the biggest grouping from the January elections. Despite its reforming zeal, pressure from its partners and its own inclinations led it into devoting its major efforts to fighting the Algerian nationalist movement FLN, which had begun its struggle for independence in 1954. Repressive policies in Algeria and France were accentuated and Mollet took France into the abortive Suez campaign late in 1956 alongside Britain. It is during this period, that of 'national-Molletism' as Werth called it, that the weakening of government authority and delegation of decision-making power to the military and their settler allies became more marked. These would of course culminate in the Algiers rebellion of May 1958 which saw the demise of the Republic. A hapless Mollet could do no more than welcome the incoming de Gaulle and serve in his government. The postwar years were then particularly traumatic for SFIO and we may expect the party to have shown considerable fractional strains.

The major stress occurred early in this period, in fact, and this is the clash at the 1946 congress when Mollet ousted Daniel Mayer as general secretary. This is usually presented as a clash between traditional Guesdists and modernisers.[26] But this is only half the picture.

In the party which arose again out of the Resistance, Blum and Mayer were determined to renew and modernise, principally by coopting various unattached leftish groups from the Resistance. A prime target was the UDSR (Union democrate et socialiste de la Resistance) which included such as Mitterrand and Pleven (later a Gaullist minister); they were close to influential intellectuals such as Camus and Aron. The hope was to enrol these, and the increasing number of socially-committed catholics beginning to appear, into a new reformist left party. The price to pay for this would have been, of course, revision of some of the fundamentals of Guesdist doctrine; SFIO needed to align its discourse with its praxis and present itself as a reforming socialist party. This did not happen and many historians lament this 'lost Labour party', as it were. The reasons for the failure are significant.[27]

The 1946 congress voted down Mayer's *rapport moral* (i.e. gave him a vote of no confidence) on Mollet's instigation. Mollet criticised the party's being in government (its deflationary policies were hitting working-class voters). Ideologically, he suggested that Blum and Mayer were lukewarm on secularism and on working-class unity (talks were going on with the PCF about a merger, though as Portelli says, many SFIO leaders had never thought through the consequences of this).[28] Finally Mollet criticised party organisation, picking up a long-standing battle over the rules and procedure. Mayer had wanted to give the new executive organ, the *comité directeur* (CD), more authority, but had been forced to agree to the re-emergence of the inefficient old CN, so as to supervise the work of the deputies. He had also been forced to include in the preamble to the statutes a reference to 'a party of class-struggle' (Blum wanted the milder 'class-action') and to the eventual goal of a 'communist or collectivist society'.

Most of this conceals more than it says, for Mollet was speaking in a code decipherable only by party initiates. The workerist and secularist critiques were an appeal to the old Guesdist certainties, as was the hatred of 'ministerialism'.[29] The wrangling about the party's self-description also fits this description, as does the mistrust of elected representatives. The bases of Mollet's appeal were thus highly ideological; he was talking in his coded language to the deep reflexes of an ideological community of activists nourished on three or four generations of such certainties.

But there was another dimension too. Mollet was concerned for the party as an organisation. Ideological dilution would weaken this by demoralising those who kept it moving, *les militants*. The proof of this is that once Mollet had been appointed secretary general, he actually allowed his motion to be synthesised (see below) with that of Mayer and gave Mayer supporters a generous minority of places on the CD. Mollet would henceforth govern SFIO with a majority based on his own Pas-de-Calais federation, in alliance with one or other of the 'big two' (Nord and Bouches-du-Rhône) and often including those who had opposed him in 1946. In government, of course, he carried out many of the reformist policies which he had condemned in 1946. This suggests that the fractional rebellion of 1946 had not just ideological aims but instrumental ones; namely, securing control of the party machinery. The main aim was to preserve this; as to the use one might make of it, that could be left to the future. In other words the Molletism of 1946 was not a left fraction imbued with a long-term project of the type postulated above. It was much more limited.

Analysis of its organisation confirms its limited nature. Graham has shown how the anti-Mayer votes were put together on very different bases.[30] Embattled Western federations disapproved of the national alliance with MRP, their strongest local rival; Northern federations and Bouches-du-Rhône hated participation in coalition government with the PCF, because their local system of power depended heavily on anti-communism. Another factor which linked the rebels appears to have been Mayer's rigidity and lack of the skills of political communication. In other words, it was very much an *ad hoc* alliance which Mollet cobbled together and as Graham says, the trick was to 'express it in terms of the traditional Guesdist language'.[31]

It is probably even a misnomer to call this Molletism, for the motion was the product of a Parisian intellectual group. Even these were fairly heteroclite, ranging from orthodox Guesdists such as Bracke, Rimbert and Commin (like Mollet a prewar member of Bataille socialiste) to trotskyite sympathisers like Dechezelles or Rous (who would turn up ephemerally in Ceres after 1970). Compared to the prewar *tendances*, this was a relatively unstructured group. Little remained of the prewar hard left, and its two charismatic leaders were out of contention, Pivert still being under expulsion and Zyromski having joined the PCF through the Resistance. It seems possible that the Parisians used Mollet as a front man for their attack on the modernisers precisely with the aim of avoiding accusations of reviving prewar *tendances*. Certainly Quilliot highlights the difficulty which Mollet had in finding a team of reliable full-time officials to run the party.[32] All of this shows the lack of cohesion and hence the improvised nature of the fraction.

Mollet did in time gain undisputed control of the party and symbolised continuity with its Guesdist past. But SFIO never had a massive or sophisticated bureaucracy, and his control depended very much on management or brokerage skills and tactical alliances with big federal bosses. As the party's government record came to resemble increasingly a much poorer version of the policies it had decried in 1946, and as in foreign and colonial affairs it came under pressure to make increasingly controversial choices, the possibility of new left fractional opposition grew stronger. In due course a policy-based internal opposition grew up, centring on foreign affairs. Its origins date from around 1954 when half the deputies defied the party whip over the EDC as their views on German rearmament diverged sharply from the Atlanticist orthodoxy of the leadership. It tended to be the same people who two years later opposed Mollet's Algerian policy and eventual surrender to de Gaulle; by 1958, under Édouard Depreux's leadership, they were publishing their own paper, *Tribune du socialisme*. But this was a short-lived fraction for at the 1958 congress they would walk out and form one of the groups that would soon become part of the new PSU.[33]

The only other significant fractional split of this period was the classic case of entrism into the youth wing, Jeunesses socialistes. By 1947 it was alleged that this had been taken over by trotskyites and that the leadership of this well-supported and quite well-funded movement was being manipulated by Yvan Craipeau.[34] It was accused of fomenting strikes at Renault. The CD broke this operation in traditional manner, expelling the youth leaders, suspending youth voting rights in

the federations and placing the movement under close CD sur-
veillance. The JS collapsed as a result, cutting the party off from some
sources of new blood. But the affair was soon over and remained a
parenthesis in the party's life. External, entrist fractions are qualitatively
different from innate ones.

We may now sketch an overall picture of fractional life in the
postwar years. The major characteristic is surely the durable absence of
a serious left fraction, for we have seen that the Mollet group was ill-
structured and limited in its aims, wishing only to return to prewar
orthodoxy and succeeding. When a left began to emerge on foreign
policy issues it came late in the day and in any case led less to a
fractional battle than to an outright split. Yet given the inevitable
shortcomings of party performance in government, especially when
measured against the maximalist ideology which Mollet had successfully preserved, the space for a left opposition was always gaping wide.
Why was it not filled more quickly?

There are a number of possible explanations. One is institutional,
and rests on the fact that the party rules meant that the CD places were
allotted not by straight proportional representation but by a system of
weighted majority, which tended to favour big alliances (i.e. usually
those already entrenched) against the small and less organised. But this
is an obstacle of degree rather than kind, and a resolute left could have
got round it by tighter organisation. The same argument holds against
another explanation, which would privilege Mollet's bureaucratic
skills. The claim that prewar *tendances* had brought havoc in the party
and that the memory of this was enough to discourage fractionalists
might also be taken seriously. Unfortunately, left fractionalists are
seldom receptive to such arguments, and indeed tend to argue that
problems arose because their predecessors did not go far enough. If
we are to seek explanations, then, we might look more profitably at
the party system.

SFIO was a natural party of government, held uncomfortably into
place amid its third force partners by domestic pressures (the Gaullist
threat) and international ones (the Cold War and its effect on the PCF).
It was almost condemned to office. And it was probably this fact which
led militants after 1947 to the conviction that in this situation there was
little point in organising to push for radical alternatives. If the main
policy choices came down to defence of parliament and militant

FIGURE 2.1   STRESS-LINES OF FRACTIONALISM IN SFIO

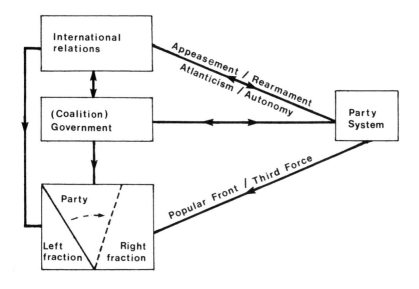

secularism at home and alignment, however reluctant, on the USA abroad, then there was not a lot left to argue about. Or at least arguments were fated to be more of degree than of kind. It was not a question of implementing revolution, but of how much the party might extract from its coalition partners. It was not a question of whether SFIO should take France into military alliances or not, but rather, what sort of alliance and with whom? Historical reality pinioned the party into the political system and in so doing it constricted its freedom for internal argument. It is significant that in the one area where France did have some relative autonomy from the two-bloc system, namely imperial and colonial affairs, the roots of an eventual split were to be found.

We would conclude this period by saying that SFIO's sustained experience of office after 1944 inserted it forcibly into a domestic and international political system which constricted its freedom of movement and largely immobilised its inner life. The result was an atrophy which threatened to accelerate and become terminal as the party began a steep plunge into a long period of opposition after 1958.

We may now in fact attempt an overall summary of the fractional patterns of SFIO over half a century. It is clear that the fraction is the norm rather than the exception, although the organisational density thereof does vary. Fractional behaviour was endemic from the start, in that the young SFIO was an amalgam of previous groups; but we can see that it is maintained by a combination of pressures at different times. Figure 2.1 attempts to summarise this process. The key stress factors are these: international tension, governmental responsibility, and the general configuration of the party system and the party's place within it. Each of these elements clearly affects any other. We might say that when all three variables are at their most conflictual then fractionalism should be at its highest, particularly left fractionalism. Thus in 1936 the party faced a hard task in government (fighting the recession) and an even harder one abroad (facing up to fascism without getting involved in work); at the same time its place in the party system was most uncomfortable, squeezed between a doubtful ally, Radicalism, and a PCF which had really begun to emerge as a serious rival. These two poles had countervailing attractions for different wings of the party. This concatenation of pressures split the party badly, with a left hardening as its disappointment with govern-ment action in all areas increased and eventually splitting itself. In the Fourth Republic the process is slightly more oblique. If international tensions are arguably as great as in 1936, the party system has a different logic, with the PCF disqualified as a result of its Cold War stance and the rise of an anti-Republican Gaullism pinning SFIO into the third force. International pressures are thus countermanded to some extent by domestic, and fractionalism held in abeyance. But eventually international pressure of a different sort (colonial not East–West) provides the momentum to release a fractional split.

At the onset of the Fifth Republic, then, the party was heir to a distinct historical pattern of which it was aware and which by now might be said to be part of its culture. During the Fifth Republic it would of course amalgamate with a series of other variegated groups into the new PS. With such a heredity added to such new diversity we could expect a priori that the new party would be as prone to fractions as its ancestor.

2.3   THE NEW PARTY AND ITS STRUCTURES

The first decade of the Fifth Republic saw a rallying of the non-communist left, but much of the impetus did not come from SFIO. Gaullist consolidation of the new institutions, reinforced by growing economic success and foreign policy initiatives that promised more autonomy, made it increasingly clear that the new legitimacy could only be challenged by an equally strong and united opposition. The left took time to see the bipolar logic which the new system entailed.[35] Defferre's abortive centre–left coalition was too narrowly based to hope for success, and it took Mitterrand's presidential campaign of 1965, when as candidate of the united left he took 45 per cent in the run-off ballot, for full realisation to sink home. Mitterrand would henceforth make the running in terms of left unity, heading the FGDS centre–left alliance in 1966–8. Short-lived as it was, its performance in the 1967 elections and its close dialogue with the PCF helped considerably to boost the idea that left unity was feasible. Other elements of the left were active too. The PSU incorporated many, particularly of the modernising, post-marxist variety; soon Rocard would come to typify these. The clubs movement, often run by senior technocrats with a problem-solving approach, mistrustful of traditional left ideology, also provided ideas and activists.[36] Dissident communists like Poperen and his group, and reform-minded catholics, saddened by the decline into impotent conservatism of the MRP (or its remains), were also in evidence. By 1971 these disparate elements would mostly have fused into the new PS, in a process described far too often to justify further repetition.[37] But what of SFIO during these years so vital to the rebuilding of the left?

In many ways it seemed to be dragged along by events. Membership shrank and little attempt was made to renew doctrine or strategy. It is true that Mollet was forced by the new electoral system for parliament into negotiating as from 1962 a number of désistements with the PCF (the best-placed candidate of right or left is given a free run on the second ballot by the withdrawal of those politically nearest him). He also began an inconclusive 'ideological dialogue' with the PCF. The party even held seminars where some new left themes (e.g. the changing nature of the working class) were aired. But none of this went far and the party's image remained much as Mandrin described it in 1969 – an old, tired machine kept alive largely by its notables. In this context it makes little sense to speak of organised fractionalism, save for the one serious attempt at renewal which was Ceres; and even Ceres thought in terms of the whole of the left and not just the PS.

Under pressure to widen its appeal, the party was beginning to water down some of the old Guesdist ideology. The preamble to the 1969 rules was thus as stern as ever on secularism, but elsewhere some modifications could be seen, when compared with the 1946 version.[38] If abolition of class was still a goal, then it was no longer evidence that classes were 'necessarily antagonist'. The 'essentially revolutionary' nature of the party now came at the end of a paragraph, not the beginning; and the meaning of this term was considerably qualified. Whereas socialism might be brought about 'by any means' in the past, by a 'party of class struggle', it was now to come strictly through parliamentary democracy. 'Collective ownership' now gave way to multiple forms of property, and in particular the rights of small individual owners were upheld. And the new rules had in general much more to say about non-economic forms of alienation (cultural and ideological) and the need to fight these.

In short when the 1971 Épinay congress drew together most of the strands of the non-communist left into the new PS, SFIO had begun to modernise its discourse if not its machinery. From 1971 it would of course be one element, possibly the most important, in a party whose unity would be quite fragile; indeed there is a case for regarding the new party not as an organic unity but as a series of fractions roped together by institutional, mainly electoral, constraints. The clash of these fractions will be seen at various points below, but let us now consider the new structures adopted in 1971 and then identify the constituent fractions more precisely.

The very structure of the new party invited fractionalism. When, largely on the insistence of Ceres, the party went back to the original straight proportional representation system for designating its leadership bodies, it was in effect condoning fractionalism. Article 5 states that PR with the highest average is used for the elections of party organs at every level.[39] Only general policy motions (i.e. overall political projects submitted to congress) confer the right to be represented. Less ambitious projects (amendments or 'contributions', which fractions used to try to submit so as to avoid being counted) do not count

FIGURE 2.2 THE PS HIERARCHY

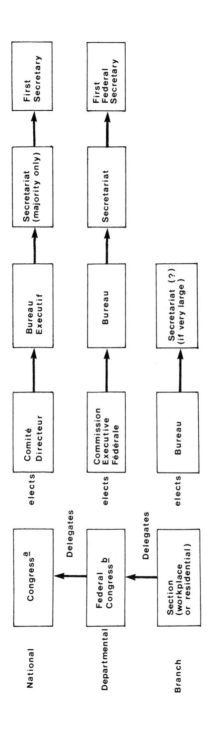

a Also elects national committees of control and of conflict settlement
b Also elects federal committees of control and of conflict settlement

for elections to party bodies. The system works as follows (see Figure 2.2). At branch (*section*) level, as congress approaches, members vote on nationally circulated motions, which are signed by those leading figures who will get the share of places on the leadership bodies proportional to the success of their motion (provided it beats a five per cent exclusion hurdle). These votes are counted up at the congress of the fédération (the departmental or county level) and it is on the basis of this *vote indicatif*, as it is called, that places are allotted on the federal equivalent of the national CD, the commission exécutive fédérale (CEF), and on its smaller bureau which meets more frequently than the (usually monthly) CEF. Places on the secrétariat, drawn from within the bureau, are not shared out proportionately but reserved for signatories of the majority motion (and its allies, if a deal is done nationally – see below). This body meets most frequently and all its members cover a particular area of responsibility. The secretariat is thus the main source of policy initiation and leadership in the fédé, as activists like to call it; the first secretary is party leader in his department and perceived as such by the public.[40]

Federal congresses send their delegates (mandated in favour of motions) to national congress (every two years) where the above scenario applies, with one exception. This is the famous resolutions committee. At congress, *votes indicatifs* are duly recorded, and seats on the national CD and BE allotted to fractions accordingly; but the resolutions committee may try to go one better and produce la synthèse. This body of fifty or sixty people brings together all main signatories of motions (i.e. fractional élites), usually in the small hours so as to lend a sense of drama. If they agree on a joint text (la synthèse) after bargaining, this will be presented to congress and usually voted unanimously. In that case posts on the secretariat are also shared out (proportionately to the *vote indicatif* again) among supporters of all motions included in the synthesis. If some fractional élites do not agree, then their motion goes back to congress on the last day and gets roughly the same amount of votes as before; but they do not join the secretariat and keep only their places on the CD and BE. Here they form a sort of official opposition to the supporters of the majority motion(s), being by definition at odds with some elements of majority views.

There is thus a structural incitement to form fractions around a motion. Fractions may be bidding for the support of a majority of the party or just staking out a more modest claim for influence; either way they have a powerful incentive to get organised, so as to secure as high a representation as possible.

Obviously all PS leaders were aware of the danger of reviving the *esprit des tendances*. We shall deal below with their attempts to regulate the problem by statutory means, but let us first obtain an overall view of how fractions function in practice.

By the mid-seventies there was observable a pattern which prevailed until 1981. After this, fractional conflict became muted in the glow of victory and the need to support the government. Fractional stresses still showed through, however, as the 1983 Bourg congress showed; and in our view the phenomenon is unlikely to disappear for a very long time.

Several major groups existed with a national structure. By this is meant that they had a Paris headquarters (usually with premises of their own), in which could be found their leaders (usually substantial figures holding national office in both party and country). These wrote the motions and represented the fraction in the public eye, and they and their helpers would sit for it on the CD, like a series of shadow cabinets, as it were. Each group had an internal communications network, parallel to the official party one. Its outer shell would be a press outlet, with the best-organised having a theoretical review and some kind of internal broadsheet too. The less visible part would be the links from provincial grass roots to Paris which ran through that crucial level of French politics, *la fédé*. A serious fraction would have half a dozen people in each department, in frequent touch with their Paris HQ (they would often be local or even national office holders). These intermediary élites sat of course on the CEF where monthly they would link with branch delegates, transmitting recommendations from above and vibrations from below. Thus if a fraction had several hundred committeed workers it would cover the territory effectively and pull out a vote at congress time.

At branch level the increasing trend was for one fraction to predominate, often causing rivals to move elsewhere. In some huge urban branches this is less so (some are permanently split three ways or more) but our research found it to be increasingly so in smaller ones. Control of the branch is of course vital as it is a key locus of, *inter alia*, candidate selection. This tended to mean that newcomers to the

PS were increasingly socialised not so much into general party ideology, so far as it exists, but into the version of the locally hegemonic fraction. Fractions were better able to do this because they were making increasing efforts to organise their own seminars, teach-ins, handbooks and so on. There was no shortage of material for this, as their Parisian leaders had recruited groups of expert advisers from civil service, university and private sector who, meeting in committees parallel to party ones, could provide policy options, polemical material or such intellectual artefacts as were required.

Before CEF meetings fractions would meet in advance to prepare tactics, and indeed even did so at branch level where control was not assured. One of our most vivid memories is of a CEF in an Eastern department, where a particularly ticklish emergency resolution was presented (this was just before Mitterrand declared his wish to be presidential candidate). The fractions and the chairman were equally taken aback and a suspension of the meeting for 15 minutes was quickly agreed. Without more ado the five fractions (for this was a resolutely pluralist department) broke up as best they could into the four corners of the room to discuss tactics.

This is of course a generalised picture. Not every fraction in every federation is as structured as we have suggested. None the less this pattern was widespread and more crucially was admitted by nearly everyone to be so, even if they deplored it and invariably blamed it on the doings of rival fractions. In the PS fractionalism had become a way of life.

2.4   THE PS AND ITS FRACTIONS TODAY

Table 2.1 shows the movement of fractional opinion through PS congresses since 1971. Not every motion represents a fraction in the full sense; short-term ploys and tactical considerations account for some motions, not to mention the numerous ones which failed at the five per cent hurdle. Beneath the shifting patterns most analysts find four durable fractions in the modern PS. To that extent the 1979 Metz congress woul be the best X-ray of the party's anatomy, with sympathy dividing between Mauroyists, Rocardians, Mitterrandists and Ceres. Compared with Épinay there have been changes, and we should note

TABLE 2.1   FRACTIONAL STRENGTHS IN PS, 1971–83 (%)

Congress of:	Mitterrand	Mollet	Poperen	Mauroy/ Defferre	Ceres	Rocard
Épinay 1971	16	33	12	28	8.5	–
Grenoble 1973	65	8	5.5	a	21	–
Pau 1975	68	3.3	a	a	25.5	a
Nantes 1977	75.8	Defunct	a	a	24.2	a
Metz 1979	40.1	–	a	13.6 + 7.9	14.3 (+3.4 for F)	20.4
Bourg 1983	77.8	–	a	a	18.2	a (5% for dissidents)

a – allied with Mitterrand in advance
Synthèses were as follows:
1971   Mitterrand + Mauroy/Defferre + Ceres   vs. Mollet + Poperen
1973   Mitterand + Poperen + Ceres   vs. Mollet
1975   Mitterrand + all others   vs. Ceres
1977   as 1975
1979   Mitterrand + Defferre (+ Ceres later)   vs. Mauroy + Rocard
1981   Unanimous motion
1983   Complete synthèse – no internal opposition

in particular the demise of Molletism, majority fraction of the old SFIO, as an autonomous force. Since 1973 its supporters have gone mainly to Mitterrand or, less frequently, to Mauroy. Poperenism also seems to have disappeared, the group having officially joined Mitterrand in 1973. But in fact it still leads a subterranean life with its own structures inside Mitterrandism; this is a new departure in fractional style and we will return to it shortly. The Defferrism of 1971 and since was, and is, a regional phenomenon, representing a Mediterranean politics typical of Bouches-du-Rhône;[41] it never had national ambitions and always sought alliances with Mollet or the Nord federation. When it put up its own motion to congress, this usually meant that there was some difficulty within the federation as to which national line to follow. This tension was defused by the device of a local motion, and then a deal would be struck as appropriate with one of the national motions at congress. With these subfractions out of the way we may concentrate on the major ones, which we shall now characterise in terms of origins and structures. Ideological differences as such are dealt with in Chapter 3.

For Roucaute, the big four fractions are contemporary manifestations of deep-lying historical trends in French socialism.[42] Rather like Rose's 'tendencies' these principles and strategies, of which the fractions are the 'bearers' (to put it in Althusserese), turn up from one generation to the next. Thus Mitterrandism continues Jaurèsism; Mauroy updates Brousse,[43] and with him most of the early utopian socialists. Ceres is heir to Zyromski and beyond him to the 'Two-and-a-Half' International of the early twenties, whose supporters strove to preserve links between the old Second International and the emergent Comintern. Poperen is said to descend, somewhat incredibly, from Pivert.[44] Rocard proves harder to place and is assigned to the category called by Roucaute 'proudhonian possibilists'.[45] For all its ingenuity in tracing historical threads, this approach is of limited use. First its categories are much too sharp and tidy, and they typify that excessively cartesian respect for categorising which afflicts many other French institutions besides the PS. What evidence proves that the Nord socialists were closer to Brousse than to Guesde, for example, given that they regularly voted Guesdist motions? How valid is the extrapolation from the peculiar domestic and international circumstances of the thirties which threw up Pivertism to the thawing of the Cold War and the incipient crisis of the PCF (not even the same party!) which produced Poperen? One could list similar objections,[46] but it would be simpler to admit that the variable which has most immediate interest for explaining fractional origins is not so much historical as organisational.

Recalling the origins of the 1971 PS, we see that all four main groups had considerable autonomy of organisation to begin with. Mitterrand had his CIR (Convention des institutions républicaines) born partly out of the clubs movement and continuing in any case his UDSR rump-party. Mauroy was widely seen as Mollet's heir to SFIO or at least to the powerful SFIO regional strengths in local government. The Poperen-ites had after a bruising passage through the PSU formed their own mini-party UGCS before joining the new PS in 1969 at Issy. Rocard was a fraction leader in the PSU and in any case came from the old SFIO anti-colonialist split. Ceres was the exception, having been always part of SFIO, but even then its cohesion, aims and sense of purpose were such as to give it a special distinct identity. All these groups then entered the new party hoping to shape it more or less according to their design.

After a decade of struggle the fractions had achieved different degrees of identity and salience. The most distinct has always been Ceres, whose ideology is more total and whose structures are more sophisticated than its rivals. Even when in the party majority it has worked to keep up its separate image. Rocardism proposes a similarly articulate ideology, but perhaps a less thorough organisation. As these two have made the running in fractional battles, this 'left/right' polarity is appropriate. Between the poles, their rivals occupy less prominent terrain.[47] As Mitterrand inherited the leadership of the new party and its apparatus, and as he always retained it, there was less pressure on his people to build up a distinct organisation or even ideology. The national prestige of the leader, emerging as leader of the opposition in a two-bloc France, was heralded by steady electoral success, local and national; many federal élites were happy to follow the leader, doing no harm to their own careers. Many new members would join on the same basis. This perhaps accounts for the uneven nature of the fraction, which in fact has several 'geological layers'. On top of the CIR core, which Roucaute rightly sees as coming from the Radical tradition, has been grafted a rather economistic marxism, defended by such as Joxe and Mermaz. Further additions include much of the Molletist–Guesdist SFIO, north and south of the Loire, and most crucially many of the new members who flowed in from 1972, often without much of a political past. Also coopted was Poperenism, which provided some of the basic ideology for the party, especially the notion of a 'class-front' (see Chapter 3). Its transformation to a semi-existence is odd. Claiming in 1973 that the PS had been transformed into a sufficiently socialist vehicle as to reduce the need for its own separate existence, the group none the less continued with its own publications, command structure and federal élites, who provide an unofficial but recognised leadership in several federations. It is as if the leadership was not certain about how socialist the party really is; the troops could thus be put in civilian uniform, but not demobilised. This clandestine existence is a curious form of existence for fractions (though not of course for foreign, entrist ones, which are something quite different); certainly it adds to the variegated nature of Mitterrandism.

Mauroyism has a loose structure, only equipping itself with a review and a structure with delegate meetings etc., in 1979; its salience depends much on the activity and alliances of its leader. Thus from 1971–9 when Mauroy was No. 2 in the PS, it cohabited happily with the rest of the Mitterrand constellation. This was also true of 1981–4 when Mauroy served as prime minister. But his departure from office and probable presidential ambitions mean that the fraction can expect to be revived from its slumbers. It is best to consider it a largely regional phenomenon, or as the survival of Guesdist local government strength in the North and those parts of the Midi where municipal socialism took root early. Certainly its national leadership of mainly big-town mayors reflects this feature.[48]

For Roucaute the fractions represent 'popular points of view about society'.[49] This may be true at the level of ideology, but he also hints, without being explicit, that the fractions somehow represent different social groups. He thus takes delight in pointing out the high represent-ation of the professions among Mitterrandists or of teachers among Poperenites. Rocardians are ritually accused of being the PS Trojan horse for the salaried middle classes. Our own findings in Chapter 4 will, we hope, shed some light on this, but we might say now that the social origins of fraction members seem of secondary importance to us. Certainly it seems hard to read off from membership of a social class or subgroup thereof an attachment to certain fractional points of view rather than others. The fractions pre-existed the new PS, and the reasons for their existence are diverse. But they are all basically groups which made different strategic responses to the question: by what means can one help the left to win office without joining the PCF? Roucaute's ideological traditions may have some bearing on the answer, but so do institutional structures. The fractions are all products of different strategies devised at different times for manoeuvring in the space between revolution and the status quo, or if one prefers, between the PCF and the right. They are held together in one party by an electoral system which dictates that more than ever, unity is strength. This is why they have finally banded together after years of separate struggle. Even the presidential functions of fraction are subordinate to this. If it is vital to capture a party as a vehicle for a presidential bid, then the capture of the PS is doubly vital because of its position near the centre of the political system as a potential rallying point. We may say then that the fundamental determinant of the fractionalism of the PS is probably the institutional one.

It needs to be seen in conjunction with another factor, however; namely, ideology. This acts as a kind of cement, holding the fraction together while at the same time making it impermeable to outsiders. We do not mean by this that fraction members need to possess fully the often complex variants of mainstream ideology which the fractions develop (this is only the case for their élites). What they will usually possess is awareness of some of the main planks of their particular ideology and a feeling of how the others are different. We should remember that ideology is not necessarily a set of crystal-clear principles, but often a much more diffuse matrix of belief which may affect its subscribers in ways which they or others might not suspect. Thus to say that Mitterrandism 'has no clear ideological focus'[50] does not mean that it has no ideology but simply that its somewhat diffuse one needs to be unearthed more carefully. We shall attempt here a cursory sketch of the main fractional ideologies, though this is developed more fully in the next chapter.

As the Rocard/Ceres battle is followed up in detail later, we shall keep our remarks to the minimum on these groups. Most Ceres supporters see themselves as on the left of the party, if not as actual revolutionaries; they see themselves as most attached to left unity and most active within the party. They believe that they stand for a more demanding but more complete type of socialism than the rest. Rocardians see themselves as more modern, beyond the 'archaic' mentality of an old left predicated on class-struggle. They see real social change as coming not from party or government but more from the efforts of a wide range of groups within civil society. They probably see themselves as more moderate and less sectarian than others.

Mauroyists affect a down-to-earth style, reflecting their belief that socialism is best served by getting results on the ground, rather than theorising. They are proud of their considerable success in local government therefore. Pro-European and admiring the welfare-state mixed economies of Northern, social-democratic Europe, they are very anti-communist and also very much attached to the party as a way of life – a reflection of the Guesdist past of the Northern region. Although close to Rocard on many issues, it is perhaps this sense of party plus their less intellectual approach which gives them a somewhat separate identity, albeit one less easy to theorise than that of Ceres or Rocard.

Mitterrandism is the hardest to pin down. Parts of it are extremely ideological, for example Poperenism.[51] This espouses a somewhat reductionist marxism (the Poperenites were the main popularisers of the notion that France was 'sociologically on the left', simply because a majority of the workforce were wage-earners!). It defines itself as marxist (suggesting that the rest of the PS is not?), and has always sought left unity; yet its desire for this is equalled only by its fear and suspicion of the PCF (and the USSR). It insists tirelessly that politics is about class first and foremost, and devotes boundless energy to hounding 'modernisers' and 'technocrats' from the new left who think differently. Much of this is done in a moralising and rather leaden-footed style which is one of the group's most recognisable features. The so-called Mitterrandist left (Joxe, Laignel, etc.) is in many ways similar except that it adds a dash of very militant secularism. Mitterrand himself is elusive; his stance comes basically from the Radical tradition (humanistic, strong on civic liberties, generously reformist on socio-economic matters in a very vague way, discreetly nationalistic and generally secularist – though not in his case overtly so). It is probably his management skills, plus the hope of influence and careers which he embodies as leader of the left, that have kept this heterogeneous group together so well over the years; it will be interesting to see what happens to it when he is gone. To some extent also the very sharpness of the 'left' and 'right' ideologies on either side of the main group mean that it is easier for it to define itself simply negatively in terms of these two; our own survey results in Chapter 4 suggest this.

Our hypothesis then is that members join not just the party but one of its fractions. These pre-existed the party and are nourished by a fifty-year tradition of fractional organisation in the party's predecessor. They are not just empty organisational shells but ideological communities, in the sense that they have a broad value-pattern with which the incomer can identify and which distinguishes them from rival groups. Membership of a fraction increases the sense of belonging, probably more so when conflict is high (usually the case outside election periods). This sense of belonging-through-struggle makes it appropriate in our view to see the fractions as to some extent communities complete in themselves. Yet they can only distance themselves from each other within certain limits, for each must work within the wider party. Up to now they have managed this balancing act successfully enough, for the PS has not known any major split. With this framework in mind we may now approach in more detail the left fraction Ceres, whose own ideology and organisation will form the subject of the next two chapters.

NOTES TO CHAPTER 2

1 H. Portelli, *Le Socialisme français tel qu'il est*, Paris, PUF, 1980, p. 9.

2 For useful overviews of the modern French socialist movement see G. Lefranc, *Le mouvement socialiste sous la Troisième République*, Paris, Payot, 1963; C. Willard, *Les Guesdistes*, Paris, Éditions sociales, 1963 and *Socialisme et communisme français*, Paris, Colin, 1969; J. Kergoat, *Le Parti socialiste*, Paris, Le Sycomore, 1983. On the labour movement more specifically see B. Moss, *The Origins of the French Labour Movement*, Los Angeles, California University Press, 1976; P. Stearns, *Revolutionary Syndicalism and French Labour*, New Brunswick (NJ), Rutgers University Press, 1971. J. Julliard, *Fernand Pelloutier*, Paris, Seuil, 1971; G. Lefranc, *Le mouvement syndical sous la Troisième République*, Paris, Payot, 1967.

3 A. Bergounioux speaks of a 'Latin model'. See 'Typologie des rapports syndicats-partis en Europe occidentale', *Pouvoirs* 26, 1983, pp. 17–30.

4 Hence Rebérioux's description of SFIO as a 'citizens' party'. See her 'Existe-t-il avant 1914 un socialisme français spécifique?' in ISER, *La Social-démocratie en questions*, Paris, Éditions de la Revue politique et parlementaire, 1980, pp. 35–43.

5 B. Graham, 'The play of tendencies: internal politics in SFIO' in D. Bell (ed.), *Contemporary French Political Parties*, London, Croom Helm, 1982, pp. 138–64.

6 A. Noland, *The Founding of the French Socialist Party*, Cambridge (Mass.), Harvard University Press, 1956. One of the best accounts of differences within the early party is J.-J. Fiechter, *Le Socialisme français: de l'affaire Dreyfus à la grande guerre*, Geneva, Droz, 1965.

7 Rebérioux, op. cit. Cf. also G. Ziebura, *Léon Blum et le parti socialiste 1871–1934*, Paris, Colin, 1968, p. 171.

8 Ibid., p. 178.

9 Ziebura (ibid., p. 188) cites the example of Marcel Déat whose federation tended to vote *en masse* and concludes that 'the whole organisational history of the PS ... is one long effort to reduce the weight of institutions and personalities ... to the advantage of social forces'. He is referring here to the interwar period, but his

remarks apply *a fortiori* to the pre-1914 era, on which some detailed federal studies are long overdue.

10   Kergoat, *Le PS*, pp. 40–67.

11   Ibid. and Y. Roucaute, *Le PS*, Paris, Huisman, 1983. Internal PS debates are also prone to use this framework.

12   See the famous 'two methods' debate between Guesde and Jaurès, reproduced in Fiechter, *Le socialisme français*, pp. 231–58.

13   P. Rimbert, 'Tu ne seras pas ministre: le XIe commandement de la SFIO', ISER, *La socialdémocratie*, pp. 29–34.

14   Fiechter, op. cit., pp. 152–5.

15   Ziebura, op. cit., p. 188.

16   Fiechter, op. cit., pp. 172–9.

17   T. Judt, *La reconstruction du parti socialiste 1921–6*, Paris, FNSP, 1976.

18   J.-N. Jeanneney, *Leçons d'histoire pour une gauche au pouvoir*, Paris, Seuil, 1977.

19   D. Baker, 'The politics of socialist protest in France: the left wing of the socialist party, 1921–39', *Journal of Modern History*, XLIII, March 1971, pp. 2–41.

20   N. Greene, *Crisis and Decline: the French socialist party in the Popular Front era*, New York, Cornell University Press, 1969, pp. 34–48.

21   J. Rabaut, *Tout est possible*, Paris, Denoel, 1974, pp. 178 ff. and cf. also J.-P. Rioux, *Révolutionnaires du Front populaire*, Paris, Bourgois, 1973.

22   On Southern socialism see J. Sagnes, *Le Midi rouge: mythe et réalité*, Paris, Anthropos, 1982.

23   Ziebura, op. cit., pp. 168–93.

24   On the néos see J. Marcus, *French socialism in the crisis years*, New York, Praeger, 1958 and Ziebura, op. cit., pp. 341–62.

25   B. Graham, *The French Socialists and Tripartism, 1944–7*, London, Weidenfeld and Nicolson, 1964.

26   B. Graham, 'The play of tendencies'; R. Quilliot, *La SFIO et l'exercice du pouvoir, 1944–58*, Paris, Fayard, 1972, pp. 170–84.

27   M. Sadoun, *Les Socialistes sous l'occupation*, Paris, FNSP, 1982, pp. 216–27.

28   Portelli, op. cit., p. 66.

29   Rimbert, op. cit.

30   B. Graham, 'The play of tendencies', pp. 152–3.

31   Ibid., p. 156.

32   Quilliot, op. cit., p. 83.

33   A key element of the split was the socialist student movement ES, most of which left over Algeria and whose leader at the time was Michel Rocard.

34   Kergoat, op. cit., pp. 79–80.

35   O. Duhamel, *La Gauche et la Cinquième République*, Paris, PUF, 1980.

36   J. Mossuz, *Les Clubs et la politique*, Paris, Colin, 1970. On the Mitterrandists see D. Loschak, *La Convention des institutions républicaines*, Paris, PUF, 1971.

37   C. Hurtig, *De la SFIO au nouveau parti socialiste*, Paris, Colin 1970; J. Poperen, *L'Unité de la Gauche, 1965–72*, Paris, Fayard, 1975; D. Bell and B. Criddle, *The French socialist party: resurgence and victory*, Oxford University Press, 1984; J. Kergoat, op. cit. For a Ceres view see P. Guidoni, *Le nouveau Parti socialiste*, Paris, Téma, 1973.

38   C. Hurtig, op. cit., p. 79 and p. 212.

39   Parti socialiste, *Statuts*, Paris, 1979, p. 13.

40   For clear presentations of PS structure see Bell and Criddle, *The French socialist party*, pp. 208–47; N. Nugent and D. Lowe, *The Left in France*, London, Macmillan,

1981, pp. 62–77 and T. Pfister, *Les Socialistes*, Paris, Albin Michel, 1977.

41 G. Rochu, *Marseille – les années Defferre*, Paris, Moreau, 1983; D. Bleitrach, J. Lojkine et al., *Classe ouvrière et social-démocratie: Lille et Marseille*, Paris, Editions Sociales, 1982, pp. 123–58.

42 Roucaute, op. cit., chapter I.

43 Leader of the *possibilistes*, who advocated an incrementalist and electoral approach to socialism, pivoting on the municipalisation of key industries and services. Cf. D. Stafford, *From Anarchism to Reformism*, London, Weidenfeld and Nicolson, 1971.

44 Roucaute, op. cit., p. 37.

45 Ibid., p. 97.

46 Kergoat is happy to call Mitterrandists, Rocardians and Mauroyists all Jaurèsians, whereas for him Joxists, Poperenites and Ceres are all Guesdists (op. cit., pp. 326–39).

47 Bell and Criddle (p. 218) find that only Ceres merits the (pejorative) term 'faction', because of its greater structuration – 'the most original intense, intellectual and best defined socialist party current' (p. 236). This qualitative distinction between Ceres and the rest must in practice depend on privileging visible organisational factors, for Rocardian ideology is as clear-cut (and arguably more original) than Ceres.

48 D. Hanley, 'Les députés socialistes', *Pouvoirs* 20, 1982, pp. 55–66.

49 Roucaute, op. cit., p. 43.

50 Bell and Criddle, op. cit., p. 223.

51 G. Pudlowski, *Jean Poperen et l'UGCS*, Paris, Éditions Saint Germain des Prés, 1975. For a trenchant restatement of Poperenism see *Le Monde* 19 April 1984 and J. Poperen, *Le nouveau Contrat social*, Paris, Ramsay, 1985.

CHAPTER 3

The Ideology of Ceres

Les national-léninistes du Ceres, dont le style vigoureux camouflait mal
l'archaïsme des mentalités.   F. Fejtö

C'est un homme du Ceres; il a la faiblesse de se laisser prendre aux mots.
                                                              R. Priouret

Il y a une grande distance entre la vérité et l'efficacité d'une idéologie, entre
ce qu'elle fait et ce qu'elle prétend faire.   J.-P. Chevènement, 1960

This chapter will examine the cornerstones of Ceres ideology as it
has emerged over twenty years. We take the concept in a very broad
sense: for us ideology is a series of principles, beliefs or attitudes
whereby a group perceives social reality. Interconnected as they are,
these shared principles enable group members to make sense of
political or social phenomena, and are likely to produce similar
reactions in group members. The principles thus seem to hold the
group together and justify its activity; in fact ideology is a crucial part of
group identity.[1]

The PS as a whole has always endorsed a broadly marxist ideology
which despite recent attenuation has been one of its most characteristic features. We have argued, however, that within this broad focus its
fractions have developed their own ideological structures which are
distinct and recongisable and which allow their subscribers to identify
and exclude. Such ideologies are mostly explicit, as is logical in a party
dominated by intellectuals. They are invariably unoriginal and much
work is devoted to proving this rather obvious fact. But this is missing
the point. The function of ideology is not to make theoretical

breakthroughs (at most it can adapt these after they have become common knowledge), but to provide identity and certainty; this means gathering the faithful and excluding the enemy or traitor. Thus successful ideology is highly operational and probably mostly fairly simple in its expression; to be overcomplicated is to risk sowing doubts.

Ceres ideological discourse when examined is shown to be just such an operational ideology, with characteristic themes sending out stimuli to their recipients. We will outline its elements as briefly as possible (far too much work in our view having gone into trying to distinguish the minutiae of the ideology and not enough into its operationality). This should enable us to set it against mainstream party ideology and show what is specifically 'left' about it.

One final point concerns the sources of Ceres ideology. Ceres ideology is an eclectic one. Its main borrowings are probably from the Gramscian type of marxism which produced Poulantzas and much Eurocommunist literature and from austro-marxism, which seems to have furnished it with some key concepts (the 'third way' between leninism and social-democracy, the importance of the national question and the links between mass movement and government). Detailed research into this question is of limited value, however, and it is pointless to accuse Didier Motchane of not being a second Gramsci. For the aim of Ceres was not to innovate in terms of theory so much as to provide a doctrinal base for action.

3.1 FROM THE REIGN OF THE MULTINATIONALS TO THE SOVEREIGNTY OF THE PRODUCERS: THE POLITICAL ECONOMY OF SELF-MANAGEMENT

The base of Ceres ideology is its analysis of contemporary capitalism and the necessary conditions for the movement towards socialism thus implied. Using concepts developed by the international communist movement and theorists such as Poulantzas, Ceres sees the capitalist system as having reached a new stage of imperialism.[2] At the centre of the 'imperial chain' stands the main centre of accumulation, the USA; the European states, EEC or not, are secondary imperialisms by contrast. Although they extract surplus value from the Third World, they are themselves exploited by US capital to a degree. The main instruments of such domination are the multinational companies (MNC) whose effects on European economies go beyond mere extraction of surplus value through repatriation of profit: balance of payments problems, inflationary trends, currency instability and increasing regional inequality are all to a large extent their doing. The future of Europe's states is indeed uncertain: the economic crisis of the seventies is really the herald of a vast restructuring of capitalism. The new international division of labour (IDL) will confine the high-tech 'sunrise' industries to North America and Japan; as for the older manufacturing industries with higher labour inputs they will increasingly be hived off, under multinational control, to the new industrialised states. Here with less scrupulous regimes and less institutional protection for labour, rates of profit are higher. The rest of the Third World will remain a source of raw materials, a market for some consumer goods and an outlet for selected investment capital.

This process is largely set in motion by the needs of the MNC (80% of which are American), but the role of the US state is also crucial. The dollar is overvalued in terms of the real performance of the US economy and it is only the sheer size of that economy, plus the military and diplomatic weight of the US, which gives the dollar its inordinate trading privileges. The US state is thus a key ally of the MNC as they seek to dominate Europe and the Third World in an attempt to shore up the falling rate of profit. But economic domination brings with it cultural and political submission. European modes of life and culture are being Americanised; consumer patterns, thought and even political behaviour are being insensibly unified in company with the internationalisation of capital.[3]

France has been spared none of these effects. The advanced fractions of French capital are today multinational in their operations;[4] older types of manufacturing capital (textiles, engineering, shipbuilding) are struggling in the face of foreign competition. Politically the role of Giscardism reflects this. If Gaullism were able to play a modernising role in the economy (by direct intervention as well as by establishing political stability crucial to growth) it has now outlived its usefulness for advanced capital. Its nationalist leanings would nowadays find more favour with the smaller, backward type of enterprise, afraid of competition. Giscardism with its commitment to internationalising the economy yet further, as seen in its acceptance of the European Monetary System (EMS), has little to offer such categories. The Barre plans with their emphasis on self-help and killing off 'lame ducks' made this clear.[5] It is in this identification with the use of 'technocratic' policies to favour the needs of multinational capital that we see evidence of the influence of stamocap types of theory on Ceres. On the political level it is suggested that governments of the right are forced, in their eagerness to help the reproduction of capital by any means, into seriously narrowing the democratic space left in French politics.[6] Their control of the media and other ideological apparatus is becoming more exclusive; soon perhaps genuine democracy (in the sense of a change of government) may be impossible.

The socio-economic consequence of these trends can be guessed. Small business and farmers will increasingly find their margins squeezed and their viability questioned. For the wage-earning classes growth may have led to an increase in income (less than that of capital owners), but this is cancelled out by increased alienation. This involves areas such as housing, transport and environment and leisure; increasingly the time, space and privacy of individuals are eroded by pressures related to the need of capital to exploit them as consumers as well as workers.

All this suggests that the objective conditions for socialist change exist in France. Socialists have to create the subjective conditions. They must attempt to combine the great mass of the dominated into a 'class-front' (the concept was forged by the Ceres arch-rival Poperen, but borrowed quite happily). The great mass of the workforce is nowadays composed of wage-earners. Workers and the white-collar grades increasingly evident in the growing tertiary sector can form the majority of the class-front, which is open to all those who have an objective stake in change. This concept of the class-front derives at bottom from PCF analyses of the 'antimonopoly alliance', which in the face of growing capitalist concentration sought to link every category of the alienated and dominated, except for the top layer of monopoly capitalists. Naturally for the PCF such an alliance would be headed by the working class and the party which is said to incarnate it, namely itself. Thus Ceres and the PS generally were obliged to differentiate their vision slightly, so as not to be seen as too close to the PCF and also not give the impression that they only represented the salaried middle class or petty-bourgeoisie in the alliance, compared with the PCF's representation of 'real' workers. Hence they stressed the wider salariat more than the manual working class and turned up their noses at some of the smaller impoverished capitalists. But this was of minor importance, for the overall effect was the same; it was suggested that nine-tenths of France could rally behind an alliance whose political expression would be the union of the left parties, against a minority of the privileged. Such a line has a high potential for mobilisation, especially when presented in sophisticated language at which the PS grew adept; it was used by all fractions of the party down to 1981. Of more interest here however is another key concept which was to bind together the class-front before and after electoral victory, namely *autogestion*. The concept was crucial for Ceres because it marked itself off thereby from not just the PCF but also from most of the rest of the PS (especially Poperen, for whom the concept was tantamount to class-collaboration). Until the late seventies it was in fact one of the fraction's best known identity-tags.[7]

If the concept is relatively new, stemming especially from May 1968, the reality behind it is much older. Without necessarily accepting Rocard's thesis that the history of the French left can be written in terms of the clash of two cultures, statists and decentralisers, it is true that since Proudhon there has been a persistent theoretical attempt to see socialism in terms of grass-roots initiatives and decision, rather than change from above led by central government. The syndicalist movement of the early twentieth century has some claims to be seen in this light and May 1968 can only really be so understood. Whatever its ultimate significance (and Ceres has hesitated on this as much as most) May meant that demands for a socialism involving a high degree of grass-roots decision-making rapidly became part of the culture of the left. If the CFDT trade union and the small PSU led the way, the PS soon followed. We may agree with Brown that by 1981 'the triumph of *autogestion* as a political slogan and theory within the socialist move-ment was almost total'.[8] Needless to say, the concept is elusive, and its elasticity fully exploited by those who subscribe to it.

We may take as a starting definition Brown's: 'direct participation by the people in the decisions which affect them at every level of the economic and political systems'.[9] Within this parameter Ceres has suggested how a socialist France might function. The economy is one area of concern but others have been discussed such as local government, education and even the armed forces. There is no space to go into detail about the many proposals, discussion of which excited activists through the decade; we shall confine ourselves to a survey of the major guidelines.

The prime component of *autogestion* is workers' self-management. Ceres sees this beginning in the enlarged public sector which would follow the left's accession to office (see below); it would thus be limited initially to a small number of large firms, a fact sometimes forgotten.[10] The new structures would go much further than the German *Mitbestimmung*, for running of the firm must be decentralised to the lowest units. If the general assembly of workers is the ultimate repository of sovereignty, it would probably leave major policy decisions to an elected works council. The day-to-day execution of these might be carried out by a professional management board under the council's control. Rotation of responsibility would be encouraged, to avoid the self-perpetuation of an administrative élite, and indeed a system of revocability of delegates to higher bodies is canvassed. Unions should remain apart from these structures, keeping their bargaining roles. At shopfloor level job-enrichment should be pursued, the aim being to move from the taylorised assembly line to the autonomous or semi-autonomous working team. On differentials, Chevènement suggests, somewhat loosely, that they be related to the hardship of the work involved. Firms' autonomy would of course have to be fitted into a national plan; here major macro-economic decisions would clearly be government's, albeit on the basis of inputs from firms. Credit policy and long-term pricing policies would be crucial instruments in creating a macro-climate which would help the transition to *autogestion*.[11] Local authorities would develop special tutelary relationships with firms, monitoring their performance and feeding it in to the national plan. In this context it is understood that self-run firms must show a profit measurable by conventional market criteria, and Chevènement is sure that the new responsibilities given to workers will increase productivity, as identification with the enterprise replaces the alienation of the past.

Such are the broad outlines of industrial *autogestion* as part of the transition to socialism. It is not as such entirely *basiste* (in the sense of absolute commitment to grass-roots power). Ceres was never

Proudhonian and even texts produced at the height of its enthusiasm for *autogestion* show that it was always concerned to articulate grass-roots demands with the wider collective needs and choices which, in its view, can only be fully seen by a left government, and hence by the parties which compose it. We should note the stress placed above on efficiency and professionalism as defined in capitalist economics, and the saliency of the planning process. Moreover Ceres was always clear that a vigorous industrial policy was necessary to help the transition to socialism. It was not simply a matter of providing the growth that even in 1967 was seen as vital for employment,[12] but also of controlling the conditions of macroeconomic activity, more and more influenced by internationalisation of the economy. Even then Ceres concluded that it was probably too late to leave the EEC and was even sceptical of protectionism. But it saw the need to stem import penetration and to preserve a French presence in areas which could be seen as strategic (not just in the sense of being vital to the security of France but also in the sense of high technology vital for the future of industries or groups of industries). The role of government in preserving such structures was irreplaceable, whether through its support of R. & D., or its direct interventions to create groups competitive on the international markets. On both these counts Ceres contrasted the interventionist policies of the Gaullist Debré favourably with what they saw as the *laissez-faire* of Giscard and Barre.

Government had in the end to make choices about what sorts of areas to preserve in the national interest and how it would raise finance to support the 'noyau dur' of big groups deemed necessary to compete in these markets. In return it would get considerable multiplier effects from the activity of these groups in terms of job creation and stimulus to smaller firms (see below, Chapter 5). It also believed, however, in stressing the virtues of this competitive public sector against parasitic activities such as property-development, which already absorbed too many resources: only government could reverse this flow of funds towards production. Other instruments of policy should also be used to support industry, especially demand management. Here social rather than individual demand should be encouraged (for services such as housing and transport) which would provide jobs for basic industry. Incomes policy should also work in this sense through a narrowing of differentials.[13] Such are the major outlines of Ceres industrial policy and they have varied little.

Clearly all this supposes an active, interventionist government, with a clear policy for industry at home and abroad: it would be naïve to suppose that sub-central levels of administration could carry out such a design (the odds on central government succeeding are already long enough). Any Ceres reflections about industrial *autogestion* need then to be seen within this framework: government is firmly in charge, so far as is possible, of macro-economic decisions. It is at the micro-level that experiments in self-management may begin. A similar mix of enlarged liberty and accountability within an overall central control is evident also in other, non-economic areas of life.

Thus in local government Ceres favours the relaxing of both administrative and financial controls, allowing authorities, especially communes, to spend their money more as their inhabitants wish. It is also keen on citizens' referenda, increased rotation of office and limitations on the holding of several offices simultaneously (*cumul des mandats*) in the hope of limiting the hold of local notables. The fraction has long favoured giving regions considerable decision-making and tax-raising powers. Much of this does militate against the centralising Jacobinism of which the fraction is so often accused, but there are limits. Thus on regions it is hard to find sympathy for any separatist demand from the French periphery.[14] Similarly on a micro-level demands for greater autonomy for communes (the smallest unit) coexist with the wish to decrease their number to something like the 500 that exist in Yugoslavia (as compared with 38,000 today); clearly this would mean many local officials losing out on their (admittedly small) prerogatives. There would thus seem to be a technocratic counter-effect to the participationist impulse. Similarly on military matters the fraction's proposal for a citizen's army based largely on reservists in territorial units (a demand made ritually by French socialists since the day of Jaurès), which Ceres saw as reinforcing the popular basis of deterrence, needs to be set against countervailing factors. These include support for the French nuclear arsenal (surely the ultimate in technocratic centralisation of defence?) and also the Ceres attitude to the conscripts' rebellion of 1975, when the national servicemen demanded the same sorts of organisational rights extended to their equivalents in some other West European states. Ceres activists, especially in Paris, initially supported the rebels and were promptly reminded by the leadership of the official PS line, which under Hernu was much closer to the status quo.[15] Perhaps the army was too serious an institution to be left to experimenters in self-management.

Even education, where Ceres once hoped to conduct many *autogestionnaire* experiments, has been the subject of revision. In 1975 Chevènement urged more teacher and parent power and greater room for pedagogical innovation. But even then he was denouncing the irrelevance of much of the syllabus from a vocational point of view, stressing the need to make the workforce of the future versatile and efficient.[16] In 1984 Education minister Chevènement was more succinct. French children needed the three Rs, technology and republican civics; teacher and parent power received no mention and pedagogical innovation was an object of sarcasm.[17]

From the start, then, Ceres advocacy of *autogestion* was tempered with demands for efficiency and awareness of the constraints towards uniformity that stemmed from market pressures and institutions alike. Ceres always stressed, to be fair, that *autogestion* was a means as well as an end;[18] it was seen as a constant process of struggle and experiment, evolving its own forms as it went along. Ceres always warned against excessive haste or optimism, denying that full self-management was ever possible in a country ruled by the right. In such a context, workplace and other struggles could only win small spaces of relative autonomy. The *autogestionnaire* process could only begin to become generalised with a left government in office, sponsoring change at every level of society. In this caution lies the sense of the fraction's otherwise arcane rebuttal of the PSU slogan 'control today to decide tomorrow', which Ceres said should be replaced with 'struggle today to control tomorrow'.[19] The implication is clear; real change can only take place in partnership with a sympathetic state. As the favourite Ceres slogan of the seventies had it, the movement from below must ally with the movement from above.

It is probably thus exaggerated to claim as does Brown that the Ceres conception of *autogestion* was 'a cross between Leninism and classical social-democracy'.[20] It is certain that the ideological battle with Rocard after 1975 (which we shall analyse shortly) forced Ceres to become clearer about some of the tensions in its doctrine between libertarian impulses and technocratic awareness of economic and political necessity, and that this awareness was more to the advantage of the latter factors than the former. But the tension was always there and arguably still is. One of the most perspicacious observers of Ceres remarked that it was always split between an *autogestionnaire* sensibility and a state-capitalist one.[21] Over the years, the state-capitalist line has indeed strengthened but the *autogestionnaire* one still remains vivid, certainly among Ceres activists.

Autogestion is in fact too valuable a concept to throw away, even if the Rocardian adversary is able to make a more seductive use of it. The reason why every PS group (except the irreducible Poperenites)[22] clung to it was that while keeping traditional socialist desire for radical economic and social change it seemed to add in a liberal if not libertarian commitment to enlarging individuals' autonomy. The mix was a heady one, especially when set by the PS against the PCF's 'French road to socialism' which to many seemed nostaligc for Eastern European models. It did not matter that no one had ever seen a self-managing society; rather, that was part of the attraction. It was a grand myth in the Sorelian sense, just out of reach yet close enough to persuade people of its feasibility and hence to mobilise them so as to attain it. Ceres saw this earlier than its rivals and this is why it invested so much effort in the concept; this also is why it was so angry when Rocard, as it were, stole its clothes. For a group which wanted an operational, mobilising ideology, *autogestion* could not be abandoned, even if some of the groups's analyses suggested contrary trends, and even if its own internal functioning (see Chapter 4) was not particularly *autogestionnaire*.

3.2 SOCIAL-DEMOCRACY AND THE PARTY – EXHUMING THE REVOLUTION?

Socialiste: révolutionnaire au bon sens du terme.
Social-démocrate: socialiste impuissant mais content.
J. Mandrin, *Socialisme ou social-médiocratie*

Un parti de masse est hétérogène par nature et tend à redevenir un parti social démocrate. Il faut lutter contre cela par la résurrection d'un parti militant.   Ceres internal document, March 1975

At the heart of Ceres' project stands the problem of social-democracy. Indeed its very existence can only be understood as a negative response to this phenomenon. We shall attempt here to say what the group understands by social-democracy, so as better to understand its socialist counter-project.

Ceres sees social-democracy more in terms of political praxis and indeed policy outcomes than of party institutions as such. It thus uses the term to describe the reformist socialist parties of Southern Europe, despite the institutional weaknesses of these which were highlighted in Chapter 1 and which, according to theorists like Portelli, render the term inapplicable to such parties. As such, Ceres critiques of social-democracy are very much those of left socialists everywhere: basically, social-democracy is a reluctance to take decisive steps towards socialism. This negative definition rests mainly on an analysis of the experiences of socialist parties in office. While accepting that a certain amount of success can be achieved by such governments operating keynesian policies in a welfare-state context, Ceres assumes that such changes will inevitably encounter structural limits.[23] These limits have to do with the very structures of capitalism itself and it is in its failure to challenge them that social-democracy is wanting. Instead of acting decisively and creating a *rupture* with the capitalist mode of production, by beginning to socialise the economy and create new political and cultural relationships (of the type described above), which would be the bases of a new socialist society, social-democracy retreats. It is now that spending projects begin to be cut or abandoned, that labour's share of national income recedes to the advantage of capital, that pressures from foreign trade balances and the exchange markets (and foreign governments?) begin to supersede the will for change – supposing that it was ever there in the first place. In short, social-democracy is the strand of the labour movement which recognises (either openly in its theory or, theory apart, simply by its conduct of policy) that there are fundamental limits to the amount of change that can be achieved. Ultimately it is not a challenge to capital, but a compromise with it. The counterpart of this in foreign affairs has been since 1947 a strong anti-communism, uncritical reliance on the Atlantic Alliance and general deference to US policy.

Typically Ceres has devoted much attention to critiques of social-democracy in office, often personalising the phenomenon. Thus in the sixties Harold Wilson and the Labour party were singled out as exemplars.[24] As Labour faded it was replaced in the demonology by another figure, the SPD, especially under Helmut Schmidt, whose clear political links with Giscard d'Estaing led Ceres to push its critiques further, making none-too-subtle analogies between German social-democracy and straight liberalism.[25] The Portuguese revolution of 1974 brought an even better target in the shape of Mario Soarès and the PSP (largely a creation of SPD finance and Mitterrandist political sponsorship). As his firm anti-communism nourished his desire to halt or even reverse the gains made by the mass movements in 1974–5, Soarès became in Ceres discourse the very symbol of social-democracy and of everything which the fraction rejected.[26]

Traditionally leninist theory explains the presence of a social-democratic stratum in the labour movement by the theory of a 'labour aristocracy'. Thus Lenin suggested that the imperialist surge prior to 1914, which enabled European capital to extract increased surplus-value from its colonies and semi-colonies, made it possible to pass on some of this extra value to parts of the metropolitan working class in the form of higher wages. The political counterpart to this reward would be acquiescence in the capitalist system as such. Social-democratic parties would become the natural form of organisation of this privileged subclass, accepting as they do that capitalism can be reformed but not fundamentally altered. Ceres has never accepted the labour-aristocracy theory.[27] If at times the group has identified social-democracy with the interests of an ill-defined 'bureaucracy',[28] it has more usually seen the real interest-group behind the phenomenon as part of the intelligentsia, which is petit-bourgeois rather than working-class. From the mid-seventies, the fraction began using a variant of this thesis to attack the presence of social-democratic elements in the PS, pointing to the increased presence of the salaried middle class, especially intellectual, within the party and describing them, oddly, as 'néo-travaillistes' (neo-Labourites). Such a caste has its origins not in imperialism but in much wider patterns of social and economic change.

Chevènement insists particularly on capitalism's power to 'integrate' disputatious elements from the lower classes, citing the paradigm of pre-1914 Germany. Nowadays the extent of integration depends on the ability to produce growth and here the keynesian techniques in use since 1945 are vital. But – and this is a deeply-felt Ceres conviction – integration also depends on capital's ability to maintain cultural hegemony. Thus the integrative role of social-democracy is 'not just the result of cleverly redistributing a few crumbs of surplus-value. It stems in the end from the bourgeoisie's ideological domination of the whole of society, from the impact of mass diffusion of a certain amount of material progress and the amazing capacity of capitalism to survive.'[29]

Againt this background we can better understand Ceres mistrust of social-democratic leaders; for office is generally held to corrupt.[30] Such corruption entails organisational consequences for the party, though; for once a generation of social-democratic leaders has tasted office, it will tend to make the party into an electoral machine, as opposed to a campaigning one. The party's intermediate levels will be filled by notables obsessed with re-election and incapable of seeing beyond their parish-pump.[31] This decline in theoretical capacity will put the party increasingly out of touch with social reality

Such is the general anti-model which Ceres erects from its reading of some widely differing European situations. We are not concerned here to criticise its accuracy or lack of originality, but rather to see how the French party, particularly in its SFIO phase, fits into the picture.

Clearly for Ceres SFIO showed most of the above defects. It has failed in government several times (1936 and 1945–7 especially).[32] Chevènement goes so far as to blame the lack of revolutionary will shown by the SFIO and the PCF in 1944 for not taking advantage of the mood in France during the Liberation to attempt 'an original socialist creation'. The party suffered from the hold of careerist, local-based bosses who virtually emptied it of any new blood; though Guy Mollet himself is generally exempted from criticism, and Ceres has, unlike others, never used the word 'Mollettism' to describe the sort of syndrome it criticises. SFIO's theoretical poverty was acute; Mollet's *Chances du socialisme* might, we are told, have been written in the Middle Ages.[33]

French social-democracy has one saving grace, however. Unlike the great majority of other socialist parties (it is never exactly specified how many, or which ones), it has always been genuinely socialist, thus revolutionary, by nature. That is the assumption on which it was founded and on which its ideology still, in 1969, pivoted. Despite this

fundamental aspiration, though, it has never actually managed in reality
to become a real socialist party; years of integration into the political
system have made it into something more akin to social-democracy.
This is a problem likely to affect any party of the left: 'all left parties are
more or less affected by social-democratic decay'.³⁴ But beneath the
rubble of years of social-democratic integration, there remains this
original socialist core, which can somehow be exhumed; this is why
Ceres socialists speak of the 'militant *resurrection*' (our italics) of the
party. This concept of a lost revolutionary essence which needs
rediscovery is crucial. For any group claiming to incarnate it stands to
increase powerfully its own legitimacy against party rivals who can be
seen as standing for other, less authentic visions of the party.

On a more instrumental level, this gambit justifies another vital part
of Ceres thinking, namely the decision to work through SFIO in the
first place. For it is not entirely clear that the decision was always
prompted by this belief in a revolutionary essence. Arguably indeed in
1964 it could be said that the rising PSU best incarnated the lost
revolutionary tradition of French socialism. Ceres has always gone out
of its way to do down this party, however, calling it 'la petite gauche',
comparing it with Jehovah's witnesses, accusing it of technocracy,
sectarianism and being impossibly purist; it was both conformist and
ultrarevolutionary at once.³⁵ Most of this can be taken with a pinch of
salt, except for one thing, which is the PSU's lack of an electoral base.
Here we come to the heart of the Ceres gambit.

For all its decay SFIO still had a number of assets, of which Mandrin
listed five.³⁶ These were its activists, voters, local and national élites and
material assets (staff, premises, etc.). Assuming the activitsts and élites
to be few in number and not generally of a quality acceptable to Ceres,
there remained the material assets of the party and above all a still
appreciable electorate, which had been twice as numerous within the
previous generation. Given the slow rate at which political change
takes place and at which parties live and die, these assets represented
something which the PSU was unlikely to possess for years. For
socialists in a hurry SFIO remained a better bet. Indeed, because it was
so weak in élites and activists it could be taken over more easily by a
'fractional struggle led by determined activists'. And since, after all,
these activists were only restoring the party to its lost identity, the
operation became doubly attractive. Thus instrumental factors

combined with the ideological aspirations of Ceres to force it to work not as an outside *groupuscule*, but from within the SFIO. Its position was 'overdetermined'; it was condemned to be a left fraction.

It thus only remained to devise a strategy for taking over SFIO, as stated baldly in the closing pages of the philippic *Socialisme ou social-médiocratie*. Many adversaries of Ceres feign horror at its alleged cynicism and leninist putschism, but all it does is to state a few home truths known to anyone who has had experience of committees. Ceres says that given the small number of activists (as compared with paid-up members who never attend meetings), a determined group can easily win control of a branch and then a federation. It suggests coordinating tactics before meetings and such devices as packing selected branches to increase voting strength. Optimistically it believes that such fractional tactics might ultimately yield control of the whole party.

None of this was illegal in terms of the party constitution and it was true that by 1969 large tracts of the party were ripe for such a take-over. Such an admission is more a comment on SFIO's decrepitude than anything else. Moreeover Ceres tactics, sharp practice though they were, were no worse than those employed by their predecessors to control what remained of the branches (e.g. mass purchase of membership cards by notables who were mayors or councillors, municipal clientelism which gave jobs to card-holders, etc.). Ceres may not have helped its image by using dramatic langauge like 'expropri-ation', but the group wanted to shock at this stage.

Ceres was, then, going to help the party to become socialist once more by taking it over. Ideologically, this would mean imbuing it with the sort of vision of socialist transformation sketched out in Section 3.1; but there were also practical implications for party organisation. From the sixties Ceres has laid down a series of consistent views about this topic.[37] Members' education should be given highest priority; Ceres motions to congress always demand higher budget priorities for this. The fraction always tries to get the post of education officer at any level and had made considerable efforts in the past to produce educational material (cf. Section 4.2). A favourite demand was for a school for party cadres. Alongside this goes the enthusiasm for workplace branches (*sections d'entreprise* – SE), again the object of frequent budgetary appeals to congress. This is not just because they have provided Ceres with many recruits and what amounts to virtual block-votes in some federations, but because of their political and ideological value. Culturally, they are a break with the electoralist obsessions of social-democracy; the very refusal to align party organisational structures on the territorial ones of representative democracy shows an aspiration to a different politics. Politically, the SE allow the party to fight the PCF at its own game; for it is at work that the PCF wins its best and most dynamic members, often through union activity. Thus the SE are potentially a way of getting through to a working class that would otherwise fall to the communists. Most SE tend to be in the non-manufacturing sector (e.g. banks and insurance) and indeed many are in the public sector (post office, railways, university, etc.). Ceres tends to dominate the SE, but there are few of them of really working-class character like the PCF's factory cells.

Active involvement of members is highly prized. Ceres has thus always insisted on small branches, ideally of twenty-five members maximum. In its early days it called for systematic rotation of office holders, a two-year maximum term of office and even at one stage permanent revocability; such claims waned, as the supply of human enthusiasm and thus of members proved finite. The mode of selecting candidates (though needless to say not the actual process) has been relatively uncontroversial in the PS, since for many years they have been selected by one-member-one-vote in the actual constituency. But Ceres had some mistrust of elected representatives and has usually called for increased accountability to branches. At one stage it even wanted a national party committee to monitor the press comments of party members; but this was dropped, probably because it was realised that the existing system (whereby office holders do need to keep the support of branches to be reselected) is adequate.

As to the legal existence of fractions within the party there has been some variation. Before 1971 Ceres stressed the need for discipline and unity in the new party.[38] But even these early pronouncements contained hints of the future. Existing fractions were blamed on the obstinacy of the majority, which refused to listen to others, and often assimilated to the ambitions of notables and their hangers-on. The best way of avoiding fractionalism would be to give every current of opinion a seat on the leadership and for free circulation of ideas to be the norm. The unspoken corollary of such ideas is of course that if these conditions are not met, then fractionalism becomes inevitable and justified. Thus Ceres would soon argue openly in favour of this. Its demand for internal PR at the Épinay congress was a deliberate endorsement of fractionalism, and in motions to subsequent congresses Ceres has often demanded the official recognition of fractions. Thus Ceres recognises that party life is a pluralistic struggle waged in the name of different conceptions of socialism; but it also believes that historically the odds are on its side.

Over the years a more explicit attempt to theorise its role as a fraction within the PS has been made. 'Ceres is not a party within the party; it's a political line', remarked Georges Sarre at a moment when the party as a whole was being forced to think about fractionalism, because relations between the fractions were worsening.[39] This is somewhat disingenuous, for we know that Ceres is perfectly aware that 'a line is worthless without a good organisation'. So how has the fraction tried to think about the organisation of its line?

Such attempts have been frequent and not always free from confusion, but it is possible to pick out some constants. First Ceres always denies that it is a party within the party. At the bitterest moments of fractional battling it warned members specifically against regarding Ceres as a surrogate, or something on which to fall back when faced with disappointment in the party as a whole.[40] Ceres must be itself, yet more than itself. It has to retain an identity as a left pole in contrast to the (social-democratic) majority. But it must simultaneously become hegemonic, spreading its values and its idea of socialism across the party. This is a deep and largely invisible process, to which congress scores are only a very crude guide. If this process went to its conclusion, we could then accept Sarre's posit that one day the group would disappear as a distinct phenomenon (simply because the rest of the party would have come to resemble it). This is of course the maximum achievement for which a left fraction can hope as we sketched out in Section 1.3.

Alongside this self-vision has coexisted another, slightly more élitist one, stated most clearly in a 1975 article but also pursued in the internal text already quoted.[41] This sees Ceres not as gradually impregnating the party, as it were, but more as standing aloof in a position of a high-quality reserve. Thus 'Ceres is not a mass organisation' and it is vital to 'prepare Ceres to assume its role as collective leader of the mass movement'. The idea seems to be that when the movement from above (left government) is faced with movement from below (spontaneous popular actions ranging from strikes to more ambitious forms of political initiatives) then somehow the party will be placed in a position of mediation between the two. Here, then, a qualitative revolutionary élite would come into its own, though the consequences of this situation (based on nostalgia for 1968 and a reading of events in Portugal) were never thought through in any detail and we cannot be clear as to what role the party would play. This second strategy which the document's author (one supposes it is Motchane) describes as 'giving the party a backbone' is not entirely contradictory to the first, hegemonic one; indeed the two could be seen as different moments of the same strategy, in the sense that hegemony would be achieved quicker in the unforeseeable revolutionary atmosphere triggered by mass action after the left's electoral victory. But the second strategy depends entirely on the mass movements occuring and so long as they have not done so, the first becomes the only option.[42] Ceres had thus to publicise and develop its ideology, and campaign and argue on the basis thereof in an attempt to expand its influence in the 'pre-revolutionary' party. All of this supposes considerable organisation.

There is also the problem of defining the limits of acceptable support. The Martinet affair showed this cruelly. For years before, and indeed after, Ceres served as a magnet for a very wide range of opposition to Mitterrand in the party, so much so that at the time people spoke of Courant II as if it were conterminous with the fraction.[43] Martinet knew this when at the *assises* of 1974 he urged Ceres to coopt the incoming PSU members into a sort of 'broad-left' fraction.[44] He linked his suggestion to a critique of the overcentralised operations of the group. But it was not so much this that worried the Ceres leaders as the thought of an alliance with men of the new left like Rocard who, though opposed to Mitterrand and social-democracy generally, stood for a socialism ideologically distinct from that of Ceres. Martinet was forced out and this was one of the first of a series of self-limitations of self-definitions by Ceres. Clearly the fraction wanted to win hegemony only on its own terms, and the Pierret episode would show the same thing three years later. In other words Ceres was not just any left fraction (some of Rocard's ideas could even be said to be more to the left, if one takes conventional criteria). It had – and with successive episodes it realised more and more that it had – a distinct ideology of its own, a subculture. This seems to be particularly inflexible and, if Ceres makes allies it does so only very conjuncturally, as at Metz. What it really wants is not allies but converts to its very widely encompassing and, at bottom, consistent ideology. It is this self-sealing ideology – which the rest of this chapter will fill in in greater detail – which gives the group one of its profoundest characteristics.

We may conclude for the moment that Ceres saw itself as a fraction, indeed as a left fraction, but destined to become hegemonic after a long and unrelenting ideological fight. It would not be dissolved into the rest of the party by a sort of osmosis, and would not merge with other anti-Mitterrand groups, left or otherwise. Rather, the rest of the party would have to become like it. It is this sense of exclusiveness and righteousness that confirms our decision to speak of Ceres as an ideological community.

3.3 THE PARTY AND THE COMMUNISTS – THE DIALECTICS OF UNITY

It is customary among adversaries to decry Ceres as communist wolves in the clothing of socialist sheep: appellations range from 'national leninists' to the curious 'paracommunists' used by a disgruntled ex-leader. Harsher critics see Ceres as the willing tools of a PCF attempt to influence the PS; kinder ones see them as naïve dreamers, anxious to wipe out the historic divisions of the French left, but blind to certain hard facts of life where communism is concerned.[45] None of these goes to the heart of Ceres' relationship to the PCF, which is complex and needs to be seen at several levels.

For analytical purposes we will distinguish the relationship with leninism as a doctrine and praxis from the relationship with the PCF as a leninist party.

Ceres was often accused of leninism, though the term is seldom defined and not always used in good faith by PS rivals. Confusion was maintained for a long time by Ceres' own reluctance to disown the term and by its frequent references to Lenin. But it would be a mistake to suppose that Ceres subscribes to all or even most of what is commonly understood by leninism.

To take points of possible identification first, it is true that Ceres analysis of capitalist imperialism undoubtedly owes much to Lenin. But Lenin's own analysis in works such as *Imperialism the Highest Stage of Capitalism* owed much to theorists like the Liberal Hobson or the austro-marxist Hilferding. Since his death his framework has sustained a host of theorists. Such theorists are often mentioned in Ceres discourse, the point being that they like Ceres are heirs to an anti-imperialist discourse that by now has no real owner. It could at a pinch be called leninist, but that does not make those who use it leninists (in the sense of endorsing the theory and practice of leninist parties).

The same is true of another apparent convergence, namely analysis of the capitalist state apparatus from a class point of view. It is plain that Ceres uses an analytical matrix running back from Althusser and Poulantzas through Gramsci to Lenin.[46] But again Lenin, though he gave a sharp edge to this problematic in *The State and Revolution* was only building on lines elaborated by Marx, as for instance in his writings on the Paris Commune. Any modern socialist should in any case address himself to such questions. But what makes him a leninist or not is the conclusions he will draw from his analysis. If he concludes that the bourgeois state is unreformable and must be destroyed in a frontal attack from the dominated classes led by a special type of party, then he is a leninist. Not only did Ceres specifically refuse such a party but it does not share the conviction that the state is totally subordinated to capital and hence cannot in any way be used to help the transition towards socialism.[47]

A more serious problem might be the concept of party, not so much its organisation which we shall treat shortly, but its function as a consciousness-raiser for the working class. In classical leninism the class will, left to its own devices, never develop more than an economistic consciousness (it will fight for material benefits but not for overall political change) or spontanism (periodic anarchic upsurges which will be crushed). Clearly Ceres, which is headed by career politicians drawn from an intellectual élite, might be expected to have some sympathy for the notion of an enlightened vanguard. But it is possible to overrate this phenomenon. Michelsian analysis might suggest that reformist socialist parties are in fact led by intellectual vanguards, even if they take care never to proclaim the fact. And some would say that the PS is a prime example of this. The best way to deal with the vanguard-complex is to see how Ceres views (in theory and in praxis) the essential function of the party: only then can we see how leninist they are on this question. For it is one thing to proclaim the need for enlightened leadership, but there is more than one way of exercising such leadership.

Probably what Ceres took from Lenin was something more diffuse, namely a sort of moral inspiration. Chevènement reminds us that there is really no organised corpus of leninism and that Stalin coined the term.[48] What Lenin represented for Chevrèment was a high capacity for analysis, great tactical flexibility and above all will-power. Chevène-ment admires him for undertaking a historic short-cut by attempting a revolution in an underdeveloped country in what, given the circum-stances of 1917, seemed a justifiable gamble. While aware that the outcome was a post-revolutionary society of a distorted type which cannot serve as a model (and which explains the fraction's mistrust of any 'thirdworldist' theories of revolution that claim to jump the stage of capitalist development), Chevènement is visibly fascinated by the 'voluntarism' displayed by the Bolsheviks. It is true that such voluntarism is not unique to Lenin and had long preceded him in history. But there is a clue here to some fundamental Ceres feelings about politics.

Ceres leninism thus far then amounts to use of some theoretical problematics associated with Lenin, plus admiration for Lenin as a practitioner, leading a revolution in a totally different country at a different epoch. We have yet to investigate Ceres' relationship to leninism as a theory of party, but we suggest that even here there is considerable divergence. In short Ceres leninism is not a very systematic affair, and it may be that the fraction was guilty of romanticism in allowing itself to be so described. One persistent adversary has different views, however, which need a separate refutation.

Lazic's method consists in juxtaposing a number of quotations from Lenin with Ceres writings, the reader being invited to guess the similarity and conclude that Ceres must be Bolsheviks. The problem is that the quotations are usually out of context and mostly irrelevant.[49] Thus we are told of a secret Ceres document which says 'without money we are paralysed', a declaration compared with the position of the early Bolsheviks! Doubtless the latter were once as indigent as

Ceres, but is there any party or fraction that would not agree with this ludicrously obvious statement? Lazic also singles out the 'voluntarism' of Ceres as being leninist; but as stated above, this quality was no more the property of Lenin than it was of historical revolutionaries as diverse as Cromwell and Gandhi. Lazic also accuses Ceres of *noyautage*. It is unclear what he means by this term, normally rendered as in English entrism, that is an external organisation secretly sending members into another one, either so as to take it over completely or else as (in Michael Crick's phrase) a kind of 'raiding party', hoping to win over and steal a few members before the inevitable unmasking and expulsion. Usually such practices are considered to be more trotskyist than anything else. But they do not in any case apply to Ceres, whose origins lie clearly within the PS and nowhere else (certainly not in some imagined Fourth International) and which has never hidden its ambition to win over the party. But then neither have the other groups.

One could make similar remarks about Lazic's claim that 'mastering the French economy' is part of the Ceres programme and that this is leninist. All socialist parties aspire to greater control over the economy than the right: the interesting variables are exactly what sort of control, by what means they seek to obtain it and in the context of what overall political aims. Other allegedly leninist themes such as the need to purge the state apparatus, the possibility of violent responses from the ruling class, the relationship of mass movements to electoral politics and new forms of producers' democracy are treated elsewhere. We would say that most of them belong to a wider patrimony than leninism and that Ceres has tried to fit them into its concept of *autogestion*. Despite its own complacency over the label, and the haste of its opponents to belabour it, there is really very little about Ceres thus far that is leninist.

Leninist theory apart, how does Ceres understand the PCF, a self-proclaimed leninist party? Ceres writings provide abundant evidence for an answer.[50]

The first point to establish precedes any written texts, however, and this is the decision to work in SFIO in 1964, arguably a moment when the future of the left seemed to promise more to the PCF. Unless we are to believe that Ceres was part of a PCF take-over bid, it is clear that by this decision Ceres opted for a relationship with the PCF that could only be conflictual. For if SFIO did survive and renew itself, then it was bound to clash with the communists. The paracommunist theory is thus something of a non-starter. One could add that virtually no Ceres members have ever left the PS for the PCF, or certainly none that mattered.[51] What is more relevant though is to study the type of conflict which Ceres anticipated with the PCF.

Ceres views on the PCF are complex and have shifted slightly, but there is a consistent core. They see the party as owing much to the special circumstances of the Soviet revolution and after; here certainly are to be sought explanations for its two most durable features, democratic centralism and fidelity to the USSR in matters of foreign policy. These two features make up what one Ceres analyst calls 'the hard core of its neo-stalinist or post-stalinist identity'.[52]

Ceres disapproves of the PCF's foreign policy deference, especially as it developed through the Afghan and Polish crises. By such behaviour the PCF helps to shore up the two-bloc system, instead of breaking it up and creating a more autonomous Europe (cf. below). Ceres also reproaches the PCF with its inability to perform a proper marxist analysis of the political and economic systems of the Eastern bloc, though its own efforts in this domain have been less than strenuous. As a rule, though, Ceres shows more interest in the party's organisational centralism and lack of internal democracy. But it always takes care to avoid the appearance of systematic anti-communism, unlike some other PS groups, for reasons that will become clear. A favourite tactic is thus to repeat some widely-shared objection to the PCF, while in the same breath attacking some weakness of social-democracy (or the right).[55] This has led some to accuse Ceres of being soft on the PCF, but by and large Chevènement's claim that 'I have no illusions about the CP' is true.[54] Most widely-echoed critiques of the party can be found in Ceres texts, and if they are not repeated *ad nauseam* as in Rocardian literature, this is not because Ceres is blind as to the nature of that party but because it has a distinct view of its role in the movement towards socialism.

What aspects of democratic centralism does Ceres then refuse? Primarily the same as the rest of the PS. Chevènement's extended soliloquy on the French left picks up at length all the objections which Léon Blum made at the Tours congress of 1920 and which were regularly echoed by such as Mollet.[55] He echoes Blum's critique of an activist élite with quasi-military discipline and a self-reproducing oligarchy; he agrees with his condemnation of communist will to dominate the unions or indeed any other party or social movement; and he resents PCF monolithism and refusal of fractions. He repeats Quilliot's 1964 analysis of the vertical power structure and how it would be bound to shape the workings of government if the PCF took office: 'a secretive, bureaucratic and extremely centralised party is likely to come up with a state that is even more bureaucratic, authoritarian and police-ridden'.[56] Chevènement also quotes with approval Linhart's analogy between the leninist conception of party and the taylorisation of factory work, whereby both are seen as producing atomisation at the bottom and unchecked bureaucratic rule at the top.

Such criticisms are frequent and often coupled with another, relating to the PCF claim to exclusive representation of the working class.[57] This aspect emerged through bitter PCF hostility to socialist workplace branches (mainly Ceres-run of course) and its refusal to collaborate with these in joint campaigns. Ceres objects to such exclusivism because it can only mean that the PS is seen as a petty-bourgeois party, however many votes it wins from workers. Hence it can only logically be a junior partner in any left alliance, as hegemony naturally accrues to the working class and 'its' party. Ceres fears that the rest of the PS might be only too glad to accept this invitation and turn the party into a flabby catch-all, trimming its socialist message to the lowest common denominator necessary to pull in votes from various interest-groups and thus rendering the whole Ceres task much harder.[58]

Fortunately however, despite all these faults the PCF is evolving. Both its foreign policy deference and its internal structures are beginning to creak under the impact of events, domestic and international. Ceres watched approvingly during the seventies as the PCF like its Italian and Spanish comrades moved hesitantly towards Eurocommunism, or national roads to socialism.[59] Ceres noted the successive acknowledgements to democratic principles given by the PCF – abandonment of proletarian dictatorship, commitment to party pluralism and to alternation of government based on free elections – and also what it saw as growing freedom within the party.[60] (Ceres was very close to the Paris federation of the PCF, which was particularly restive at the time.) It also thought the ties between PCF and the CGT union were loosening. And Chevènement could find various one-off examples of defiance of Soviet foreign policy to claim that PCF decisions were made in Paris not Moscow. He concluded that by the mid-seventies very few of Lenin's twenty-one conditions, laid down as guidelines to communist postulants for membership of Comintern, were still applicable to present-day parties.

Not that the PCF or its fellows had definitely destalinised, however. They were shaking off the Russian mould but still uncertain of their new identity. To help them find this identity – and indeed part of their very healthy identity-crisis is already due to its pressure – the PS is necessary. We come thus to left unity and the heart of the Ceres project.

The aim of unity is not just to win power and begin the movement towards socialism on the basis of the common programme of government (CPG). It is also to change the nature of both parties. Always conflictual – Ceres willingly accepted the communist Fajon's tag that 'union is combat' – unity was to be lived out not just in the voting booth but at all times. Both parties should act and campaign together on as many issues and in as many arenas as possible – supporting strikes and opposing closures; for Allende, against Pinochet; for tenants' rights, against fare increases; and so on. Such action would, in addition to increasing the left's audience, affect both parties. On the one hand the PS would be hardened against its innate tendency towards social-democracy and become more the sort of party Ceres sought; on the other the PCF, by rubbing shoulders with an equally dynamic but more democratic partner, would be slowly forced to democratise, taking in more of the *autogestionnaire* aspirations of the PS. The word 'forced' is employed deliberately, for there is nothing indulgent towards the PCF in this tactic; rather, it is an aggressive and voluntaristic belief that the PCF can be beaten at its own game of activism. The PS can become leader of the alliance, though it must never dominate the PCF entirely;[61] the two are linked umbilically, but the cord has only a certain amount of elasticity. The need for unity demonstrates *a contrario* why Ceres is so concerned about possibly disunity; for in this case the PCF will simply restalinise and the PS become more social-democratic. Unity is thus essential to the group's whole project.

It will be objected that this is a naïve view of the PCF and that recent history has largely shown this to be the case. Some might also discern a tendency within Ceres to concentrate on the texts of the PCF at the expense of its political practice (though the rest of the PS is guilty of this). In fact the extent of PCF commitment to democracy for France could only be known if it governed alone or as dominant partner. As for intra-party democracy, the crackdown on such as Fiszbin and Elleinstein – precisely the sort of communists Ceres sought to encourage – and the gradual exodus of critical members since 1980 show the limits to that. Ceres prediction of PCF behaviour was only half correct. In its blithe voluntarism the group thought that a dynamic PS could kick the PCF towards change. But what happened was the reverse. As PS strength grew within the union (thanks in no small way to Ceres efforts), the communist leaders grew more worried both about falling behind (electorally at least) and about the pressure which this put on them to change the party so as to make it more attractive – something which could best be done, argued internal critics, by adopting an open conflictual democracy as in the PS. Their reaction was what one would expect from men who have learned their politics in a traditional way inside a very rigid machine. Discipline was tightened and a harsher line taken towards the PS.[62] Hoping to put the brake on the process of unity and resolved to fall back on its traditional strengths in union and town hall, the PCF wanted to ride out the storm and hope to catch up with the PS again. In foreign policy it moved back towards the USSR, provocatively so on Afghanistan, complacently so over Solidarnosc. Support might shrink as a result of all this, but the hard core would remain.

Ceres was bound to suffer from this move, for in its view the result could only be the 'social-democratisation' of the PS, hence a strengthening of the Rocardians. Yet from the first public split between the PS and PCF in September 1977 right down to the presidential campaign in 1981 and indeed since, Ceres has continued to call for left unity. Unlike Mitterrand, though, it wanted the PS to commit itself to a new programmatic deal with the PCF and indeed to a 'compromise about power' (i.e. taking PCF ministers into government if the left should win). Ceres claimed that the PS could still by sheer activist pressure force the PCF to accept such a deal on its terms. Mitterrand, less optimistic, spoke of unity but without a programmatic deal and Rocard was harsher, wanting the PS to appeal to communist voters over the head of the PCF, without concessions and on a take-it-or-leave-it basis.

He was confident they would vote for the only real chance of getting rid of Giscard, namely a socialist presidential candidate (hopefully himself). In truth Mitterrand and Rocard both wanted the same thing – communist votes with no concessions on their part; but differences of style were crucial. Rocard's bluntness may have proved less effective in the end than Mitterrand's lyrical rhetoric, making much of his own role as founder of left unity, even if he promised little concrete. Only Ceres stood for a deeper conception of unity, with increasing difficulty as the PCF hardened its presidential campaign in a desperate attempt to stop a Mitterrand victory.[63]

In the end Ceres got by its own standards the worse possible result. The PS won a big electoral victory in May and June 1981 but very much on a catch-all basis and not a strongly socialist one.[64] Arguably it was more against the PCF than with it, for the crucial factor was the big drift of PCF support to Mitterrand on the first ballot, as voters sanctioned the dog-in-the-manger attitude of the party leaders. Certainly neither party had been transformed as Ceres hoped. The PS was still a party of public-sector intellectuals, with little institutional weight among the working class or the labour movement, even if it had pulled in over 40 per cent of the working-class vote. Much of its support came from people who wanted moderate change, not the ambitious aims of the *Projet socialiste*. The PCF, far from democratising and derussifying itself, now seemed more sectarian, internally repressive and russophile than ever. The only argument on which Ceres could fall back was that its continuing relentless decline would soon force it to consider again the sort of changes which the fraction urged.

Eventually Mitterand granted the Ceres wish to see the PCF in government, but not as an equal partner; the four minor posts it received were more designed to limit its room for obstruction than to recognise it as a serious influence. Little before the PCF departure from government in mid-1984 suggested that the party was evolving as Ceres hoped. On the face of it, Ceres ideas of mutual renewal of PS and PCF seemed to have been squeezed out, on the one hand by a leadership bent on preserving itself and the only conception of a communist party that it can understand and, on the other, by an alliance between the PS majority and a large section of the French public prepared to settle for a programme of moderate reform. Between them, stalinism and social-democracy seemed to have blocked the path of left socialism. The

Ceres motion to the Bourg-en-Bresse congress in 1983 contained several pages, but it devoted to the topic of left unity precisely six lines.

If the hopes which the fraction invested in the Ceres–PCF relationship have been showed to be unfruitful, the question of this relationship is still not exhausted. In particular we need to deal with claims that Ceres has been used by the PCF in various ways. One claim is that Ceres actually acts as a sort of recruiting ground for the PCF, initiating members into marxism and preparing them, doubtless unwittingly, for defection to the PCF. Lazic alleges this in connection with one of the best-known departures from Ceres, that of Exbrayat and Berenger (teachers' union activists) in 1977 and a Ceres boss in Toulouse, Destrem.[65] Our research has found no evidence of regular drift into the PCF via Ceres; in most federations it amounts to one or two isolated activists. In fact the reverse is more likely. Michel Charzat believes that some 10 per cent of what he calls Ceres cadres have had PCF experience.[66] If true, this would suggest that Ceres has at least helped make the PS into the sort of party which can attract non-stalinist communists.

We may also ask: in its anxiety to demarcate itself from the PS majority, has not Ceres at times given the impression of being too close to the PCF line, even to the point of *suivisme* (uncritical copying)? This charge is frequent, and Lazic is well to the fore.[67] He deals mainly with the period 1975–7 (the most agitated in Ceres and party history) and the examples he takes are: (1) attacks on the leaders and tactics of the PSP; (2) *ad hominem* polemics against Schmidt, Soares, etc.; (3) over-generosity to the PCF in the battle over heads of lists for the municipal elections of March 1977; (4) acceptance of direct elections to the European parliament in the wake of the PCF's volte face in 1977; and (5) appeals to Gaullists to join in a national alliance with the left (cf. Chevènement's article in *L'Appel* of June 1976). We shall take these in turn.

The Portuguese events after 25 April 1974 are dealt with more fully in the context of Ceres' European vision (see Section 3.4). For the present we may recall that Ceres sought in Portugal the same sort of alliance as in France, namely a broad front of the dominated classes led by a united left (PSP + PCP). It thus supported those left elements of the PSP who thought as it did.[68] It could thus only be wary of Soarès' leadership of the PSP, which was highly mistrustful of Cunhal and the PCP, more so in the eyes of Ceres than of the Portuguese right. Ceres condemned Soares' failure to pursue left unity and further the rapid social change already taking place, predicting that the most likely outcome of his failures would be a restoration of liberal capitalism. The fraction disapproved of PSP vote-winning on an anti-communist basis, especially when it neglected the more spontaneous organs of popular power which had arisen in factories and localities and which Ceres saw as *autogestion* in action. It was inevitable that the PCF would use similar critiques against Soarès' anti-communism, even though Ceres texts were also critical of PCP attempts to manoeuvre into positions of influence close to the ruling Armed Forces Movement and exert a covert influence from above. Ceres did not believe in the likelihood of a PCP putsch, since the party was powerless in the north of the country and did not control the army or other key parts of the state apparatus. Thus 'the risk of a "people's democracy" has always been greatly exaggerated'.[69]

Now it is possible to claim with hindsight that the PCP was preparing a coup and that thus Soarès' tactics were correct. But this reading depends on abstracting Portugal from its situation on the map; in 1975 there was little possibility of a sustainable coup led by communists in a NATO country so far from Eastern Europe. Thus, stalinist as the PCP was, its room for putschist manoeuvres was cramped and to that extent Ceres was entitled to ask about the feasibility of a PSP alliance with it in pursuit or consolidation of social change. The alternative was an alliance between the PSP and the right, and what has happened since 1975 in Portugal has shown that Ceres warnings were well-founded.

But even leaving aside the unregenerate nature of the PSP, it is clear that to ask Ceres not to support the left wing of a sister-party is to deny its very *raison d'être*. What it recommended for France (viz. left unity) could only be prescribed for Portugal, and vice versa, if it were to be consistent. The only alternative was, as stated, alliance between socialism and the right; and Ceres had seen too much of that in France to countenance it. If this stance gave the PCF a weapon against the rest of the PS, then this was unfortunate, but inevitable. The space in which left socialists work can be very narrow, and they will often find themselves in a situation where they either show knee-jerk loyalty to the party (in which case the party's right is strengthened) or stand by their beliefs (in which case they are called disloyal or crypto-communists). There is little room to manoeuvre, and much depends on the way in which the left line is presented.

We would concede that on occasions Ceres did present its line badly, thus facilitating charges of crypto-communism. Lazic's point on the Euro-elections is valid here. Ceres' about-face did seem like *suivisme*. The fact is that it has always despised the EEC in general and the Strasbourg Assembly in particular. Once it saw Mitterrand was determined to support direct elections, Ceres decided that it was no longer worth making an issue of it (especially as the fraction would gain some MEPs and some cash). But the leaders timed their decision badly; had they gone through the motions of protesting for three months longer, it would have been harder to accuse them of *suivisme*. In any case the substantive point in all this – hostility to the EEC – has never been abandoned, but merely continued by other means. Similar considerations are valid for the *ad hominem* attacks on Schmidt, etc. which by their repetitive exaggeration are often reminiscent of PCF diatribes; once again we need to distinguish between (an unfortunate) style and substance (highly relevant to Ceres' whole critique of social-democracy).

Lazic's claim of excessive generosity in the municipal elections also needs some qualification. Firstly, many observers feel that the PS as a whole was very greedy in the battle over candidacies.[70] Ceres was concerned to stop PS mayors from fielding exclusively PS lists or from demanding a greater share of the list than the local *rapport de forces* warranted (both of which practices were against official party policy and the whole spirit of the CPG). An internal document lists such PS notables as Delelis at Lens and Loo at La Ciotat, plus the *locus classicus* of this form of abuse, Hernu at Villeurbanne.[71] But Ceres also protests against the 'excessive demands' of the PCF in places like Paris and Bastia and supports the PS against the PC at Albi. It is true that the latter, like Paris, is a Ceres stronghold, and this gives us a clue to the fraction's real attitude. Generally faithful to the spirit of the CPG, with united lists wherever possible and the headship going to the partner with the best local scores, the fraction did not hesitate to criticise either partner for sharp practice but its main interest was in its own positions. This may be regrettable but it does not amount to *suivisme*.[72]

Nor does Lazic's final point, which shows total misunderstanding of the nationalist culture of Ceres; this, as we show in Section 3.4, is far more than tactical opportunism. The attempt to lure Gaullists fits into a deep cultural matrix which has bred a long-term strategy. If anything it is the PCF who are following Ceres here.

Let us now sum up on this question. Ceres position as a critical left fraction meant that it would at times be bound to make points similar to the PCF. But it sometimes combines these points with a critique of that party. Where it falls down sometimes is in not distinguishing itself sufficiently from both PCF and the PS right. It tries to avoid making the PCF presents at its own expense, as in the municipal elections. At bottom one can only accept the thesis of *suivisme* if one accepts that Ceres is really no different from the PCF. But we hope to have shown that its whole political project refutes this.

Can we agree overall that Ceres had no illusions about the PCF? Although some Ceres, particularly the more idealistic kind, often admire communist militants as if they were in a class of their own,[73] and although some of Lazic's points contain a limited amount of truth, we must keep in mind the group's overall aim of transforming the PS. Ceres were not paracommunists or uncritical russophiles. They believed they could force the PCF to change by being more activist than it. In this they underestimated the PCF apparatus and the lengths to which it was prepared to go. Their voluntarism also misjudged their own party, the PS; for thus far it has never looked capable of mounting the sort of militant effort Ceres demands. Ceres also overestimated public demand for change – unlike Mitterrand whose 1981 campaign seemed to have watered down party ideology to about the right mix for electoral acceptance. In short the story of Ceres' relationship to the PCF and the left union is one of over- and underestimation; and these errors are not the result of conspiratorial malevolence but of voluntarism.

3.4   FRANCE, SOCIALISM AND THE WORLD

Il y a un lien entre tous les terrains et tous les champs . . . Il n'y a pas un rapport de forces commercial, un rapport de forces monétaire. Il y a un rapport de forces global.   J.-P. Chevènement, *L'Appel*, June 1976

The Ceres chief here expresses one of the deepest held views of his movement. Ceres has always started its analyses from one prime fact, namely that politics takes place in nation-states.[74] The French nation has undergone a long historical development and acquired a certain role in the world-system. Ceres has always sought to understand France's objective international position and has striven to articulate its project for domestic change with the role that France might play in world affairs. The interweaving of the domestic and foreign dimension of Ceres socialism is of the tightest, and it seems to us that such is the fraction's insistence on the international dimension that it could be said to precede (in logic, and arguably in time) the type of change which Ceres seeks within France.[75] At any rate the link is strong and has never varied. We shall here examine the Ceres view of the international system and how France fits into it, then the possible relations between a socialist France and her partners: such relations will be, as Chevènement's remark illustrates, interlinked. International political economy will be inseparable from diplomatic and military relationships, as well as from cultural ties.

For Ceres the modern world begins in 1945 in Yalta. The agreements between the wartime allies (from which France was excluded) meant a cynical division of Europe into two suzerainties, Soviet and American. Ceres views of the Soviet system were mentioned above so we shall concentrate on Western Europe. Its nations enjoy what amounts to limited sovereignty:[76] 'French capital, like German or British, must, if it is to remain imperialist, have the support of US imperialism and thus remain subordinate to it. It is constantly competing or even conflicting with US capital, but cannot break free of its support/domination in military, monetary or economic matters.'

US military domination is assured essentially through NATO. The patterns of economic dominance are those described in Section 3.1 above, and cultural influences will figure in the next section. European integration in the shape of the EEC has done little to counterbalance these domineering trends. Always sceptical of what it saw as a free-trade area ruled by liberal market principles, Ceres felt that European integration could lead in one of two directions.[77] Either it would reinforce the (largely invisible) US penetration of national economies or – and this was the less likely – Europe might begin to develop a higher degree of political cohesion as a result of economic integration and begin to show signs of political autonomy. In this case the US would riposte by threatening to withdraw its military protection. The only way for Europe to progress then was not on liberal and Atlanticist, but socialist and independentist, lines.

At the heart of the European equation stands, however, not so much America but Germany; and here Ceres reveals some very French behavioural syndromes. German economic strength, albeit dissociated from the wish to assume a major diplomatic or military role, roused some deep fears. By the mid-seventies Ceres was wont to speak of a 'mark zone' (used more or less synonymously with the EEC). Its opposition to French membership of the EMS was due to fears of the French economy being 'locked in' to that of a too-powerful neighbour.[78] But the problem goes beyond economics. For German economic strength has as yet no real political autonomy, Ceres often describing Germany as a 'sub-imperialism' or 'staging-post for US imperialism'. The reason for this is the real political and military weakness of Germany. Yalta made it clear that a divided Germany is the rule;[79] it will not be allowed to realise its full potential through unification since the USSR would regard this as an unacceptable security threat. Strong as unitary pressure remains (and it is probably growing), it will not succeed – certainly not through war, for as Chevènement reminds us, either superpower would probably prefer to destroy Europe than cede its part of Germany to a rival suzerainty.[80] This dangerous and frustrating division of Germany will then last for a long time yet, and probably the only way in which some progress can be made on German unity – without France being disadvantaged either – is in the wider context of a dissolution of the two-bloc system. This aspiration lies at the heart of Ceres foreign policy and hence at the heart of the whole political project.

The fullest formulation of Ceres' grand design took place in the mid-seventies notably at the movement's Tenth Colloquium.[81] Here emerged the so-called 'geographical compromise'. Although political developments in Europe (and Mitterrand's own diplomacy since 1981) have weakened the bases of such a strategy, we may still say that it encapsulates Ceres desiderata well. The 'geographical compromise' was a Southern strategy: put at its crudest, it postulated the emergence of like-minded left governments in France, Iberia, Italy and Greece. Developing links of an economic, diplomatic and even military nature, extending its collaboration to take in 'progressive' states in Africa and the Middle East, this socialist community might prove to be the beginnings of a socialist pole in Europe. It might begin to exert a socialist influence on Northern Europe and contribute to détente between the superpowers in Europe as a whole. Concocted in the heady atmosphere of 1975 with the PCI expecting office in Italy, Portugal in leftist effervescence and the left in Spain and Greece awaiting its chance as the dictatorships crumbled, the geographical compromise was a strong brew, even if on inspection some of its contents were rather doubtful.

The founding concept is the notion of a Southern Europe juxta-posed to a Northern one. If it is easy to conceptualise common features which give a Southern identity to Italy, Greece and Iberia, France is more of a problem. Apart from the cultural fact of its Latinity, its recent socio-economic mutations would put it in the eyes of most analysts in the Northern camp. This latter is assumed to cover West Germany, Benelux, the UK and Scandinavia. It is an area of developed monopoly capitalism, with fully-fledged national bour-geoisies and large urbanised working classes; politically it is marked by the ascendancy of social-democracy and an Atlanticist foreign policy. This schema has the advantage of clarity even if it does miss out awkward states (Ireland in the North, Switzerland in the South?) which do not fit very well. But the main aim of this is to enable Ceres to make a counter-definition of Southern Europe. For as Ceres admits, the latter is above all characterised by the negative features shared by its states in contrast to the better developed North. Thus the South is industrially underdeveloped with a large peasant sector. Such development as has occurred is mainly outside-directed, funded by North European and North American capital, with an underlying tendency for German capital to replace American as dominant investor. The business class which has arisen from this is a weak parody of a national bourgeoisie, what Poulantzas would call a mere 'bourgeoisie intérieure'. The working class is of recent peasant origin, hence less integrated than the disciplined social-democratic battalions of the North. The economy of the Southern state is weak, with a feeble currency, high import dependence (especially for oil and raw materials). In addition we may expect political weakness, democracy being feeble as the state emerges from prolonged periods of *régimes d'exception*. In short, if imperialism is a chain then South Europe is near the bottom end of it, exploited by the North which itself is exploited by the USA. Now the advantage of France is that it occupies a special position with one, if not to say one and a half feet in the South; as such she can lead the latter out of capitalist dependence.

This is very much a mid-term strategy. The alliance of left governments might agree on a strategy which has three geographical axes. Towards the South special relationships would be sought with 'progressive' North African states, though Ceres stresses how few and how volatile these are. In practice this would have meant seeking deals with Algeria, Libya and pre-Camp-David Egypt. The economic dimension of this axis will soon be seen. The strategy towards the North is more ambiguous. Given the weight of German investment in the Southern economy, there is no question of a sudden rupture (by nationalisations, withdrawal from the EEC, etc.). Rather the aim will be to strengthen the Southern pole gradually in the hope of convincing the North (mainly German social-democracy) of the advantages it can gain from this. For Ceres believes it possible to wean Germany from its Atlanticism towards a more European-based international policy.[82] As for the Eastern axis, Ceres holds that the gradual emergence of a Southern socialist pole will increase détente in so far as it weakens what the USSR sees as an aggressive Western bloc. Moreover it might help the political liberalisation of Eastern Europe in that the USSR would henceforth feel able to slacken its political hold on its allies. This military–strategic dimension of Ceres thought is given a sharp twist by the hint that the Southern pole might eventually become neutralist or at any rate leave NATO; here the role of French nuclear forces becomes crucial and will be discussed below. Thus far, then, we have a strategy for the creation of a sort of Southern bloc with France effectively, though not entirely openly, postulating for the role of bloc leader.

There is also an attempt to underpin this grand design in the best traditions of 'high policy' with some economic bases. The South has some trump cards which can be played to advantage by coordinated action. First is its demographic potential which promises big markets and high demand. Second is the fact that any industrialisation drive would be able to rely on some key natural resources; the region is self-sufficient in phosphates, oil, iron and cotton and its main shortfall, non-ferrous metals, could be made good through agreements with African producers. The major weakness lies in agriculture, with grave deficiencies in cereals and livestock. Here Ceres proposes rapid land reform done with productively gains in mind, plus strenuous efforts at regional production of fertilisers using the above-mentioned resources. Thus would be created big food industries which could become a major export asset. On a more technical level, industrialisation would be accelerated by inter-governmental coordination of R. & D., intensive training programmes and technical transfer from France and Italy, the two most advanced states of the bloc. A final element of this development programme is that of international financing. Aware of the strength of the dollar and mark and the consequent weakness of Mediterranean currency Ceres suggests an alliance with Arab oil producers (and possibly with a wider circle of commodity producers) in a concerted effort to challenge the hegemony of the dollar. A key stage in this might be the creation of a pan-Arab currency (a sort of Mediterranean écu?) to facilitate trade.

Such are the economic props of the grand design. As for its military dimension, Ceres has taken up some equally characteristic positions.

If the superpowers each dominate their imperialist zone, their hegemony ultimately rests on military strength. Thus any challenge to their politico-economic superiority cannot escape the military dimension. Ever since its inception, which coincided with de Gaulle's attempts to create a relative autonomy in this sphere, Ceres has understood this. Its thinking has been dominated by these questions: What sort of threat does the Warsaw Pact pose to Western Europe and to France? What sort of defence collaboration does France need with Europe and/or the US? These questions come down to asking about the whole relationship of France to the Atlantic Alliance.

Unlike many socialists marked by the Cold War Ceres has never taken a hawkish line on Warsaw Pact intentions. Its analysis ranges from serene optimism to cautious mistrust, depending on the overall tenor of East–West relations. In the late sixties as détente set in at its strongest, Ceres could write that Soviet will for peace since 1954 was so evident that soon a European conference might be held to dissolve both NATO and the Warsaw Pact.[83] In 1983, after Prague, Kabul and the collapse of détente, Ceres refused to see the USSR as fundamentally aggressive. Pointing out that with the exception of Afghanistan none of the current conflicts in the world was due to Soviet instigation, the fraction wrote that if there was a consistent Soviety policy towards Western Europe then it was one of attrition.[84] 'In Europe [Soviet] strategy is less one of war than of "victory without war", via steady neutralisation of the enemy.' In other words the USSR is much less likely than the USA to unleash a conflict over Western Europe; at most it would hope in the long run to wear down Europe by diplomatic/ military pressure, 'decouple' it further from the US and then 'Fin-landise' it. Recognising the need to resist such Soviet pressure 'whenever French interests are threatened', Ceres doubts, however, whether attempts to punish the USSR by economic sanctions, so as to warn it off further Afghanistan-type adventures, serve much purpose. If indeed 'the road to peace in Europe runs through Moscow', then dialogue must be kept open (though this does not exclude a firm posture when required). Thus Ceres views on the USSR as a foreign policy problem have been fairly consistent. Like the statesmen of previous Republics they have, while disliking the regime always been ready to look at the map and appreciate the need for an interlocutor in the East beyond the German (and nowadays the American) just across the frontier.

Cold War socialism believed in a major Soviet threat and sought the answer in the Atlantic Alliance and acceptance of the US nuclear shield in return for conceding political and military leadership of the Alliance. De Gaulle, doubting the strength of US commitment to the defence of Europe, built up French nuclear capacity both as an insurance for the future and to give France more autonomy within the Alliance.[85] Hence the withdrawal of French forces from the NATO integrated command structure in 1965–6. Ceres was quick to approve such moves and its defence policy should be seen as an attempt to push them to their logical conclusion. An early commentary accused the General of not going far enough by remaining in the Alliance.[86] Since then Ceres has rarely stated its ultimate aim so bluntly; but admission of the necessity to stay in the Alliance for the time being is usually qualified with escape-clauses of various kinds.

Ceres has never believed that the US would risk its own cities in defence of Western Europe.[87] What it might do is fight a 'limited' nuclear war in Europe, and this has been a Ceres fear from the early days of flexible response to the arrival of the Euromissiles in 1983 (see

Chapter 6). In this case Europe must rely on its own defence potential as a deterrent to US and USSR alike. Clearly such potential must be mainly nuclear, the group never having had much faith in enhanced conventional defence, at least, in the view of one commentator, until very recently.[88] Unlike the majority of the PS and PCF, Ceres endorsement of French deterrence was swift and total. Believing in 'la dissuasion du faible au fort' or the 'tear-off-an-arm' theory of deterrence, the group holds that French possession of strategic arms gives her a credible deterrent in that it raises the price of invasion beyond limits worthwhile to the aggressor. Such is Ceres confidence in this ultimate deterrence that it is more than ready to abandon battlefield nuclear arms, in the hope of making absolutely clear the distinction between conventional and nuclear warfare.[89] Even the arrival of 'surgical' first-strike weapons like Pershing II and SS-20 has not undermined belief in all-or-nothing deterrence.

But Ceres has also paid attention to the growing doubts as to the credibility of French deterrence – a question which grows more acute as the weapons systems of the superpowers gain in sophistication. How far can a medium-sized power (not that Ceres would openly accept such a label for France) make the financial and technological effort to stay in the nuclear race? Ceres rejects the British solution to this dilemma, namely purchase of a US-produced system on terms of what it sees as technological and political subordination and hence renunciation of an independent nuclear capacity. Another solution might lie in nuclear defence collaboration between France and other European states, and Ceres has toyed with this possibility since the beginning. In 1967 it wrote that only 'a Franco-British nuclear force' could provide a serious mid-term alternative to the Atlantic Alliance.[90] Since then doubts have increased as to the will or capacity of the UK to free itself from dependence on the US, though the door has never been closed. Of late, increasing attention has been paid to Germany as a possible partner, not least since Mitterrand seems to be thinking on similar lines[91] (cf. Chapter 6) notwithstanding the fact that in international law Germany is forbidden to possess nuclear weapons. More serious than this legal constraint is the political problem of persuading Germany to exchange an American nuclear shield for what would be in effect a French one (albeit German-financed). Still more problematic is the fact that a transnational deterrent would presumably need a transnational authority to make it credible and that Ceres is more than anyone in the PS opposed to such supranationality.[92] For the moment, then, the fraction calls for modernisation of the French deterrent but has never abandoned hope of somehow broadening its economic and ultimately political base beyond France.

Ceres has always tried to avoid two traps.[93] One is increasing French reapprochement with NATO, in the hope of recoupling the US more firmly to Europe – a hope which Ceres regards as illusory if, as it says, Chicago will never be sacrificed to save Berlin or Belgrade. The other is what it and the rest of the political class in France call pacifism; by this is meant not renunciation of all violence as a means of defence but the type of unilateral nuclear disarmament and/or enhanced reliance on conventional defence now espoused by most of the PS sister-parties in the Socialist International.[94] Ceres has been one of the earliest and harshest critics of this policy, which in its eyes can only lead to a neutralised Western Europe.[95] 'A neutralised Europe would be a dominated and broken Europe. That is not a political project but an expression of tiredness or fatigue. Turning into a sheep never made the wolf go away . . . This movement is an incoherent expression of the loss of its values by Western society.' Clearly this refusal of 'pacifism' has cultural undertones as well as strategic justifications.

Ceres has, then, been quite consistent on defence matters and not even the moves of the Mitterrand presidency or the Euromissile crisis have signficantly altered them. They see France as having at worst an autonomous role and at best that of bloc-leader and protector if the Southern strategy took wing. Many details of the strategy could be criticised exhaustively and we shall shortly make some of the more salient points. But foreign policy critiques are often underpinned by one argument, namely that Ceres are latter-day Gaullists, if not to say out-and-out nationalists; in moments of anger we have even heard the word 'national-socialists' used. We should perhaps first investigate this charge.

What prompts it is not just Ceres acceptance of the nation-state as the framework of political action, but the positive relish with which the fraction identifies with France.[96] Historically socialists have handled class problematics more readily than national ones; class, not nation, was held to be the major bond of loyalty for the working class, and not even the regular body-blows which this concept has taken, from 1914 to the Falklands, have seriously dislodged its grip on the culture of the European left. In many ways it is hard for a socialism based on class to assume a spatial and cultural dimension the nation, which was, as Poulantzas shows, created contemporaneously with that capitalism which they aim to supersede.[97] Many socialists believe in the international solidarity of the class (whatever this is supposed to mean in practice) and feel that any socialists integrated into their nation are somehow betraying an essential dimension of socialism; this they feel essentially because they see the ruling class as having captured not just the state apparatus but also the whole cultural patrimony which the nation represents. Hence the particular resentment which some feel at the effortless patriotism of Ceres.

We might suggest several reasons for the group's strong and deliberate nationalism. The first and least convincing is an intellectual argument. Faced with a PS generally in favour of European integration, yet seeking also the social transformation of France, Ceres might be said to have seized on the contradictions of this. As the group argues endlessly, the stronger the supranational movement, the more likely it is to be anti-socialist and US-dominated. By contrast, then, socialist policies are best served by resisting integration and using the instruments still available to national governments. While this European dimension may be part of an explanation, it can in no way explain the intensity of Ceres feeling about France.

A more plausible explanation might be the formative experiences of Ceres leaders. These were mainly *énarques*, that is specially trained élites from one of the oldest and most sophisticated bureaucracies in the world. It was moreover a state with long *dirigiste* tradition, whose role in the French economic miracle after 1945 was crucial and which was busy, while the future Ceres was training at ENA (École Nationale d'Administration), preparing a second modernisation of the French economy, purging French finances, encouraging capitalist concentration and dragooning French industry on to the export markets. It is no accident that the Ceres project for French leadership of a Southern bloc makes reference to the power and experience of the French state. Whatever else they learned the young Ceres were steeped in knowledge of the state and its workings;[98] and this knowledge was inseparable from a certain veneration. Significantly, most of them had experience in the diplomatic service or similar branches of the service at a time when de Gaulle's drive for an autonomous world role for France was at its peak. This public service background perhaps explains why Ceres never believed leninist notions about the irredeemably capitalist nature of the state apparatus but also why it saw itself not as a privileged élite but as genuine public servants devoted to the general interest, the *res publica*. If many pages of the famous lampoon *L'Enarchie*[99] are filled with sarcasm towards the greed and ambition of the young bourgeois passing through ENA, we should not forget that the work ends with the thought that a minority at least of the *énarques* are truly committed to the public interest and that they will one day be 'the hussars of socialism'. Like Marx and Lenin, then, the Ceres leaders see themselves to some extent as revolutionary *déclassés*, with the exception that service to the state, even in its present capitalist form, is seen as a revolutionary virtue. Some years ago in a television programme where public figures were asked to choose their favourite historical personage, Chevènement's choice fell on Rossel, ephemeral commander of the citizens' army in the Paris Commune. The choice tells us much about Ceres. Obviously a patriot (the Commune's anti-Prussianism and Jacobinism are well known), Rossel was a civil engineer by trade and from all accounts previously fairly apolitical. Ceres has a vision of a genuinely detached professional, educated indeed bourgeois, but devoted to the public good to the point of dying for it – a model of what the true public servant should be.

Linked to this are questions of character. The Ceres leaders, in their writings, in interviews and in the reminiscences of friend and foe alike come across as men who are intellectually and politically ruthless. They can at times use very dirty tricks (like their opponents) but their devotion to their goal never varies. In their way they are idealistic and almost puritanical. Their admiration for these aspects of French Republican culture is quite logical. Now such characteristics are often the preserve of nationalists also; like the revolution, the nation is a higher ideal calling for effort and sacrifice. There is no reason why if such temperaments are socialised early enough into nationalist as well as socialist ideology, both should not take root. In our view some such process probably affected the young Ceres during their academic career at Sciences-Pô and ENA.

With this we come inevitably to an ill-known but controversial episode, namely the alleged involvement of Motchane and

Chevènement in the student organisation Patrie et Progrès. This allegation (which Chevènement denies) is often made by opponents and occasionally revived in print.[100] Patrie et Progrès was on the populist right: describing itself as socialist it seems to have stood for firm government with a certain amount of economic intervention and redistribution of income, bolstered by a strong nationalist culture. It was run by pro-Gaullist *énarques* at the height of the Algerian war, and seems to have had an audience at Sciences-Pô. Motchane's brother, Jean-Louis, was one of its leaders and some of its members were in favour of *Algérie française*. Detractors also like to point out that Chevènement wrote a student dissertation on the French nationalist right and Germany under the supervision of the old-style Maurrassian nationalist Raoul Girardet. But on inspection this document evinces no particular sympathy for Maurrassism or indeed very much else, being one of the bland, even-handed treatments of the topic which were deemed necessary for academic success in 1960.[101] The point of such inferences is that Ceres leaders were during their student days marked for life by a hard nationalism, if not to say fascism.

This is absurdly exaggerated. Had they really been affected by this type of nationalism the young Ceres would have ended up not in the PS but the OAS. Nor would they have gone on to acquire their encyclopaedic if not to say pedantic marxist culture. What they drew from Patrie et Progrès was most probably a heightened sense of the political importance of the national community and how important a mobiliser it can be. But the French left already knew this of course: and here in our view lies another major source of Ceres nationalism.

Much of the French left has been for most of the time nationalist and internationalist. It has tended to see no conflict between the two. As a recent analysis has it, 'an implicit belief in France's unique revolutionary role in world history is a constant if unavowed factor in the political culture of the French left'.[102] Ceres was and is happy to avow it. It sees itself as successor to the *levée en masse* of 1793, the communards of 1871 and the resisters of 1943–4. Such people were fighting not just to defend the territory, nor even to push through a programme, but for a model they believed universal and exportable. The Blanquists of 1848 and the Zyromskists of 1936 thought that what was good for socialism in France was valid for Poland or Spain. They were ready to go to war to defend this model or on occasion to export it. This aggressive socialism has usually prevailed over its more pacifist and less patriotic rivals. Ceres belongs to this current and this alone makes any comparison with the Pivertists an irrelevance. Now crucially this strand of French socialism became weak after 1945 as French governments, aided and abetted by SFIO leaders, tied France in to Atlanticism and European integration. In this they enjoyed little popular success as France, despite losing an empire, could still not find a role. De Gaulle's populistic pursuit of independence showed how to fill the void and began to draw support from the left. Ceres strove to emulate him; by reviving the patriotic tradition of the left the fraction was thus both effecting a return to orthodoxy and giving itself a vital – probably the most vital – part of its identity.

A final relevant point is Ceres awareness of the political appeal of nationalism. If Gaullian independence was so popular with the French and indeed at the base of the Fifth Republic consensus,[103] any left that wanted to supplant de Gaulle would somehow have to assume this heritage. Thus perception of political advantage to be gained, combined with the sort of predisposition analysed above, made Ceres try and pull the left towards nationalism. This is why it makes sense to Ceres to try and appeal to Gaullists disgruntled with the deviance of Giscard *and* Chirac from received orthodoxy to join in a national pact which would ally an independent foreign policy with a growth-oriented economic package (whose non-socialist elements could if required be stressed). We are also now better able to understand Ceres' relation to Gaullism; for if it endorses most of Gaullism's foreign and defence thinking, then it has always been critical of its economic designs.[104] These they see as no more than a slightly more *dirigiste* version of liberal economics, incapable of providing a material basis for the sort of independence de Gaulle sought. Gaullism is fundamentally flawed; its domestic project can never match up to its foreign one. Only a socialist France at home can guarantee an independent France in the world. The link between high policy and socialism, nation and class is complete.

We have attempted to show why Ceres has elaborated a nationalist strategy for the transition to socialism and why in the light of this it postulates the role of a bloc-leader for a socialist France. It remains to criticise concisely the very model of the geographical compromise on which the strategy is founded.

The fundamental weakness was the assumption of a community of like-minded governments in the South. Plausible as this may have seemed in the excitement of 1975, history took a different path. The PCI's historic compromise came to little, and it seems as far from power as ever. The mass movements in Portugal peaked rapidly and were replaced, thanks to their own contradictions, external interference and the role of the PSP, by a succession of governments dominated in turn by the PSP and the right; these have sought to reverse the gains of 1974–5, using monetarist medicine to weaken an already sick Portuguese economy. When in Spain the PSOE eventually came to office, domestic economic constraints and the tensions of the post-détente era blunted the audacity of a party which under Gonzales had already begun to deradicalise. Thus the whole basis of Ceres strategy was vitiated.

There were always likely to be problems in any case with an alliance of (relatively deprived) Latins and Mediterranean progressives (a very dubious category) against rich Northerners. Not least because France herself, though postulating leadership of the deprived, is nowadays much closer to the rich. The one thing she has in common with the South is a Latin heritage, and in fact much of the appeal of the strategy has to do with this dimension, less measurable than economic factors perhaps but surely no less potent.

Probably the most sensible way to see the whole project is not to take it over literally, but as an aspiration. It does try to suggest how France might enlarge her freedom to manoeuvre in the economic, military and diplomatic fields. The details are less relevant than the ideological message. This is strong and optimistic and we may suppose that it has considerable mobilising power inside the party, and perhaps outside. Certainly it is an essential part of the Ceres ideological matrix, of which the nation can now be seen to be the centre.

3.5 IDEOLOGY, HEGEMONY AND THE ENEMY WITHIN

The preceding sections of this chapter have been highly ideological in character in that their subject matter is informed throughout by an underlying set of principles which reflect and give coherence to the aspirations of those who subscribe to them. Much of this process is perhaps unconscious, but Ceres has been prepared to make an issue of ideology as such. It has sought to make explicit the posits of the ideology of PS rivals and to expose what it claims are the material interests behind them. Since the late seventies much Ceres work has been devoted to this theme, making for some turgid reading. But since the fraction considers this work to be so important we are obliged to follow it.

Like most left socialists Ceres has been influenced by Gramscian notions of hegemony, and like them it has interpreted this complex and open-ended concept, which cannot be fully examined here, to suit its own aims. Ceres takes the term to mean the widespread consent across the social spectrum which accrues to the ideology of a dominant class or class-fraction. Conventionally such supremacy is distinguished from dominance based on repression, using those means of violence which are held to be the legitimate armoury of the state; though as Anderson reminds us, political control of the state apparatus, repressive parts included, is structurally interdependent with hegemony in the ideological field.[105] What this involves, when translated into political practice by socialists, is usually that if they are to win power and govern successfully they must win wide acceptance of their fundamental principles across a large layer of society. That means more than securing a majority for an electoral programme, but somehow ensuring that socialist principles become the everyday 'common sense' of society instead of the liberal-bourgeois ones currently in the ascendant. Thus ideological struggle must be paramount.

So far a the PS is concerned we may add a rider to this. Because of its fractional nature, each fraction will by definition offer a differing version of socialist ideology. That much is obvious; but it is also the case that being a highly intellectualised party, there is an inbuilt tendency to maximise and exploit ideological differences for purposes of identification and exclusion.[106] Thus the ideological battle inside the party will be as strong within it as the battle between the party and the right; it may even on occasion assume an autonomy which proves difficult to control.

Alongside its Gramscian heritage Ceres has an extremely instrumental approach to ideology. It believes that if certain themes are correctly orchestrated, they will produce a high degree of mobilisation. *Autogestion* and nationalism would be prime candidates for this role. Such a view fits in with what we have seen to be the voluntaristic temperament of the leadership and its conviction that economic and social constraints can in the end be transcended by popular surges in alliance with determined political leadership; it is no exaggeration to talk of an attachment to risk and daring as values in themselves. In short Ceres' awareness of the importance of hegemony, its instrumentalism and the very nature of the PS were bound to lead to major ideological battles about ideology. So it would prove after 1975.

Generally Ceres had had a fairly clear field until the presidential campaign of 1974, having by then elaborated a recognisable and operational ideology. It was perceived as standing for a new type of socialism that broke with the past errors of social-democracy; stressing self-management, a renovated and dynamic party, full commitment to left unity, this socialism sought an unashamed reconciliation with the patriotic tradition. This was distant enough yet close enough to the other fractions' version of socialism for all to coexist happily at a time when the PS as a whole was growing in members and votes – a period which peaked with Mitterrand's narrow defeat in 1974. Mitterrand drew conclusions from this, mainly that as the party would probably soon be a certain candidate for office, then it was time to excise or control the more adventurous bits of party ideology which might just deter the few per cent of voters needed for victory. Soon after the Rocardians joined the PS and Mitterrand took them into his majority at the Pau congress in 1975, pushing Ceres for the first time into the minority. The effect of this was to trigger an open ideological battle, which would pivot on the Ceres–Rocard exchanges. After a slow start the battle picked up rapidly after the failure to win the parliamentary elections of 1978 and had sunk to very low depths by late 1980 when with presidential elections in sight the party swung together behind Mitterrand. At times it was reminiscent of the later stages of a fight between two heavyweights, with the punches becoming cruder and more wayward, under the eyes of a referee (Mitterrand) who favoured first one contestant, then the other, before walking off with the prize money. We shall then concentrate on the Ceres–Rocard duel since it encapsulates Ceres views on the role and importance of ideology.

The debate really took off with Rocard's 1977 congress speech on the two cultures.[107] Here he distinguished two traditions on the

French left. The dominant one is Jacobin and statist, looking to the action of an enlightened state to provide change. In so doing it underestimates the value of the second tradition which from Proudhon has seen change not as government-led but arising from the initiatives of groups in civil society and more generally from 'social movements'. These latter conduct the 'social experiments' from which will emerge viable social and economic forms of organisation: in the past cooperatives and mutual aid societies would be good examples, while today the women's movement and environmentalism seem promising. This is of course a very simple presentation of an argument that theorists like Touraine or Rosanvallon and Viveret would handle with great sophistication. But Ceres' reaction was prompt. Mindful of Rocard's lukewarm attitude to the CPG and left unity generally (on the statist grounds elaborated above) and fearful that he would influence Mitterrand, the fraction lashed out. Soon an ideological war was raging in which Ceres caricatured Rocardism as virtually excluding any role for the state in the transition to socialism and the Rocardians riposted by presenting Ceres as arrant statists and crypto-totalitarians.

It is not our aim here, for we are concerned not with ideology as an end in itself but with its uses, to explore in detail the many square kilometres of print where the champions of the enlightened state take on the heralds of civil society. More interesting is the outcome of the dispute in policy terms. For on reflection it is plain that Ceres has never scorned civil society as a force for change: its whole concept of the 'movement from below' shows this. Neither do the Rocardians conceive of the economy in neo-Proudhonian terms as a system of exchanges between sovereign groups of petty commodity-producers, under the benign eye of a state which is by now largely residual. On the face of it it would be astonishing if a fraction with its fair share of *énarques*, led by an *inspecteur des finances*, were entirely sceptical of the macro-economic tools available to government. To demonstrate this we need only consider the principle arena of change, the economy. We have argued elsewhere that the fractional debate on the economic policy of a left government was a hollow affair, particularly with regard to its most frequently evoked aspect, nationalisation.[108] Both sides allowed it to be suggested that there was a crucial choice between two opposing lines: central planners versus market liberals. In fact there was considerable agreement on the main planks of what eventually became PS policy in 1981–2. Both sides admit the need for adequate instruments of macro-economic policy, including control of credit and of the major industrial groups; both agree that the French economy will remain mixed with the major part of it in private hands and with the market playing a determining role (the 'democratic planning' proposals of both sides are quite clear on this). Where the two differ is on the mode of nationalisation, with Ceres seeking full public ownership and the Rocardians content with purchase of majority shareholdings, and above all perhaps in the emphasis given to different parts of their discourse. Thus Ceres spends much time extolling the virtues of the public sector and less on the future of private capital (though fully admitting its vital role in innovation, job-creation, etc.). The Rocardians have an inverse weighting. The other area of disagreement is short-term measures. Rocard warns of the dangers of job-creation via deficit financing and the probable inflationary and balance-of-payments effects of overheating consumer demand.[109] As with nationalisation, this is a question of degree not kind. Both sides are telling the public how much can be expected from a left government in a fairly short time; Ceres has chosen a bullish approach compared with its bearish rivals. It is here that we need to situate Ceres' obsession with *rupture* – an ill-defined break with capitalism which is supposed to take place within the first three months or so of left government. Presumably a series of measures, of which the nationalisations are seen as the most important, the concept has for Ceres a symbolic or a mobilising value. Whether Rocard's lower-key approach to socio-economic change constitutes a fundamentally different version of socialism is something that we can only know in practice (i.e. through a Rocard presidency). For the moment we will conclude that the differences lie between the two varieties of a socialist economic project rather than between two vastly different projects, a socialist one and a liberal one.

Similar considerations arise from fractional versions of what a new socialist economy might look like. Seizing on the affection of some Rocardians for Ivan Illich and their doubts about nuclear energy, Ceres accuses them of seeking a zero-growth economy where 'small is beautiful'. Motchane in particular has enjoyed sneering at such 'bucolic christian daydreams'. Equally Rocardians have chosen to see Ceres as champions of an all-or-nothing productivism, seeking growth irrespective of social or environmental consequences. In truth both fractions know well that growth is a *sine qua non* of successful socialist government; they also know the constraints of the French economy, especially in the energy field and this is why no official text to congress from either will be found to condemn civil nuclear energy. It is true that Rocardians enthuse about changing long-term consumer habits (e.g. by replacing shoddy throw-away goods with better quality products) but Ceres texts can be found which say similar things.[110] Once more it is a question of emphasis, both sides seeking to maximise their difference from the other, in what remains a narrow economic space.

Moving from the economy to a moral level, we find that the rivals have chosen to argue in terms of individual rights versus collective ones. Picking up some of Rocard's critiques of Soviet bureaucracy, Ceres has hinted that its rivals are really born-again liberals, both economically and politically. As such they are not really part of the socialist camp. Against them stands a Ceres which incarnates an older, firmer commitment to collective solidarities and recognises that group freedoms are the best (only?) guarantee of individual ones.[111] It is further suggested that the new individualism is not just a by-product of May 1968 but that it has foreign roots: in fact it is an American import. It originates on the West Coast of the sixties, and imperceptibly such individualism has become conflated with sexual and other forms of permissiveness ('the liberation of desire'). Capitalism was quite happy to encourage such hedonism, for of course it turns back on serious politics; there is a sort of pleasure/authority trade-off. When Ceres really wants to wound, Calfornian drug-culture is dragged, none too subtly, into the equation; the retailers of neo-liberalism are assimilated to dealers in dangerous drugs. At the limit the Ceres caricature of Rocardian socialism, the 'American left', might be encapsulated in the heroes of the film *Easy Rider* – individualistic, self-indulgent and politically impotent.[112]

As if this were not enough, attacks are made from other angles than the transatlantic. Picking up Rocardian interest in autonomous groups within civil society, Charzat assimilates this to the mainstream of nineteenth-century liberal thought or even to Christian social thought as exemplified by organicist theorists like Le Play.[113] The *Projet socialiste* does not hesitate to consign interest in intermediary groups and the support for decentralisation which this usually involves to the tradition of the French right from de Maistre to Marshal Pétain![114] The Rocardians tried in vain to have this section deleted from the text. Rocardism thus stood condemned from yet another angle; not only was it American but anti-Republican and clerical.

The final nail in the Rocardian coffin was a methodological one. Seizing on growing Rocardian criticism of the 'totalitarian' nature of the Soviet state, especially by Jacques Julliard, Ceres attacked this as a flabby concept which conflates regimes of different origins and characteristics.[115] But some Rocardian critiques went further, hinting that 'scientific' marxist analyses were at bottom responsible for the human and political errors of stalinism. Ceres took this to mean that Rocardism was anti-scientific, in the sense that no valid conclusions could be drawn from history or social science as to how to analyse capitalist society and prepare a political response. Hence the insertion into the *Projet socialiste* of stern strictures emphasising the attachment of socialists to the spirit of scientific enquiry and the numerous side-swipes at the 'irrationalism' of enemies.[116] Sometimes this is linked to the revival of fringe religion, and in general readers are not allowed to forget that Ceres' enemies are in some way connected to religion, unlike the fraction itself which is firmly in the secularist Republican lineage.

Ceres thus built up an image of Rocardism (hardly ever mentioned directly) as a sort of antipole. As recently revived phrase has it, it is 'the enemy within'. Objectively or subjectively – one is never quite sure – it is an accomplice of Giscardism, part of the 'liberal–libertarian alliance'. Both are said to favour the market, not socialism; both accept the dominance of America and neither is properly Republican, nor in the last analysis, French. At times the clash is painted in the language of World War II, with appeals to join the resisters. Their enemy can only be the collaborators . . .

What are we to make of this depiction? We will not attempt a detailed critique, for its grosser elements render that task superfluous. More interesting are the motivations behind it. For if Ceres goes to such ridiculous lengths to disfigure opponents, there is more to it than passion engendered in the heat of the moment.

Ceres has given a sociological justification for its polemics.[117] According to this, Rocardism is the attempt of the new salaried middle class to secure a political role and accompanying material advantages for itself. Hence it adopts a reformism compatible with Giscard and pursues a mythical French version of Northern social-democracy, at the expense of the left alliance (in which it would take second place to the workers). This is a modified version of the 'labour aristocracy' theory. While useful polemically, it glosses over the fact that the leaders and followers of Ceres are in sociological terms very little different from the Rocardians or indeed any other fraction – certainly not to the point where one could base a theory on it. Unless of course one shifts the argument away from social origins (which are measurable) to the secret thoughts of leaders (which are not).

More serious are questions of power. Rocard was a potential party leader and president; his followers were numerous and able enough to form the backbone of a government and fill the more important positions in the state apparatus. All this would happen at the expense of Ceres. Questions of power and careers are always extremely important and it has never been the intention of this study to minimise them. But power has first to be won and then to be used in the service of an ideology. Ceres had doubts about Rocard on both these scores. On winning, it may have been that Rocard's abrasive approach to the PCF and left unity might still have allowed the PCF to demobilise enough of its voters to stop a PS victory. To that extent the Mitterrand line (not openly hostile to the PCF apparatus, but sending increasingly reassuring signals to floating voters) was preferable, even though Ceres knew that Mitterrand's real feelings on this topic were nearer to Rocard's than their own. Even more serious was the prospect that a Rocard victory would signal the end of an attempt at a French socialism, with the key factor of growth sacrificed to the constraints of counter-inflation policy and balance-of-payment precautions. To sum up, Rocard might never win in the first place, despite the opinion polls, and if he did there would be less likelihood of even a partial attempt at Ceres policies than with Mitterrand. Either way he was the man to stop, and in a party like the PS, ideological war was the best weapon.

There are other reasons also. Ceres hated Rocard long before he became a national figure.[118] It despised him for leaving the SFIO and helping to start up the PSU, where *autogestion* and other modernising themes were first aired during the sixties. His return in 1974 was

regarded with amused irony; here was a Johnny-come-lately trying to
take over a successful ship which Ceres had done much to launch. But
it is not simply that Ceres dislikes Rocard's opportunism or even that it
despises the political judgement of a man that it has always regarded as
a loser whatever his short-term popularity. At stake is loyalty to a
certain conception of party. Ceres actually loved the SFIO; to read
Socialmédiocratie is to perceive, beneath the *énarque* jibes, a genuine
affection for the party, to some extent because it was so antiquated. For
traditionalists – and Ceres are such – the party's sheer capacity for
survival was proof that it represented something durable and was
worth saving. Also what SFIO incarnated was not just the socialist and
working-class tradition but also the Republican one. Like the Radicals
before it, it was a vehicle for values such as belief in rational approaches
to politics, a rather puritanical suspicion of blatant individualism and a
strong notion of solidarity and mistrust of any metaphysical approach
to politics. Rocard helped Ceres realise that this was a part of its
identity. The catholic influence within Rocardism of men like Viveret,
especially when combined with Rocardian reverberations from dissidents within Ceres' own ranks, in which catholics played a large part,
provided a sort of trigger. Rocard was not just a political opportunist
with some wrong ideas; he and his people actually did not belong to
the same family. The war with Rocardism thus helped Ceres to harden
its identity, probably not in a way it would have anticipated. Ideology
thus has the capacity to surprise those who think they are using it.

In conclusion, Ceres awareness of the importance of hegemony led
it to pick an ideological fight with Rocard. Given that political
differences between the two were initially blurred by the fact that both
claimed the new creed of *autogestion* as their own, Ceres felt it had to
maximise these differences and did so to the point of caricature. The
process was partly deliberate, partly involuntary. The element of
choice stemmed from the fact that the fraction needed to reinforce its
self-definition if it were to survive the modernisers' challenge; to paint
oneself in bright ideological hues is the best way to reinforce those
feelings of belonging (and of exclusion of the other) which are central
to fractional existence. (The Rocardians for their part did the same.)
The involuntary element lay in the consequences of this choice,
notably in the militant re-espousal of the Republican tradition,
especially its rationalist secularism, which had hitherto figured little in

FIGURE 3.1   CERES IDEOLOGY: A MATRIX

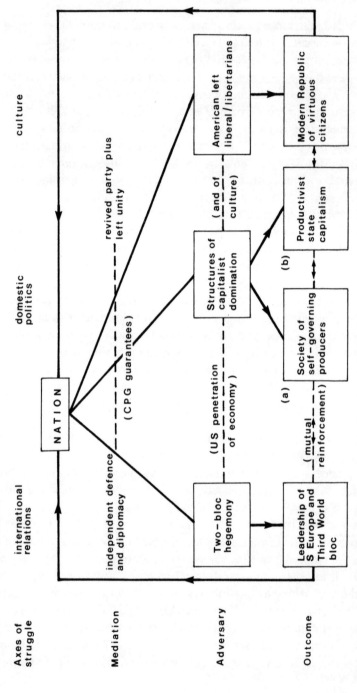

Total outcome: A socialist nation, reconciled with itself, playing a progressive world role

Ceres discourse. The battle of ideas confirmed that such ideas revolve round communities and that the PS fractions illustrate this well.

3.6 CONCLUSION

Figure 3.1 attempts a diagrammatic summation of the considerable ground covered in this chapter. We suggest that within the Ceres ideological matrix, the nation is the starting point and the final goal; its transformation from the framework of bourgeois capitalism which it is at present to a socialist community of producers is the result of constant struggles. Led by the forces of progress within it (the class-front and its political spearhead, the left union), the French nation affronts various adversaries as it seeks its self-realisation. In foreign affairs it must break the two-bloc hegemony; at home it must fight the hold of (mainly multinational) capital and the cultural destruction sponsored by it and its allies. All these struggles are linked in time and in purpose. Out of them will emerge an independent France (model and bloc-leader) which has at home rediscovered her Republican self, and in the field of economy and society developed a new mode of production (the two versions of this, *autogestion* and state-capitalism, can be seen as superseding each other in time). Each one of these effects strengthens the other and thus France; the circle is complete.

Any one element of this matrix could be isolated and criticised separately and we have done this on occasion. Such exercises are of limited relevance, however, for what matters about Ceres ideology is its comprehensiveness. It offers a global, overreaching explanation of the world. As such it well fulfills its mythic function as a mobiliser, as Ceres is well aware: 'Utopia is far away and this distance somehow establishes its legitimacy; but it is also very close. Its project must be understandable and feasible; it cannot be seen to depend on the sacrifice of whole generations.'[119]

What distinguishes it then from mainstream party ideology and what makes it left?

In order to answer this question we need an operative definition of mainstream PS ideology as it emerged after 1971. This is in fact more elusive than seems apparent; party texts are the official guide to it, but we need to complete these by reference to the statements (and

actions) of leaders, notably Mitterrand. With this in mind we may
postulate the following. Despite use of marxist terminology (which we
see to be a rather adulterated legacy from its Guesdist past), PS ideology
is fundamentally reformist in scope. Economically it promised more
state intervention, but always within the context of a mixed economy;
in so far as it contemplated a new mode of production, socialism, this
remained far away in the mid to long term. Although it spoke of class
or even class antagonism, it did not think in terms of class war, with the
eventual victory of one class over another; and it always combined
such rhetoric with commitment to increasing democratic participation
and civic liberties generally, including property rights. In foreign affairs
it took due heed of Gaullian independence and even allowed itself
some thirdworldist, anti-imperialist flourishes; but its pro-European
and generally pro-Western aspects were equally visible. In terms of
party alliances, it favoured the left alliance with the PCF, but not at any
price; and it always strove to keep open the door for centrist or
disgruntled right-wing voters. Probably the traditional bit of Guesdist
baggage which it had most difficulty in hiding was its secularism,
especially in education policy.

In short here was an ideology governed mainly by the party's place
in the political system. It had to keep faith with some of the left
tradition, so as to retain its older voters and attract PCF deserters. Yet its
aura of youth, change and modernity, often presented in an informal,
unideological way, was vital if it were to reach out on its right towards
the new salaried midle class with its 'cultural liberalism'.[120] Such a
compromise ideology is always the lot of reformist parties, simply
because of their place in the party system and the nature of the social
groups which they must of necessity attract.

We may thus better situate the Ceres ideology, and we can see that
several factors place it on the left of the main one (just as Rocardism
could be put on the right).

First is its aspiration to a qualitatively distinct style of socialism
(symbolised by the anxiety about rupture), beyond what the social-
democratic majority seeks; the content of this socialism has undergone a
mutation (in a more statist sense),[121] but not the conviction that social-
democracy can and must be left behind. Second are the instruments of
this transformation, the party and the left union, which are dialectically
associated; this element is crucial to the left project because it is the

only means of avoiding the slide back into social-democracy. The third element is the hardest to fit into a left framework, yet it is the most characteristic, namely nationalism. From the start Ceres strove to reconcile its concept of a new society with a new concept of belonging to the nation and a new international role for it. How far nation can be synonymous with progress and socialism is something which readers – and history – will decide.

In conclusion we hold that Ceres secreted a comprehensive left ideology, distinct from the majority PS line, yet not so incompatible with it as to justify claims of paracommunism, etc. But if such an ideology is to fulfil its role of mobilising, it needs the support of an organisation. To this we now turn.

NOTES TO CHAPTER 3

1   J. Plamenatz, *Ideology*, London, Macmillan, 1970, p. 31.
2   On Ceres economic theory generally, see Parti Socialiste, *Socialisme et multinationales: colloque de la fédération de Paris*, Paris, Flammarion, 1976; CERES, *L'enlèvement de l'Europe*, Paris, Entente, 1979 and *Le Ceres par lui-même*, Paris, Bourgois, 1979, pp. 90–117; M. Charzat et al., *Le Ceres – un combat pour le socialisme*, Paris, Calmann-Lévy, 1975, pp. 142–53; D. Motchane and J.-P. Chevènement, *Clés pour le socialisme*, Paris, Seghers, 1973, pp. 174–85; J.-P. Chevènement, *Le vieux, la crise, le neuf*, Paris, Flammarion, 1974, pp. 71–120 and the following numbers of *Frontières/Repères* – 13 January 1974; 31–2, March–May 1976 (on MNCs); 34, July–August 1976; 36, October 1976; 37, November 1976; 40, February 1977 (industrial policy); 43, May 1977 (nationalisations); 52–8, April–November 1978.
3   A vintage declaration (*Cahiers du Ceres* III, 1968, p. 12) sees the result of American cultural domination of Wilson's Britain to be such that it has turned the British political class into 'a people of sub-Americans'.
4   *Repères* 31, March 1976, pp. 10–26.
5   'La droite américaine', ibid. 49, pp. 48–69 and 58, November 78, pp. 46–61.
6   'La Démocratie menacée', ibid., 50, Feburary–March 1978, pp. 4–60.
7   For a useful survey of the concept see B. Brown, *Socialism of a different kind*, New York, Greenwood Press, 1982. The PS line is in *Quinze Thèses sur l'autogestion*, Paris, 1975. For typical Ceres views see Chevènement, *Le vieux*, pp. 133–241; Motchane, *Clés*, pp. 240–94; *Les Cahiers du Ceres* XI, January 1972 (special number); 8e. Colloque du Ceres – *Autogestion, programme commun et problème de la transition* (supplement to *Frontières* 18, July–August 1974).
8   Brown, op. cit., p. 67.
9   Ibid., p. 53.
10   Chevènement, *Le vieux*, p. 181.
11   Ibid., pp. 190–204.
12   *Les Cahiers du Ceres* III, 1967.

13   Ibid., VII, February 1970.

14   In general the furthest Ceres is prepared to go corresponds to the party line on devolution. Thus on Corsica it supports the idea of a special statute, but within the French state (cf. J.-P. Chevènement, *Etre socialiste aujourd'hui*, Paris, Cana, 1979, pp. 57–79).

15   P. Krop, *Les Socialistes et l'armée*, Paris, PUF 1983. For Ceres views on the armed forces see J.-P. Chevènement and P. Messmer, *Le Service militaire*, Paris, Balland, 1977; *Frontières* 24, July–August 1974, pp. 22 ff; 28, December 1975, pp. 41–6 and *Repères* 43, April 1977, pp. 39–46.

16   Chevènement, *Le vieux*, p. 217.

17   *Le Monde* 24 August 1984.

18   Chevènement, *Le vieux*, p. 147.

19   Ibid., p. 119. Cf. Ceres 8e Colloque, op. cit., Motchane, *Clés*, pp. 152 ff.

20   Brown, op. cit., p. 76.

21   Marc Wolf, interview with author, Mons-en Baroeuil, March 1981.

22   J. Poperen, *L'Unité de la gauche*, Paris, Fayard, 1975, pp. 374–7.

23   Thus on Sweden (*Frontières* 11, November 1973, pp. 32 ff.) Ceres admits that SAP government has brought the highest living standards and best protection against risk in Europe and that material inequalities have been considerably reduced. But there are limits and future progress is impossible 'without overturning the traditional organisation of society'.

For general views on social-democracy see J. Mandrin, *Socialisme ou social-médiocratie*, Paris, Seuil, 1969; J.-P. Chevènement, *Les Socialistes, les communistes et les autres*, Paris, Aubier Montaigne, 1977; Charzat et al, *Le Ceres – un combat*, pp. 191–211. D. Motchane, *Clés*, pp. 90–124; CERES, *Le Ceres par lui-même*, pp. 195–254.

24   *Les Cahiers du Ceres* II, part 2, January 1968 and VII, February 1970, p. 21.

25   'Les mérites de Monsieur Schmidt', *Volonté socialiste* (new series) 13, August 1976.

26   'Are not Soarès and the majority of the PSP the caricature of some weaknesses that the PS must avoid? The inability to match electoral success with mass action and failings which mean that they give up as soon as the problem of breaking with capitalism is raised.' (*Volonté socialiste* 31, May 1977).

27   Chevènement, *Les socialistes*, pp. 171 ff.

28   Mandrin, *Socialisme*, pp. 25 ff.

29   Chevènement, op. cit., p. 175.

30   Mandrin, op. cit., p. 52.

31   Ibid., p. 70.

32   Chevènement, op. cit., p. 116.

33   Mandrin, op. cit., p. 37.

It is important to distinguish Ceres dislike of Mollet's politics from its admiration of Mollet the man (cf. the obituary in *Repères* 26, October 1975, pp. 39–40). It is true as Ceres says that he did in the end reluctantly come round to some form of left unity and that it was he who gave Ceres its chance to make a political name in the first place. Beyond this, Ceres admired Mollet for his total loyalty to his party; and it is possible that certain of his nationalist and secularist ideals were closer to the underlying culture of Ceres than the latter cared to admit, initially at least. Some of our case studies will suggest in fact that culturally Ceres and Mollettists were not always the enemies which they seemed to be.

34   Charzat *et al.*, op. cit., p. 203.

35 Mandrin, op. cit., p. 148.

36 Ibid., p. 162.

37 *Les Cahiers du Ceres* IV, 1968 (special number on socialist parties). See also Ceres motions to congress, usefully reproduced in CERES, *Le Ceres par lui-même,* pp. 59–88. Cf. also Motchane, *Clés,* pp. 186–227; Chevènement, *Le vieux,* pp. 118–32.

38 *Les Cahiers du Ceres,* op. cit., p. 35 states that 'the existence of organised tendencies within a movement does not prove that internal democracy is practised – rather the opposite'.

39 *Le Point* 10 May 1976.

40 Internal document on organisation, n.d. (*c.* April 1977).

41 'Le Ceres – un autoportrait', *Repères* 28, December 1975, pp. 20–5.

42 The second line seems only to have figured prominently during the effervescence of the mid-seventies.

43 There were of course only two substantive motions at Pau – Mitterrand's being no. 1.

44 G. Martinet, 'L'avenir du courant de gauche au sein du PS', internal document, n.d. (summer 1974).

45 For the hardline view see A. Salomon, *Le PS: mise à nu,* Paris, Laffont, 1980; B. Lazic, *L'Echec permanent: l'alliance socialiste-communiste,* Paris, Laffont, 1978. Mauroy once hit below the belt in a CD meeting by saying that Ceres was dangerous 'because it comes from outside'. For the second view cf. G. Martinet, interview with author, Paris, 1980.

46 Cf. Chevènement's admiration (*Les Socialistes,* p. 49) for Lenin's *Break-up of the Second International* whose analysis of the causes of World War I stems directly from Lenin's theory of imperialism.

47 For Ceres views of political action and the state see Motchane, *Clés,* pp. 129–85; Charzat *et al., Le Ceres, un combat,* pp. 223–73; *Repères* 52, April 1978, pp. 6–17. Cf. also the interview of Chevènement and Motchane with Henri Weber in *Critique communiste* April–May 1975, pp. 32–40.

48 Chevènement, op. cit., p. 161.

49 Lazic, op. cit., pp. 155–7.

50 Chevènement, *Les socialistes,* passim; CERES, *Le Ceres par lui-même,* pp. 220–53. See also the following numbers of *Frontières/Repères:* 18, July–August 1974; 21, January 1975, pp. 12–17; 23, May 1975, pp. 38–47; 26, October 1975, pp. 4–13; 27, November 1975, pp. 4–7; 41, March 1977, pp. 4–18; 46, October 1977, pp. 34–65; 53–4, May–June 1978, pp. 92–105; 64, June 1979, pp. 10–19.

51 Michel Charzat believes the opposite. He reckons that some 10% of Ceres cadres (his phrase) have had experience in the PCF. (Interview with author, Paris, July 1981.)

52 T. Bondoux, 'Vaincre la division', *Volonté socialiste* (new series) 98, March 1981.

53 A typical example is Chevènement's interview with *Volonté socialiste* 91, November 1980, where he derides Marchais's view that the USSR is simply helping a fraternal government in Afghanistan and his praise of the Polish government's 'spirit of negotiation and conciliation' in its dealings with Solidarnosc. He then adds that the Labour minister's advisers have just pointed out that the right to strike in France is in fact much more restricted than commonly believed.

54 *Volonté socialiste,* op. cit.

Ceres views on the USSR are scattered across the fraction's texts but the general line is clear. Despite some disagreement Ceres tends to see the USSR as state-capitalist. This mode of production preserves some essential features of capitalism (wage labour producing surplus value) but this value is appropriated not by a bourgeoisie but by the ruling élite of state and party functionaries (there is some hesitation as to whether these constitute a class capable of reproducing itself). Aware of the historical difficulties of Soviet development, Ceres regards as positive the disappearance of private ownership of the means of production and the development of productive forces by the regime, but criticises the lack of democracy. It is felt that this might change in view of the growing economic strength of the USSR.

In foreign affairs the USSR is not seen as irretrievably expansionist. Its imperialism (some of the fraction refuse this term) is military/diplomatic and not based on the export of capital. If it extracts surplus value from its Comecon allies it does so by price mechanisms of 'unequal exchange' (cf. Barrat-Brown's analysis).

Ceres thus does not make an issue of the 'totalitarianism' of the USSR but could not be said to be uncritical. Anti-sovietism has its uses in internal PS debate, and the fraction is well aware of this.

See Charzat et al., op. cit., pp. 156 ff.; Motchane, Clés, p. 139; Mandrin, Le socialisme, op. cit., p. 266.

55 Chevènement, Les socialistes, pp. 176 ff.
56 Ibid., p. 148.
57 CERES, Le Ceres par lui-même, pp. 230 ff.
58 Repères 55–6, July–September 1978, p. 9.
59 A dissenting note was struck by Guidoni (Repères 65, July–August 1979, pp. 20–7) who suggested that a successful transition to democratic socialism by the communist parties might cut the ground from under their more fragile rivals.
60 '[The PCF] shows more evidence of internal democracy than the need to impose iron discipline' (Chevènement, Les Socialistes, p. 146).
61 A very weak PCF would be as bad as a very strong one, for there might then be no necessary counterweight to the social-democratic tendencies inherent in the PS. Presumably the right balance involves a PCF strong enough to threaten but not to forge ahead.
62 For a detailed account of this period see R. W. Johnson, The Long March of the French Left, London, Macmillan, 1981.
63 On the campaign see Projet, December 1980 and February 1981; Pouvoirs 14, 1981; Le Monde, L'Election présidentielle, 26 avril – 10 mai, 1981, Paris, 1981. Journal of Area Studies 4, 1981.
64 J. Jaffré, 'France de gauche, vote à gauche', Pouvoirs 21, 1982, pp. 5–28.
65 Lazic, op. cit., p. 173.
Lazic speaks of a 'véritable exodus' towards the PCF in 1977, which on inspection amounts to six people. He also implies, by suggesting a link between Roland Massard's departure from both Ceres and the PS, that he was joining the PCF. This is nonsense and Lazic is silent about the real cause of Massard's departure, namely Hernu's seizure of Villeurbanne town hall from the PCF, who were entitled to head the list. The operation has more in common with a smash-and-grab raid than with a political alliance (of which the PS was supposed to be part).
66 Charzat believes that Destrem never ceased to be a member of the PCF – which suggests that the latter was worried enough about the fraction to have tried to place someone on the inside (interview with author, July 1981).
67 Lazic, op. cit., p. 165.

68 *Repères* 25, September 1975. On Portugal generally see the following numbers of the review; 23, May 1975 (special number); 26, October 1975, pp. 40–5; 27, November 1975, pp. 62–75; 28, December 1975, pp. 26–34; 30, February 1976, pp. 42–8; 46, October 1977, pp. 76–9.

69 *Repères* 25, op. cit., p. 7.

70 V. Wright, *Conflict and Consensus in France*, London, Cass, 1979, Chapter 1.

71 'Municipales', internal document, n.d. (*c.* July 1977).

72 It is possible that Ceres' failure to give better support to Massard (which made him very bitter) is due to tacit trade-offs within the CD over other towns where the fraction was better placed. If so this shows that the fraction is less concerned with feathering the PCF's nest than its own – exactly like its rivals in the party.

73 P.-L. Séguillon, 'Le 23e. congrès du PCF', *Repères* 64, June 1979, pp. 10–19.

74 In 1983 Ceres could still write 'democracy is for the time being and for a long time to come only practicable in nation states' (J. Mandrin, *Le Socialisme et la France*, Paris, Sycomore, 1983, p. 194).

75 'France's mission in the world – that was the real question asked of Frenchmen during the presidential election, *the question which subsumes all the others and which gives our project its true meaning*'. (Ibid., p. 196, our italics.)

76 *Repères* 33, June 1976, p. 93; Parti socialiste, *Socialisme et multinationales*, op. cit.

77 *Repères* 33, p. 56. More generally see CERES, *L'Enlèvement de l'Europe*, op. cit. This title is incidentally lifted from the June 1976 number of the Gaullist *L'Appel*, where Chevènement made his appeal for the patriotic vote.

78 J. Sandeau, 'Brême – pavane pour un boa-constrictor', *Repères* 58, November 1978, pp. 46–55.

79 'The European balance between East and West has been established for thirty years on the division of Germany . . . So long as there is no volatility in Central Europe the risk of war is nil (Chevènement, *Les Socialistes*, p. 287).

80 Ibid., p. 288.

81 'Dossier du Xe. Colloque', *Repères* 33, June 1976, pp. 44–120.

82 'The aim will not be to break with the North but to exert joint pressure so as to draw it gradually into a Mediterranean strategy', ibid., p. 83.

83 M. Lancier, *Cahiers du Ceres* I, 1967. On Ceres defence views in the 1970s see *Repères* 42, April 1977, pp. 7–47 and 47, November 1977, pp. 26–78.

84 J. Mandrin, *Le socialisme et la France*, p. 224.

85 The insurance argument has two pillars, first the idea that the limited French deterrent can still make the price of aggression too high. This is known as 'la dissuasion du faible au fort' or the 'tear-off-an-arm theory', and had always been endorsed by Ceres. The second, unavowed but possibly more credible, rests on French capacity to escalate a conventional war into a nuclear one by firing a missile, undetectably, at either of the main protagonists. See D. Johnstone, 'The French left and the Bomb', *New Left Review* 146, July–August 1984, pp. 5–37.

86 M. Lancier, op. cit.

87 J. Mandrin, op. cit., p. 211.

88 J. Howorth, 'Consensus of silence: the French socialist party and defence policy under F. Mitterrand', *International Affairs* 60, Autumn 1984, pp. 579–600.

89 J.-P. Chevènement, *L'Appel*, June 1976, p. 47.

90 M. Lancier, op. cit.

91 J. Mandrin, op. cit., p. 221.

120 Keeping left?

92 D. Motchane, preface to *L'Enlèvement de l'Europe*. See also Ceres contribution to party special congress on Europe at Bagnolet, December 1973 in *Frontières* 11, November 1973, pp. 46–60. For the PS and Europe in general see M. Newman, *Socialism and European Unity*, London, Junction Books, 1983 and J. Bound and K. Featherstone, 'The French Left and the European Community' in D. Bell (ed.), *Contemporary French Political Parties*, London, Croom Helm, 1982, pp. 165–89.

93 J. Mandrin, op. cit., p. 218.

94 See D. Hanley and H. Portelli (eds), *Social-démocratie et défense en Europe*, Paris, forthcoming.

95 Mandrin, loc. cit.

96 'We are not, whatever Giscard may have said, a second-rate nation. And other countries know that well ... Please forgive us our weakness, but when someone says "France", we do not sigh condescendingly ... when France is humiliated or vilified we do not feel like laughing.' (Mandrin, op. cit., pp. 195–6.) There are a number of similarly emotional reactions in this text.

97 N. Poulantzas, *L'Etat, le pouvoir, le socialisme*, Paris, Seuil, 1977, p. 132.

98 A former Ceres economic expert told us that 'Chevènement and co. knew more about the state when they were twenty than I did when I was forty'.

99 J. Mandrin, *L'Enarchie*, Paris, Table Ronde, 1968, pp. 47 ff. and 151–2.

100 'La patrie de Chevènement', *Valeurs actuelles*, 5 September 1983.

101 J.-P. Chevènement, *La droite nationaliste devant l'Allemagne*, Paris, IEP (mémoire), 1959.

102 D. Johnstone, op. cit., p. 11.

103 P. Cerny, *The Politics of Grandeur*, Cambridge University Press, 1980.

104 'La décomposition du gaullisme', *Repères* 38, December 1976.

105 P. Anderson, 'Antinomies of Antonio Gramsci', *New Left Review* 100, January 1977, pp. 5–80.

106 P. Garraud, 'Discours, pratique et ideologie dans l'évolution du PS', *Revue française de science politique* XXVIII, April 1978, pp. 257–76.

107 *Repères* 45, July–August 1977, pp. 44–65. The debate between these two lefts is immense and the following are offered simply as representative introductions to both protagonists. For Rocardism or the *deuxième gauche* generally see M. Rocard, *Parler vrai*, Paris, Seuil, 1978; P. Rosanvallon and P. Viveret, *Pour une nouvelle culture politique*, Paris, Seuil, 1977; A. Touraine, *L'Après-socialisme*, Paris, Grasset, 1980. For a general overview see H. Hamon and P. Rotman, *La deuxième gauche*, Paris, Ramsay, 1982. Ceres' attitudes are found in Chevènement, *Etre socialiste*, pp. 79–93; *Le Ceres par lui-même*, pp. 255–76; M. Charzat, *Le syndrome de gauche*, Paris, Grasset, 1979 and in *Repères* 55–63, 1978–9 which cover the period of the Pierret split.

108 D. Hanley, 'Les variables de Solférino: thoughts on steering the socialist economy' in S. Williams (ed.), *Socialism in France from Jaurès to Mitterrand*, London, Pinter, 1983, pp. 136–54. The main thesis is that the differences between fractions have less to do with hard and fast economic issues than with cultural ones, especially nationalism.

109 M. Rocard and J. Gallus, *L'Inflation au coeur*, Paris, Gallimard, 1975.

110 Chevènement, *Le vieux*, p. 199.

111 Parti socialiste, *Projet socialiste – pour la France des années 80*, Paris, Flammarion, 1980, pp. 142 ff.

112 The origins of this curious tag 'American left' appear to lie in the subtitle of *Repères* 49, January 1978, 'La Droite américaine'. This dealt largely with Giscard, so

presumably it seemed logical to describe his 'objective allies' in the same coin.

113 Charzat, *Le syndrôme de gauche*, op. cit., p. 197.

114 *Projet socialiste*, pp. 26–7.

115 Mandrin, *Le socialisme et la France*, p. 204.

116 Charzat, *Le syndrôme, passim*.

117 Ibid., pp. 137–210.

118 Chevènement, *Le vieux*, p. 14.

119 Mandrin, *Socialisme ou social-médiocratie*, p. 110.

120 G. Grunberg and E. Schweisguth, 'Profession et vote: la poussée de gauche' in J. Capdevielle (ed.), *France de gauche, vote à droite* Paris, FNSP, 1981, pp. 139–65.

121 Perhaps not too much should be made of this since to a large extent other sections of the party have followed suit in the light of disappointments at socialist performance in government. The only serious *autogestionnaires* at the 1983 Bourg congress were the supporters of Motion III and these 'dissident Rocardians' scored a bare 5 per cent.

CHAPTER 4

The structures of Ceres

Les trois sources du Ceres – l'Eglise, l'appareil d'état et le gauchisme
décomposé.   Organisation Communiste Internationaliste

Un pot-pourri communo-gauchiste qui ne correspond, selon moi, à
aucune
réalité politique.   F. Mitterrand, 1975

On rentre au Ceres comme on rentre en religion, ou au PC.
                                            Ceres activist in Brittany

4.1 THE HISTORY OF CERES – FROM THINK-TANK TO
FRACTION

At some time in December 1965 or January 1966 – survivors'
memories vary – a group of young activists began to meet regularly to
discuss socialist politics. They met in the apartment of Jean-Pierre
Chevènement or in that of Ghislaine Toutain, a student who soon
became the group's (unpaid) secretary. Of the initial half-dozen, most
were civil servants from the top training school, ENA. As well as the
two leading spirits Chevènement and Didier Motchane, they included
Alain Gomez (now head of a major nationalised group after a career as
a captain of industry), J.-L. Chartier, a treasury official who has since
been a regular contributor to Ceres writings and Loic Hennekine, now
a career diplomat. Another key figure was the *énarque* Jacques
Vidal who would die prematurely but seems to have been particularly
dynamic.[1] The group soon swelled to twenty or so, most of them
in the SFIO and mostly active members of the branch in the
14th *arrondissement*. Their concerns were simple and have hardly
varied since. How could the left unite and win power? What sort

of socialist party was needed to spearhead this unity and the subsequent government?

In mid-1966 these intellectuals received a reinforcement that would prove crucial. This was young postal inspector Georges Sarre. Like many provincial postmen, *montés à Paris*, Sarre came from an old socialist family. He was also active in the trade union FO (Force ouvrière) and a born organiser. He set up a friendly society for postmen, l'Amicale des postiers socialistes, recruiting on a personal basis.[2] This would bring Ceres (the group had now adopted this title) a core of keen and hardworking militants and enlarge its scope beyond its intellectual base. The other major Ceres organiser, the academic Michel Charzat, joined shortly before the 1968 riots. For the time being activity remained intellectual, with pieces appearing in left-wing papers like *Combat* and discussion papers being published as from 1967. These *Cahiers du Ceres* were published with money supplied by Guy Mollet himself, and printed in Arras where he was deputy-mayor; he was pleased to welcome some intellectual talent into a party whose death was now regularly predicted. These texts were written by sub-committees, subject to the approval of an open meeting of all Ceres members.[3] By now too Ceres could afford an office in rue Beauregard, thanks to the subscriptions which it levied, illegally, from members.

As confidence grew, the group began to organise a series of colloquia on themes germane to the left. They would become a characteristic feature of Ceres life and some 13 would be held by 1983. One of the most successful was on industrial policy, being held in April 1968 and attended by Mollet and Mitterrand. In 1967 the group had already put down its own motion to the annual SFIO congress. It contained all the themes of Ceres policy:[4] left union with a government programme, economic transformation using nationalisations and planning, creation of a truly socialist party and in foreign affairs, anti-Americanism and mistrust of the EEC.

The May events of 1968 (on which Ceres analyses have varied somewhat) confirmed its belief that advances towards socialism were possible and its doubts about the existing left's ability to seize such chances. They also let to Mollet's withdrawal of support because of Ceres' excessive activism and hence to a rethink of group strategy. Thanks mainly to Sarre it was now drawing support from beyond the original intellectual core, but clearly there were limits to how far it could now hope to influence the party leadership. The way ahead seemed obvious: Ceres would have to organise seriously so as to win over and transform the party, with all the strategic choices and struggles which this entailed. From think-tank the group would have to become fraction. Thus began a career which was to have deep effects on French socialism.

The first actions were taken in Paris where in 1969 Ceres proved strong enough to win control of the federation. It would also gain another major recruit in the shape of Pierre Guidoni, SFIO student leader of the national student union UNEF who would become one of the chefs historiques of the group. Already like-minded groups were busy in the provinces and links would be forged with them in the period down to June 1971. One federation even went over to Ceres before Paris, that of Savoie.[5] In Paris Ceres inaugurated a dynamic new political style and built up its support elsewhere in France. Like all groups of the non-communist left it knew that institutional pressures were forcing left and right into two united blocks, however conflictual that unity. For the non-communist left it was a question of being as strong and united as possible, so as better to bargain with the tougher and more powerful PCF. What activists wondered was: when would this unity occur and on what terms?

The socialist unity congress of June 1971 at Épinay-sur-Seine would of course give the answer, as most of the non-communist left came together to found the new socialist party. It will be recalled that Ceres held the balance of power among the constituent groups, as the delegates lined up thus:

Savary –	Mollet	34%	(Guesdist 'left' of SFIO)
Defferre –	Mauroy	30%	('right' of SFIO)
Mermaz –	Pontillon	15%	(Mitterrand's CIR, plus some votes
Poperen		12%	'loaned' from SFIO)
Ceres		8.5%	
Others		0.5%	

Ceres used its weight with some skill, seeking in the resolutions committee an alliance with the Mitterrandists and the Defferre–Mauroy axis against the Molletists and Poperen – a deal that had probably been worked out in advance. As a result Ceres got places on the secretariat of the new party with Sarre taking charge of workplace branches (SE) and Chevènement taking education and research. Ceres had also had institutional success, for the congress had accepted the system of straight PR for the election of leadership bodies, thus making Ceres' position secure; the Molletists had sought a weighted majority system which would have killed small groups. The party also accepted the idea of workplace branches with full voting rights, *pari passu* with territorial branches. Programmatically the party also committed itself to seeking agreement with the PCF with a view to forming a government. Observers agreed that the new party was to the left of its predecessor, thanks in no small measure to Ceres. As Charzat put it, 'Épinay was neither a conspiracy nor an accident, but the meeting of our will with that of Mitterrand'.[6] The fraction could be well pleased with its new saliency, as well as with the useful organisational bases acquired.

Progress went ahead till the mid-seventies, both in organisational terms and in terms of influencing the party line. The 1972 programme *Changer la Vie* had Ceres inputs. Chevènement's research department had done much of the drafting and Ceres pressure ensured that the PS commit itself to the nationalisation of nine major industrial groups, plus nationalisation of other firms on the request of their workforce with parliamentary approval. This latter contribution was due to Marc Wolf, Ceres leader from Nord. If other parts of the programme were less enthusiastic about wholesale *autogestion* or less hostile to the Atlantic Alliance than Ceres would have wished, the fraction's influence had still been considerable; Charzat claimed that it was 'the spearhead of socialist renewal and of left union'.[7] In June 1972 the PCF and PS signed the CPG; Chevènement had been one of the main negotiators, dealing with the economic chapters.

Organisationally these were years of growth, with Ceres attracting recruits individually and sometimes *en masse*, as happened with the arrival of Gilles Martinet and his supporters in 1972 from the PSU, which had remained outside the new PS as an aloof bastion of principled socialism. The group brought experience and skill, access to the media (Martinet was a senior figure on the influential left weekly *Nouvel Observateur*) and most of all, enough capital to enable Ceres to launch a monthly, *Frontières*. The group was now recruiting some of its ablest provincial élites, many of whom would be its mainstays in years to come and who would usually be found on the national CD – Groscolas in Nancy, Natiez in Nantes, Chanfrault in Haute-Marne and so on.[8] The upswing of the PS as a whole during the seventies helped

Ceres as well. Although it did less well than other fractions out of the general election of 1973, Chevènement and a handful of others did get elected deputies. The Grenoble congress of 1973 with its easily achieved *synthèse* showed that no one in the PS desired a quarrel yet. But the presidential campaign of 1974 showed a change in attitude. Mitterrand made very little use of Ceres on his campaign staff, but did draw considerably on the resources of PSU leader Rocard, already identified as a danger by Ceres. It was thus no surprise when he and Mauroy later set up the October *assises du socialisme*, where Rocard and his supporters joined the PS, stripping the PSU yet further. Ceres was deeply suspicious of this whole operation (which aimed to pull in many other components of the *deuxième gauche*, such as CFDT members and people from associations), fearing for the CPG and left unity.[9] The fraction's fears grew as, on the one hand, Mitterrand's control of the party increased commensurately with his national prestige (he absorbed the Poperenites and Molletists as of 1973), and on the other, relations between PS and PCF worsened in the light of the by-elections of 1974 which showed the PS to be the indubitable winner in the alliance. Could Mitterrand be veering away from left unity?

Ceres began to feel unwanted, and internal tensions showed for the first time as the Pau congress of February 1975 approached. The Martinet group wanted Ceres to ally with the incoming Rocardians in the hope of keeping the whole party more on the left: they were even ready not to submit a motion so as to stay in the majority. Ceres knew better what separated it from Rocard, whom it now saw as its most dangerous rival in the party. It also knew the value of motions in terms of assessing fractional strength, and suspected that Mitterrand would either make Ceres submit to an unacceptable text or else refuse the *synthèse* and force the fraction into opposition. To these tactical and political differences were added legal and financial battles about the control of *Frontières*. After months of threats of writs and counter-accusations the split was confirmed, with Ceres continuing to publish under the name *Repères* and the Rocardians (whom Martinet had now joined) launching the new *Faire*. A vindinctive, acrimonious atmosphere persisted thus for several months before the Martinet group left, and it still leaves a nasty taste in the mouth of those who remember it.[10] One internal Ceres document accused Martinet, quite seriously, of trying 'to create a sub-tendency within the left current'!

At Pau Ceres now spoke for a quarter of the party, with delegates from 93 out of 95 departments, even without Martinet. Mitterrand forced the group out of the majority, while keeping in all other groups including Rocard's. Political differences between him and Ceres had not grown any wider but he wanted to show the world – especially the PCF – that he was in charge and that the party was not about to be pulled any further to the left. Hence his denunication of the 'double language' of Ceres and of its fractional behaviour:[11] 'it's high time you obeyed the decisions of the party and not the authority of some fraction or tendency'.

Mitterrand was also furious at the growth in SE numbers, which he put down more to Sarre's massaging of the figures than to real growth in workplace militancy (a charge Ceres has always denied). Doubtless he was aware, as Charzat claims, of the anger of PS notables, threatened in their hold on their fiefdoms by this new type of action.[12] Be this as it may, Mitterrand wanted to affirm his authority and while Ceres might have been allowed to stay in the majority in return for a fairly public humiliation (a price which some claim Chevènement was ready to pay), the fraction delegates were not ready for this. A period of opposition thus began.

Initially Ceres seemed to profit from its new situation. The Nantes congress of 1977 saw it reach its peak at a time when the left was rising inexorably in the polls and victory in the 1978 general election seemed a formality. Even the bureaucratic harassment of the left fraction in which the Mitterrandist majority indulged – one could never speak of a proper purge – did nothing to halt its progress and may even have brought it extra sympathy. Nantes also saw Rocard's speech on the 'two cultures'; and the congress could be seen perhaps as a photograph of the fractional cleavages in the PS at the time, with a 'hard left' confronting an apparently more moderate socialist majority. But the break-up of the PS and PCF over renegotiation of the CPG in September 1977 led to a virtual civil war between the left partners and allowed them to snatch defeat from the jaws of victory in March 1978. Clearly as the champion of left unity Ceres was bound to be particularly hard hit.

After the defeat the PS became a fractional battleground for the next three years, with the presidential election of 1981 drawing up the battle lines of the protagonists. Rocard argued for his modernising, liberal-tinged socialism and aimed at floating voters, with no concessions to left unity. Ceres accepted the challenge and embarked on the ideological escalation analysed above. Mitterrand hung as ever in an intermediary position. It was clear that the Metz congress of April 1979 would see no holds barred.

Ceres preparations for Metz were interrupted by an internal crisis. As the leadership tried to sort out its tactics in a colloquium at Évry late in 1978, some long-standing discontent came to a head. Some younger Ceres challenged the hardening tone of the leaders, which had begun to sound very Guesdist. Their main spokesman was Christian Pierret, newly elected a deputy, but the group also included some of Ceres' ablest intellectuals such as Hugues Portelli and Michel Beaud, plus the Nord leader Marc Wolf. They challenged the leaders on several points: *suivisme* with regard to the PCF (including reluctance to criticise the USSR); increasing use of Gaullist-type nationalism; over-rigid economic theory (especially the motor role of the state) and the internal functioning of Ceres (cries of 'democratic centralism' were heard). The dispute involved questions of generations, careers, and hitherto unsuspected cultural differences, notably the gap between the traditional secularism of certain Ceres leaders, which had surfaced increasingly during this period of polarisation, and the catholic background of some, although not all, of the dissenters, which had shaped their political outlook (more detailed examples are given in the case studies in Chapter 5). From all accounts the protestors did well at Évry, but in a second meeting at Épinay, held in the famous gymnasium where the 1971 congress had taken place, the Parisian leaders had organised things more tightly. Admission was restricted, the *service d'ordre* appears to have been particularly heavy and the debates took place in an angry atmosphere. Eventually the protesters walked out and the 'Pierret split' was confirmed. Another motion, 'F', would be presented to congress alongside the Ceres one ('E').

There were in fact numerous motions, Mauroy having decided to throw in his lot with Rocard, and doing this via presentation of his own motion in the first instance. Marseille, being split between Rocard and Mitterrand, avoided the dilemma by presenting its own text, and a feminist one brought up the number to seven. Only this latter and the Pierretists failed to beat the five per cent hurdle, so no one had a clear majority.

Mitterrand made a *synthèse* with Defferre to which Ceres was later added, somewhat irregularly, after the congress. Rocard and Mauroy were forced into opposition for their *lèse-majesté*. Ceres, though back in the majority, had been badly wounded in the struggle, having lost half its support and some of its ablest élites. In future too its image was likely to seem more sectarian and less broadly appealing than before. In some ways the Pierret crisis had provoked a sort of decantation, revealing a deeper identity.

It remained for Ceres to extract what it could from its presence on the secretariat. The fraction strove to mobilise all possible support against Rocard, mainly by the device of writing, under the auspices of Chevènement (back in charge of research), a *Projet socialiste*.[13] This text, duly approved by the party majority was in some ways the equivalent of Labour's 1982 programme, that is it marked the high point of an ambitious socialist intent to promote, mainly by governmental means, a new economic system, predicated on high growth and redistribution. This orthodoxy could then be used against any attempts to present a more liberal image of socialism to the electorate in 1981. In the event this proved unnecessary, as Rocard refused to challenge for the party's nomination. And Mitterrand's own '110 Propositions', on which he based his presidential campaign, took considerable liberties with the *Projet*, as he sought to reassure doubtful voters as to the nature and extent of the changes promised. During all this time, party membership and activism stagnated and relations with the PCF worsened, as everyone awaited in a kind of paralysis the outcome of the election. The campaign itself did something to heal wounds but many (not just Rocardians) saw it as a lost cause and were really thinking of *L'après-Mitterrand*.

With the help of Chirac's 'premeditated treason' Mitterrand of course won and for Ceres and the rest a new period began. The June 1981 general election brought it a rich crop of deputies compared with the previous pittance. Although the leaders had not figured prominently (again!) in Mitterrand's campaign, they and the other fraction bosses got their rewards in terms of government posts, which Mitterrand shared out in proportions remarkably similar to their shares of the vote at Metz.[14] We shall analyse Ceres' role as a government fraction in Chapter 6, but for the present we may note its prominent identification with the early reflationary phase of economic

FIGURE 4.1   THE STRUCTURE OF CERES

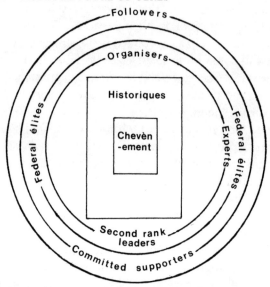

policy in 1981–2 which accorded broadly with its demands. But as the government was blown off course by import penetration and balance-of-payments problems and retreated to more austere policies, Ceres protested with the resignation of Chevènement in February 1983. As Finance Minister Delors's deflationary policy bit harder, the fraction stepped up its campaign for reflation, bolstered if necessary by protectionism. At the Bourg congress of 1983, Ceres put up its own motion (unlike 1981 at Valence, which had been unanimous in the flush of victory). Ceres scored 18 per cent and managed to effect a synthèse, including some of its points in the final text and retaining its presence on the secretariat. As the right got stronger during 1984, ranks began to close in view of the 1986 general election, and when in the summer Mitterrand appointed Laurent Fabius as prime minister, Chevènement returned to government, albeit as Education minister.

Ceres was thus back in office (though its lesser ministers had never in fact resigned), alongside the rival Rocard who had never left it. In calling back the head of Ceres, Mitterrand was admitting a fact of life in the PS, namely the durable existence of a left fraction which represents something permanent and is likely to do so for the foreseeable future.

4.2 HOW CERES FUNCTIONS – AN OVERVIEW

It is best to regard Ceres as a series of concentric circles, strongest and most coherent at the centre but losing coherence progressively as the circles widen (cf. Figure 4.1).

The innermost group consists of some half-dozen people, the so-called *chefs historiques* (the analogy, never discouraged by Ceres leaders, is with the founders of the Algerian FLN). They are the founders of Ceres and incarnate its continuity and internal legitimacy.

Jean-Pierre Chevènement (b. 1939) is the *primus inter pares*.[15] Born in Belfort into a family of primary-school teachers of socialist tradition, he made his way through the education system by hard graft, very much in the tradition of the Third Republic provincial scholarship boy of modest origins. Though nowadays at home in the world of Paris politics, he is genuinely proud of his provincial, lower-class origins and not above stressing them on occasion for partisan purposes, much as British Labour ministers are sometimes heard to rediscover their Northern accents. Studying at Sciences-Pô and the ENA, Chevènement did his military service in Algeria at the end of the French occupation. Back in France he combined work as a civil servant (in the foreign trade divisions of the Finance ministry) with political work as founder of Ceres. He has also worked briefly as a lecturer at Sciences-Pô. Since election as deputy for Belfort in 1973 he has been a political full-timer, combining this post with various national offices in the PS (notably head of research). In 1983 he became mayor of Belfort. His government career since 1981 has included spells at Research and Technology, Industry briefly and Education.

Chevènement is a dark, stocky man on the shortish side, with a shock of brown hair hanging down from a large forehead. He has a strongly featured face and an intense gaze. A slightly squeaky voice offsets perhaps the impression of quiet determination and competence which he otherwise exudes. Although articulate in argument and quick on his feet when dealing with generalities, he is not loquacious by nature, being at bottom a reserved, if not a shy man. Lately his public speaking has improved, but he still cannot hold a large audience in the manner of a Rocard or Mauroy. Chevènement has always known what he wanted and shown great determination in pursuing it. He has never confused resolution with idealism, though, and has over the years shown much tactical skill and suppleness to keep Ceres and himself in a good position. He thinks a long way ahead and as the fraction's *présidentiable* has had his sights set on the 1988 election from the mid-seventies. If a quantitative analysis of his vocabulary were made, as once was done for de Gaulle, it is a safe bet that the most frequently used word would turn out to be 'volonté'.

Very different is the man whom some see as his *alter ego*, Didier Motchane. Some years older then Chevènement and from a more comfortable background, his passage through Sciences-Pô and ENA seemed much more natural and indeed he is the best educated of all the Ceres, having picked up several other diplomas as well. He has worked as a career diplomat, including a spell in London, which is said to have done little to enhance his appreciation of the 'Anglo-Saxon world', but has been for many years a political professional, living by journalism and his posts in the PS. These have included responsibility for Third World relations and culture. Since 1979 he has been a Euro MP, with a high place on the PS list, but a less than enthusiastic attender at Strasbourg. But the public face of Ceres is Chevènement; Motchane's part in the division of labour is intellectual. He has overall responsiblity for Ceres press and it is above all he who moulded the very operative Ceres ideology, piecing it together from often sophisticated sources and working it into a usable synthesis. His impact as a Ceres educator was also considerable, especially in the growth period of the seventies, and more than one activist has told us of his ability to hold audiences spellbound by the clarity and immediacy of his analyses. A number of ex-Ceres recall his contradictory nature – capable of being genuinely inspiring and generous as a mentor, but implacably hostile once political disagreements were established. He is a complex man, probably not easy to get on with. Small and with a limp left by a childhood illness, he retains a certain detachment about politics and responds to questions with a polite and amused contempt. One sometimes feels that this vastly cultivated intellect derives more pleasure perhaps from its ability to dissect or analyse than from anything else.

Motchane is interested in ideas and tactics, but not organisation. This is the province of two men, Michel Charzat and Georges Sarre. Charzat combined for years his work as a political scientist with service to Ceres. He helped considerably with the development of Ceres ideology, which probably owes him its borrowings from austro-marxism (on which he wrote a thesis) and some of the more forgettable aspects of the anti-Rocard crusade such as 'néo-travaillisme'. His major contribution is organisational, however, for he it is who is really master of the Ceres national network. He knows the inside of each federation, its problems, personalities and perspectives. Like all the *historiques*, he has put in many hours of meetings and seminars all over France in order to create the network in the first place. Talking to him, one feels that this is his main interest; and certainly discussing the affairs of such and such a department is one of the few things which brings some animation to his serious and rather staid exterior. His efforts have been rewarded in other fields. Besides holding posts in the PS secretariat (public sector policy and local government) he has been a Paris councillor since 1977 in the East End of the city, where he won a deputy's seat at the second attempt in 1981 (he himself resides in the somewhat more luxurious 16th *arrondissement*). As a deputy he has played a major role in the nationalisation legislation since 1981 and now chairs the High Commission for the Public Sector. His adversaries always acknowledge his tenacity and capacity for hard work. His wife Gisèle, an academic and also a Euro MP, is a powerful personality and a fiery orator; many believe her to enjoy the confidence of the *historiques*.

Georges Sarre is another provincial who has followed a pattern that has become classic since the Third Republic, namely upward social mobility through employment in the public service. Joining the postal service in his native Haute-Vienne, where he was born into an old socialist family, he rose through the ranks to inspector. He did his military service in Algeria and also found time to take a sociology degree. The 1968 riots had a sharp impact in the big sorting centres where Sarre now worked and did much to enlarge the horizons of the trade-union activist towards the *autogestionnaire*, mass-movement philo-sophy that would eventually become the Ceres line. The *amicale* for socialist postmen, especially provincials, which Sarre created would be vital in widening Ceres influence, not least because many postmen, having learned their politics in Paris with the Ceres would then return to their native regions as *missi dominici*. Sarre's PS career began with his appointment as secretary in charge of the SE in 1971, but this career avenue was somewhat blocked when Mitterrand fired him at Pau. But

Sarre seems to have benefited from the peculiar indulgence to be found in the upper reaches of the French civil service, whereby officials can be more or less indefinitely on secondment ('en mission'), that is be paid while not actually required to work in their ministry. According to one of our informants, Sarre was still enjoying this privilege as late as 1979. He had used the time to become a Paris councillor as early as 1971 and led the PS list in the mayoral contest of 1977, disastrously. He duly picked up his deputy's seat in Eastern Paris in the 1981 landslide, having missed out in 1978 and earlier in 1973 in his native Limoges, where the local party, furious at his change of union from FO to CFDT in 1972, preferred to hand over a totally safe old SFIO seat to the PCF – an eloquent measure of its displeasure. Today Sarre chairs the PS group on Paris council, but did not lead the municipal list in 1983: he has responsibility for local government on the PS secretariat. Neither a theorist nor a good orator, he is an indefatigable organiser and committee-man, popular with Ceres militants, socialising easily and knowing how to retain his common touch when required. He seems visibly pleased with his status as a deputy, clearly enjoying the trappings of office.

The other man counted as an *historique* is Pierre Guidoni. This chemist's son from Narbonne, again from a socialist family, joined Ceres from a background in student unionism and rose quickly to be elected a Paris councillor in 1971. He was an administrator with Gaz de France for some years. His role in the inner councils of Ceres seems to have been fairly free. He oversaw the fraction's student operations (see below) but has also written on international affairs and had national PS responsibilities in this area and for local government. From 1978 his trajectory has been much less Parisian, with his election as deputy for Narbonne and latterly his ambassadorship in Madrid, where he had the hard task of persuading his friend Gonzales that Mitterrand was not really obstructing Spanish entry to the EEC. This itinerary has led to some speculation about Guidoni being estranged from the other leaders and, being unable to find a role, choosing exile. Whatever the truth of this and whatever his future in the fraction, he has been renowned in the past as a hard fighter in internal squabbles. More than one ex-Ceres describes him as the most sectarian of all the *historiques*. A tall, slightly drooping figure, with longish, lank hair and a craggy nose he certainly lacks neither articulacy nor confidence.

Such is the central Ceres group; it effectively decides fractional policy and tactics (alliances with others, day-to-day operations in the BE). On a deeper level it fulfils various symbolic functions. It is the visible symbol of Ceres' existence (it is invariably one of the *historiques* who will appear on TV or comment in the press). The inner group also serves as a focus of loyalty; much of its time is taken up with travel around France, speaking and meeting people. All the Ceres intermediary élites outside Paris will know personally one or more of the *historiques*; they are the living symbol of Ceres vitality. Their closeness amounts to empathy, formed by years of common struggle and profound agreement on their political goals. Ex-Ceres have described them as 'un petit intellectuel collectif'. Bizot tells a joke about how they once came to see Mitterrand, who remarked that there were four of them to one of him. 'Don't worry, we came on our own', was the reply.

They cannot of course perform unaided, and rely on an inner circle of several dozen, maybe a hundred people. This can be divided into several segments. First are what might be called second-generation leaders; these were rising young men like Wolf, Pierret or Portelli, who were very good theorists and, in the case of Pierret, a high-class organiser and tactician. To this category could be added some of the trade-union cadres like Pierre Héritier of CFDT or Gérard Desseigne of CGT, who joined after building up a reputation in their unions. The position of this group, halfway between the *historiques* and the advisory/organisational role of the rest of the inner circle, was always uncomfortable, with a strong chance that the new men might rise high enough in the hierarchy to threaten the leaders. So it proved, with most of them departing with Pierret and never being adequately replaced, in terms of intellectual calibre at least (though the entry of CFDT leaders like Garnier and Coffineau after the *assises* partly plugged the gap). More relevant today is the second element of the inner circle, the organisers who link up with the federal élites. Much of this work, which involves circulating material and organising meetings, is now conducted by Thierry Bondoux, an *énarque* but not one with great political ambitions. He was long helped by some postal inspectors, usually seasoned union men, often doing a stint in the Ceres office between shifts. These have included such as M. Ekevarria, or Georges Mingotaud and Francis Borie, whose devotion to Ceres is matched only by their amiability. The sort of enthusiasm which Ceres could evoke in its best days is still best apprehended by talking to militants like these. Ghislaine Toutain's efforts in the early days were invaluable also. Sometimes in Ceres parlance, these two layers are referred to as 'le secrétariat élargi', but fractional self-descriptions tend to vary a lot so far as organisation is concerned, so it is better to stick to the outline used here.

One of the most important people in this group is the least known, Jean-Paul Escande, who is treasurer. This senior banker (head of a nationalised bank since 1982) has long presided over the finances of Ceres usually making a virtue out of necessity.

At another point on the first circle comes another sector, the experts. Usually these people, drawn from activists in the civil service or academia (though sometimes from the business élite), man the specialised commissions, which shadow policy parallel to those of the party at large, thus providing the leaders with the material for their policy options. In the late seventies Ceres ran some seventeen commissions, covering everything from agriculture to civil liberties to education. Each might have an attendance of a dozen. Probably the best was the economic one, which before 1978 included such as Michel Beaud and Daniel Lebègue (both served on Mauroy's staff after 1981) and Third World experts like J.-C. Hourcade. This group provided the most interesting and original Ceres work (e.g. the 'geographical compromise') but broke up in 1978. Their loss has been cruelly felt, as evidenced in Ceres publications. On social affairs, Ceres could call in the expertise of *énarques* like Nicole Questiaux (later Mitterrand's Social Affairs minister) and Jacques Fournier (later general secretary to the government). Foreign policy expertise remains considerable, owing much to past contacts. Michel Suchod, now a deputy, worked at the Quai d'Orsay for years and there are still some early Ceres there who, it appears, still contribute material.

The input of these experts was advisory, not dynamic. What really keeps the Ceres motor ticking over is the departmental élites, who may number from 500 to 1,000 or to put it another way, between half a dozen and a dozen per department. They will attend the periodic *collectifs* in Paris, relaying questions and requests from the federations and taking back the Ceres line as it emerges from the centre. They will usually be CEF office holders and often in local government as well. They will usually provide congress delegates, and Ceres draws from them its mayors, deputies and *conseilleurs généraux*. They run Ceres in their federation and are ultimately responsible for its progress or decline. While obviously committed to the overall logic of the fraction, they are by no means passive tools, manipulated at will; the case studies show this. In fact the stronger Ceres implantation the greater their autonomy will be.

That said, the atmosphere of a *collectif*, which might be held as frequently as once a month and which might gather several hundred people from all over France was usually, according to past participants, fairly deferential.[16] If there was debate, it was on an agenda set by the leaders, who intervened frequently and did the summing up. Former provincial leaders say that the main opposition to the leaders came from those federations where the local Ceres had its own power base. Our own experience of Ceres gatherings suggests that the relatively small numbers involved make for a personal style of leadership; in a gathering of a few hundred people, such as the congress delegates' meeting, the chiefs and their lieutenants will circulate on the floor when not speaking, arguing, cajoling and usually winning their way by persuasion. This is as much emotional as rational, and the parallels with parent/child relationships are irresistible; the Ceres father can usually obtain compliance without using a slap on the bottom. It is not so much democratic centralism as paternalism.

The last circle of Ceres support has two zones of different intensity; neither can be quantified with much precision. In the first are those Ceres who are loyal and active, probably to the point of attending meetings and maybe giving financial support. They will have varying degrees of political sophistication, but very often will be followers of a group or leader hegemonic in their area; this leader will have recruited many of them. The final group consists of those who vote Ceres for congress but are not active; the basis of their vote may well be problematic and their support conditional (this is of course true of all other fractions). This completes the description of the structures. It is hazardous to attempt numerical precision, but if we take the figures for the Bourg congress, then out of a membership of 210,000 Ceres spoke for some 38,000. Bearing in mind the frequently low turn-out for the *vote indicatif* (figures are rounded up) this probably means a few hundred inner activists, a few thousand slightly less committed ones and the rest made up of followers of one sort or other. In other words an 'active minority' does the work and others follow. But there is nothing which allows us to suppose that other fractions are very different.

One good guide to the way Ceres operates is the preparation of congress motions. Ceres always prides itself on the *autogestionnaire* nature of the process, with inputs coming in from branch level; rival fractions are always pilloried for the undemocratic way in which they let their bosses simply write the motion. The Ceres image is a romantic one in fact, for though there are indeed grass-roots inputs and though the final text is agreed by a general meeting open to all members in theory, there are other considerations. First the themes on which branches base their contributions are circulated in advance. Thus for Pau, branches were asked for the following:[17] analysis of the recession (in accord with the Eighth Colloquium of Ceres); reinforcement of left unity; strategy of 'rupture', control and *autogestion*; building a real socialist party. Secondly, the general meeting (in Paris) is subject to the style of management described above. Thus although the inputs come from below, the output is what the *historiques* want.

The same is true of the lists for the CD (comité directeur) which accompany motions. Here again guidelines are given as to distribution by age, sex, region, profession, etc., which means that the final list is certain to be what Paris wants (especially the top two-dozen names which is all that Ceres can usually hope to see elected). Ceres colloquia are much the same. From academic exercises at the start they were widened to involve activists from all over France and become, in the eyes of many, mini-congresses with their own debates and con-clusions. As with general meetings, the conclusions usually went the way Paris wanted (the exception being the abortive Évry revolt). When he became Research minister Chevènement organised a series of colloquia across France, building up to a national *assises* in Paris. Cynical observers noted the resemblance to the traditional Ceres exercises with their apparent decentralisation masking conclusions that had been drawn in advance.

Ceres then has a special style. 'Democratic centralism' is unsuitable to describe it, if only because the fraction lacks the rigid apparatus necessary to impose such a practice. There is an element of democracy in that decisions are, on the surface at least, public and therefore conflictual. But given the restrictions which operate, it might be more relevant to talk of 'guided democracy' in the sense used in African politics. Our own preference would be for 'benevolent paternalism'.

Resources

We turn next to the least known part of the activity of any party or fraction, its resources. Given the secrecy which surrounds such operations in general, what follows is necessarily speculative; but the broad outlines of Ceres resources can none the less be guessed.

Not all resources need in fact be monetary. At federal level, especially if it is in control, the fraction will enjoy access to facilities such as duplicating, postage and telephones and maybe secretarial help. These days most federations are better equipped than constituency parties in the Labour party, in no small measure because of the membership fees levied (these are banded according to income, but in 1984 a white-collar professional could pay around £15 per month, compared with £7 per year in the Labour party), and all fractions can usually get some access to their facilities. If Ceres has federal control, then the full-time official (*le fédéral*) will be its appointee, and his role can be considerable in recruiting and guiding members; most *fédés* can now afford one such appointee. Similarly if Ceres controls a town hall, facilities and maybe staff can be made available, one or two people being paid out of municipal funds but spending some time on fractional work. The same logic has held for ministerial staff since 1981, for Ceres must have benefited from control of certain ministries; but we are not able to quantify this. These parameters are of course true of all PS fractions.

One possible source of income might be the press. But it is doubtful if at its peak *Frontières* ever sold more than 5,000 copies, which is not enough to make big profits. *Le Crayon entre les dents*, an abortive student magazine, was a huge white elephant.

Ceres relies to some extent on *ristournes* (pay-ins) from members elected to public office, especially parliament; this is over and above what they are supposed to pay the party at large. But prior to 1981 Ceres deputies and big town mayors were a rare breed; this was an area where the fraction had never pulled its weight in comparison to rivals. Another means of moneymaking in French parties is the *bureaux d'études*. These are consultancies, usually in areas of town management such as planning and quantity surveying, which local authorities hire at rates well above par. The financial difference is then filtered through to the party behind the bureau by various laundering devices. Most parties have a bureau, and the PS one is Urba conseil. More than one informant told us that Ceres ran just such a bureau in the early seventies, and indeed one mayor had some extremely rude things to say about being approached by Ceres on this topic. The truth of the matter is impossible to establish, but the most likely surmise is that some senior Ceres figures did consultancy work on an *ad hoc* basis (not always for Ceres town halls, be it said). This need not involve setting up a bureau as such.

Another venture of the seventies was political tourism, under the auspices of a travel agency Solstice. The idea was to combine business with pleasure for activists by visits to such progressive states as Cuba, Algeria or Yugoslavia, with political discussion alternating with the more traditional gastronomy and sunbathing. Some of these package tours did in fact occur, thanks mainly to the hard graft of some younger Ceres, but the scheme foundered through lack of proper organisation and support. It is unlikely to have made much money. Hostile critics sometimes speculate about clandestine financing of Ceres. Such claims are impossible to verify without scrutiny of the accounts. But it has been suggested to us several times that the thirdworldist and anti-imperialist line of Ceres, plus its strong Palestinian sympathies in a party which usually inclines the other way, have on occasion led certain oil-rich states to lend a hand. If this is true, it should be pointed out that, somewhat surprisingly, it also applies to the Rocard group which has in the past probably used its leader's radical PSU past to some advantage. It is also believed that Alain Gomez's success in business may have enabled him to help out his old comrades; but like all the other speculation, this cannot be verified.

In any case none of the above probably amounts to a fortune and in the last analysis Ceres relies like the rest of the party on money from its supporters, again over and above what they subscribe to the party. Some federal Ceres had regular subscriptions (*stricto sensu* illegal), even by banker's order. Ceres Nord of the early seventies even published accounts. Thus in 1974 it had an income of some £750 p.a., over three-quarters of which came from subscriptions (around £4 per month per head). Varying amounts of this seem to have been sent on to Paris, but on average around a fifth. Nord was clearly one of the better organised

Ceres federations, and it might have been sending around £150 a year to Paris. If the others did as well, Ceres might thus have been receiving around £10,000 a year in subscriptions. But a more realistic guess would be around half that figure. It is true that the irregular inputs from other sources listed above cannot be quantified and that we are far from having a full picture of Ceres financial operations. But it is a fact that internal documents before 1981 often read like an extended begging letter and that even if the odd federation was comfortable, the central operation ran on a shoestring. Certainly in respect of the vast sums which Michael Crick believes Militant to control, Ceres resources are slight indeed.

This is seen by the working of the Ceres office. Although visitors will usually find half a dozen people working in the rather dingy succession of apartments where the fraction has made its home, it is doubtful if more than one or two have ever been paid as full-time secretaries or administrators. Most of this work is done voluntarily by people holding jobs with a certain autonomy (teachers, or postmen, or sometimes the parliamentary assistants which French deputies are allowed); considerable inputs are made by wives and girlfriends. At low moments in Ceres' history the telephones have even been cut off for non-payment of bills.

Press and publications

Regular Ceres publications fall into two categoriese, a theoretical journal and a weekly broadsheet of short-term perspective. The latter is *Volonté socialiste* which began in 1969 and has had several reincarnations, always with the same title (which makes numbering difficult). The format has changed little. It is basically an eight-page pamphlet which vulgarises basic Ceres doctrine and applies it to current problems, domestic and international. These days its management seems mainly to be left to younger activists. More care is taken with the theoretical journal, which began life as the *Cahiers du Cérès* in 1967. These numbers are now collectors' items. Their successors, *Frontières* and *Repères*, were better produced and represent the peak of Ceres achievement in this field. Well written, with readable and sophisticated articles on a whole range of issues, an educative section and the odd critical contribution from an outside source (usually trotskyite or PSU), these were a very good read. To them should be added the educational

pamphlets produced in 1974–6. Written by specialists on themes such
as the women's movement, agriculture or local government, they are
well documented and thorough, and not at all sectarian in approach.
One of them, a *Bibliographie socialiste*, bears comparison with the
booklists for courses at Sciences-Pô though of course it is aimed at
ordinary party members and not full-time social science students![18]
These publications did not survive the 1979 split when most of the best
writers left. The main journal then became *Non!* and aimed at a wider
focus than just Ceres members; some names from the broad left, such
as Régis Debray, were coopted on to the board. The result was
disappointing, far too much weight being given to 'American left'-style
polemics; and since 1981 a further change has been made. Now the
review is *En jeu*, in a more popular format, with shorter articles and
illustrations. It is certainly more readable than *Non!* and its broad-left
editorial board again shows the intention to reach out to a wider
public.

Overall supervision of the fraction's press is Motchane's, assisted
increasingly by P.-L. Séguillon, long the assistant editor of *Témoignage
chrétien hebdo* and nowadays presenter of a news programme on TV. A
committed catholic, who combines his faith with a marxism of
thirdworldist tinge, Séguillon typifies the sort of catholic at which TC
hebdo aims and who was long believed to be the stuff of which Ceres is
made – erroneously as we have shown. A trained Arabist, he
sometimes acts as a sort of Ceres ambassador in dealings with certain
Third World states.

Internal discipline

In order to understand fully the functioning of Ceres we need to
consider the question of its internal disciplinary structures; for these
have arguably existed.

The two key moments of this problem are clearly the Martinet and
Pierret splits. The first had several elements – a financial wrangle over
the review, political disagreements on left unity, and tactical ones (on
alliance with Rocard, and on whether to put down a motion). But
there was also a disiplinary question, related to the Étudiants socialistes
(ES), then controlled by Ceres but about to be disbanded by
Mitterrand. Ceres' most forceful student leader was Patrice Finel, a
Martinet supporter. This fact, plus his alleged mishandling of Ceres

student operations, made him a prime target. In a general meeting of 29 June 1974 he was given a public warning (public inside Ceres, that is). A similar assembly on 20 October concluded that between Finel and Ceres 'disagreement was fundamental and irremediable'. Finel and friends were thus in effect expelled and joined Rocard at Pau.[19]

The presentation of the charges is interesting. The document quoted says that Finel 'placed himself outside the *courant*' both by breaking party rules and 'by a constant action of denigration and division inside Ceres'. Thus party and fraction discipline were cleverly amalgamated. He was accused of 'fractional activity [*activité fractionnelle*], based on a strategy, the verbal leftism of which cannot conceal its irresponsibility or even opportunism'. He had led the ES into 'adventurism'. This included a variety of offences such as trying to set up popular mobilisation committees during the 1974 campaign and trying to form a personal clientele within the ES leadership, so as to detach it from Ceres.

What is striking about this is firstly the language. Phrases like 'adventurism' or 'placing oneself outside the party' are very much those used by communist parties when expelling dissidents. There is also the conflation of two offences – breaking party rules and breaking Ceres solidarity (there could be no written Ceres rules obviously). Clearly Ceres sees itself, perhaps even unconsciously, as being of similar structure to a party; for it is hard otherwise to explain the use of the word 'fractionalism' to criticise Finel. It is after all odd to hear a fraction accuse some of its members of forming a faction!

The Pierret split was similarly revealing, political and tactical disagreements blending with generational and cultural clashes. But central among the objections of this group was its analysis of Ceres functioning. Some survivors have spoken of 'Stalinist show trials' where they were arraigned by Chevènement in front of a general meeting. Doubtless these descriptions from men who are no political innocents owe something to poetic licence, but they give an idea of the envenomed atmosphere. The split actually occurred in the Épinay colloquium which, according to several different participants of very opposing views, had the following features. First, delegates' cards were issued by Ceres HQ in Paris; without these no admittance was possible, and to make sure of this there were *gorilles* ('heavies') manning the corridor giving entrance to the debating room. Pierret supporters claim that such cards were simply not sent to known oppositionists. Needless to say this is illegal in terms of party statutes and, more to the point, it broke the unwritten rules of Ceres practice whereby branches send their own delegates. By these means the *historiques* were able to win the day, though in purest Ceres tradition no vote was ever taken. It was clear that the Pierrists would have to go and found their own fraction; it is perhaps an exaggeration to say that they were expelled, but they were certainly bureaucratically marginalised and forced out.

This was the last serious internal crisis, and since 1981 victory and office have been strong healers. The fraction's militants, many of whom now have fifteen years' experience, seem to have settled into a consensual frame of mind, and the crises of the seventies can be seen for what they were, growing pains. The crises were a sort of decantation process whereby a different left, less attached to strict marxism and secularism, more open to social movements and cooler towards left unity and nationalism emerged, leaving Ceres to occupy the more traditional space of the left. But the crises also tell us much about the workings of Ceres. Its leadership seem to have behaved very much like a party executive, indeed like a PCF one. Is the fraction then after all democratic centralist, despite its claims? We have seen its views on this topic in Chapter 3; we can now examine its practice.

Democratic centralism may be apprehended on two levels, theory and reality. In the theoretical model, policy is elaborated by duly elected leaders on the basis of inputs and arguments from below; but once such policy is finalised, members are expected to support and implement it. On the face of it this seems not entirely different from parties like the PS. In reality the second part of the theorem holds good, but the first less so. Party leaderships have long since insulated themselves against pressures from their own grass roots by a series of mechanisms which assure them virtually unchallenged rights to make policy and perpetuate themselves in office. Such mechanisms are both institutional and cultural. The first variety includes such devices as forbidding lateral communication between branches, filtering candidacies to higher office, tutelage of branches by full-time officials, and so on. All these structures combine with the Michelsian advantages already accruing to the leadership by virtue of its better access to information, superior communication skill and experience of management. But these structures would not work so well without cultural support. In big parties of this type, members must accept willingly the logic of these structures, if not their letter; in the last analysis the party (i.e. its leaders) always knows best. If you yourself have doubts, they are probably wrong and should be suppressed. Such a culture might be particularly deep-rooted in areas where parties of this type have achieved hegemony (e.g. certain workplaces or 'red' municipalities). How does Ceres measure up to this model?

Judgement is restricted by the fact that Ceres activity is paradoxically in some ways less visible than that of a communist party; having no real official existence it is obviously not in a position to issue public warnings or expulsion notices. But we have some facts on which to base an analysis. Ceres leaders are not elected; their legitimacy is based on charismatic or indeed paternalistic authority. It thus fails to fulfil one of the basic criteria of democratic centralism, namely the holding of formal elections, however meaningless these might be. That is a rather disingenuous point, though. For Ceres' cohesion depends not on institutional or bureaucratic factors but on ideological ones;[20] it is, as we remarked, primarily an ideological community. In fact Ceres does not possess – and it is hard to imagine its possessing – the institutional means to enforce rigid discipline. Resources are crucial here. Without a network of full-timers in the federations, Ceres depends on its departmental élites for its efficacy. So long as these are not paid by the centre (like PCF *permanents*), then their potential relative autonomy must be high. If they wish, such élites can actually encourage dissidence or splits. And this autonomy is increased by the fact that there are always other fractions available for dissenters; whereas the PCF expellee faces a political wilderness (unless he joins the PS?). In short, resource constraints, plus the pluralist structure of the party, set severe limits to the application of intra-fractional discipline. The Finel affair confirms this; all that the leaders could do was establish disagreement and create such an unpleasant climate that the minority left. Compared with the disciplinary weapons available to PCF bosses this is extremely modest.

It is true that one feature of Ceres life seems *a priori* to bring it near to democratic centralism, and this is the leaders' monopoly of policy-making. Against this we would argue that the other fractions elaborate their options in exactly the same way. What is striking about Ceres is that it goes to great lengths to be seen to consult its grass roots,

arguably much more so than its rivals. The reason is ideological; having
set so much store in the past by *autogestion*, the fraction cannot dissent
too much from the logic of this theory, at least on the surface. This is
the price to be paid for the ideological cohesion of the group.

Ceres' charismatic paternalism has then helped to build up an
ideological community. After years of struggle the fraction has thus
achieved a sort of stability and durability, with its own principles and
values and a structure of loyalty to its leaders. Its future will always
depend on consent and not coercion, however. Even if its leaders are
attracted by the efficiency of the democratic centralist model they will
be unable to enforce it, so long as their resources are modest and the
pluralist structure of the party offers other options to dissidents. This
restriction is at bottom a function of the reformist space in which the
party has chosen to work. Paternalism, even of authoritarian style, is
not democratic centralism.

Party discipline and Ceres

It is also relevant to consider the relationships between Ceres and
the party majority from a purely disciplinary point of view (as opposed
to a political/strategic one). In general this centre–periphery relationship is in fact governed by political criteria, ultimately by *rapports de force*.
The key variable appears to be whether Ceres is in the majority or not.

If it is, then it is visibly harder for the majority to weaken it or
eradicate it (as some have perhaps at times dreamed of doing). But if
Ceres is in internal opposition, then attack is much easier. The
seventies show this pattern clearly. Until Pau Mitterrand felt he needed
Ceres as allies; thus his criticisms remained verbal. At Grenoble in 1973
he warned about 'parties within the party' and made the famous crack
about 'making a fake CP out of real petty-bourgeois'. But administrative
or disciplinary sanctions against Ceres were few, and the offenders had
usually visibly broken party rules (cf. Chevènement's six-month
suspension from office in 1970 for publicly accusing Savary of cheating,
or Groscolas's suspension at Nancy for setting up an illegal federation).
No credible party leadership could let such things go. But such cases
were few and, as Laignel shows, the PS prefers to solve such cases at
federal level or failing that, via an *ad hoc* arbitration and conciliation
committee of 'wise men'. It is rare for cases to go to the national
conflicts committee (maybe a dozen per year).[21] But between Pau and

Nantes one senses a real desire to go on the offensive, especially from one of Ceres' earliest enemies, the party No. 2, Mauroy. The reasons were as much tactical as ideological (in the sense of fundamental disagreements about the nature of socialism). Ever since the near-miss of 1974 the Mitterrandists sensed victory was near, and best secured by sending signals of moderation to the few per cent of floating voters required. This meant putting the left fraction firmly in its place; beyond and through Ceres the PCF was of course targeted.

The attack combined specific shows of strength with attempts to change party rules so as to weaken fractions in general and Ceres in particular. The most spectacular gesture was the forbidding of a Ceres colloquium on the municipal elections of 1977 arranged at Reims for 10–11 April 1976, to precede the official PS special congress at Dijon. Preparations for this were in hand, including the hiring of a special train from SNCF and the purchase of a delivery of wine from Hérault ('l'année spéciale Ceres') to refresh delegates, when Mitterrand had it cancelled in a vote at the CD of 3–4 April.[22] Ceres knuckled under, and strove with reasonable success to extract from the party a text which would stop notables from running municipal lists without the PCF. Its internal circulars simply recommended activists to do the business of the cancelled congress at federal level. Significantly, the CD approved the regular Ceres colloquium set for 19–20 June, which duly went ahead.

The institutional offensive had already begun at Pau. Here Mitterrand effectively destructured the ES and youth wing (MJS), which were stripped of their Ceres leadership and placed under the tutelage of Mitterrand aides (principally Edith Cresson), until they were felt to be safe from Ceres control. This type of purge is endemic to socialist parties with youth wings. Linked to this was the sacking of Sarre from his post of responsibility for the SE. These gestures thus went further than the symbolic, in striking at some of Ceres' real power bases.

The CD of April 1976 marked a real attempt to change the institutional bases of fractionalism. At the Suresnes congress of March 1974 which finalised party rules, Mauroy's propositions would have weakened proportionality. Henceforth, CD members would be selected by the resolutions committee, which would make a *synthèse*, 'taking into account' the indicative votes. In other words, CD places would be shared out on the basis of a deal between fraction bosses. To some extent this happens anyway, but Mauroy's scheme would have replaced proportional representation with a straight majority system. Thus small groups might well lose their representation. Fortunately for Ceres, enough others felt threatened to refuse the proposal and the weight it would give to the big federations. Mauroy did not give up, however, and the above mentioned meeting of the CD requested Gérard Jacquet to draft a code of good conduct for the *courants*. Mauroy meanwhile gave an idea of what he understood by this, in a letter to Marc Wolf which set out his conditions for a *synthèse* in Nord federation;[23] fractions could not have their own press, public meetings, subscriptions or educational activities, or make declarations at variance with the party line.

Jacquet's report to the BE formed the basis of the latter's propositions to the special party convention on the rule book, delayed by electoral pressure till November 1978. Most of these propositions were duly incorporated into the rule book, which now treated the problem as follows.[24] *Courants* may meet in party premises on three conditions: that this be announced to the party authorities in advance, that meetings be open to any PS member, and that they be not advertised outside the party. They are then announced in internal party circulars.

As regards press, the official *Le Poing et la rose* was to have a polemical column reserved for each fraction (four pages out of twenty-four, as compared with the recommendation of two). There was to be a polemical bulletin published every 2 months, open to fractions according to their national strength; this never saw the light of day. In return, fractional literature was supposed to cease publication. It was recalled that *L'Unité* was open to all party members. Somewhat desperately, the text then seeks to draw a line between doctrinal and political questions, accepting that the former may be aired in the 'theoretical reviews' which may be associated with fractions. But political questions fall into two categories: those where there is a clear PS line (which must not be disputed publicly) and those where there is not (here 'great prudence is recommended'). Editors of fractional reviews were urged piously to bring them together into a single party-run publication.

Organisationally, Mauroy's points are recalled, as set out in the Wolf letter. It was pledged to give all fractions firm representation on party commissions and seminars, and in a final paragraph added by the convention the leadership promised not to use powers accruing to its office to discriminate against any fraction.

These rules are still in force and they represent the last attempt by the leaders to settle the fractional question by administrative or legal means. How successful were they?

The short answer is: hardly at all. Practically every proviso sketched out above is a dead letter. Thus fraction meetings are held outside party premises, if activists want to exclude rivals. When they do take place there, to avoid breaking rules, information notice of them may not be available in time to would-be attenders who are not fraction members. More to the point is the fact that by now few militants would *want* to attend rival meetings; this exclusiveness has become part of their mentality.

The provisions for the press were a joke. Even had the polemical bulletin ever appeared, it was utopian to suppose fractional publications would cease. Indeed the rules admit this, with their desperate attempts to split off doctrinal questions from political ones, and their pious talk of a merger. To take one obvious example, how can one distinguish whether debates about nuclear postures in Europe are doctrinal or political? Even when the party does have a line, there is seldom a watertight interpretation of this line, as it is frequently a result of compromise to begin with, and as political language is as elastic as most other varieties. The real question is: who decides when an opinion is divergent from the party line or not? And this is a question of *rapports de force*.

The rules were asking the impossible here, as they were with the organisational provisos, which are of course ignored, not least the last one. For it is clear that leadership-minority relations are not governed by the goodwill of the former, but again by *rapports de force*.

This examination of legal relationships between centre and periphery shows fraction to be a fact of life in the PS. Indeed the evidence suggests that the object of the offensive was probably not so much to kill Ceres as to cut it down to size. The leadership sensed that Ceres represents something in party and country, even if it alienates others. Conceivably also such people might be useful as future allies (and such would be the case at Metz soon after). Hence Mitterrand never drove in really hard against Ceres (cf. his authorisation of the June colloquium and indeed the rumours that he would have offered a *synthèse* at Nantes but for pressure from his own supporters show this).[25] Ceres for its part understood the warning and knew how to set limits to its autonomy. The conclusion from all this is that there are structural limits to the sanctions which socialist party leaders may take against their lefts; they may huff and puff at times for the benefit of public opinion, but their relationship is perhaps as much one of complicity as of conflict.

4.3   STRENGTHS AND WEAKNESSES – AN AGGREGATE ASSESSMENT

This section seeks to assess Ceres' implantation within its own party. We will begin with some national aggregates to highlight the more obvious features of Ceres performance, concentrating on the departmental level, given its importance in party activity. Ceres departmental strength since 1971 is shown in Table 4.1 and a five-point typology has emerged which is tabulated in Figure 4.2. No indicative votes were taken in 1981, and the 1983 figures reflect a different situation in that the party was in office; hence they were not taken into account, so as not to disturb our analysis of the decade-long evolution.

We distinguish first some twenty-seven departments where Ceres has shown consistent strength, that is where congress scores are well above its own national average.[26] The differential used was five per cent; but the table shows most of the scores to be well above that. We also took accounts of Motion F scores with regard to 1979 figures, simply because most Pierret supporters had been Ceres supporters until shortly before; their presence thus shows evidence of a considerable Ceres penetration. At the other end of the scale we find sixteen departments which are consistently poor (more than five per cent below Ceres' national average). In the middle come some twenty-seven departments where Ceres scores are prosaically average (±5%). The two final categories were harder to isolate and some approximation was necessary; these are the eighteen departments where Ceres has been losing strength over a period of time (usually since 1973–5) and conversely the eleven where, against the trend, some slow gains have been occurred. Needless to say none of these categories is absolutely tidy and all show exceptions or variations. But they do have

FIGURE 4.2 TYPES OF CERES FEDERATION, 1971–81

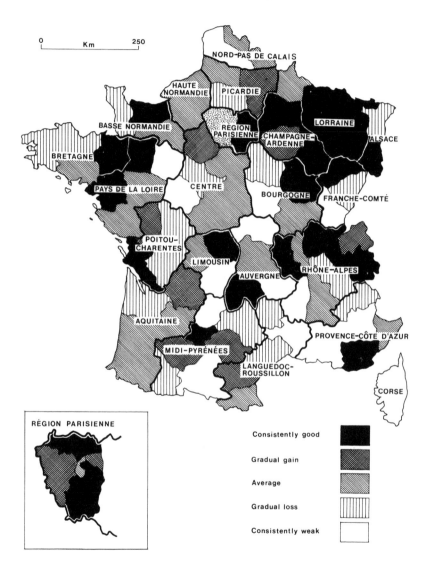

0 Km 250

NORD-PAS DE CALAIS

HAUTE
NORMANDIE   PICARDIE

BASSE NORMANDIE

RÉGION
PARISIENNE   CHAMPAGNE-
ARDENNE

LORRAINE

ALSACE

BRETAGNE

PAYS DE LA LOIRE   CENTRE

BOURGOGNE

FRANCHE-COMTÉ

POITOU-
CHARENTES

LIMOUSIN

AUVERGNE

RHÔNE-ALPES

AQUITAINE

PROVENCE-CÔTE D'AZUR

MIDI-PYRÉNÉES

LANGUEDOC-
ROUSSILLON

CORSE

RÉGION PARISIENNE

Consistently good

Gradual gain

Average

Gradual loss

Consistently weak

TABLE 4.1   CERES STRENGTH PER CONGRESS, 1971–83

Department	Épinay 1971 (8.5)[a]	Grenoble 1973 (21)	Pau 1975 (25.4)[b]	Nantes 1977 (24.2)	Metz 1979 (14.4)	Bourg-en Bresse 1983 (18.2)
01 Ain	–	50	42.8	31.8	21.9 (8.1)[c]	15.5
02 Aisne	–	–	22.6	22.6	24.9	30.8
03 Allier	7.4	25	18.5	11.1	7.6	17.5
04 Alpes de Hte.-Provence	–	12.5	22.7	6.9	0.5 (0.5)	8
05 Htes.-Alpes	–	50	50	30	18.2	26
06 Alpes-Maritimes	–	13.8	28.6	23.4	11.2	17.4
07 Ardèche	–	15.4	16.7	21.4	7	12.8
08 Ardennes	15.7	21	34.6	26.1	14.7 (8.6)	19.2
09 Ariège	–	6.5	7.4	14.5	11.3 (0.2)	16.3
10 Aube	5.8	11	21.4	40	25.3 (3.5)	37.3
11 Aude	16.8	12.3	18.9	13.3	16	9
12 Aveyron	24	30	33	20	11 (1.1)	11.1
13 Bouches-du-Rhône	2	4.9	4.5	2.4	1.8 (0.7)	2.3
14 Calvados	34.8	25	33	29	17.8	19
15 Cantal	–	50	50	37.5	24.6	19.5
16 Charente	–	33	36.8	23.1	13.7 (0.5)	19
17 Charente-Maritime	18.8	25	41.3	35.1	15.3 (7.9)	20.9
18 Cher	4.6	14	25	27.8	19	31
19 Corrèze	–	56	17.6	11.8	7.8 (2.4)	7.1
20 Corse	–	14.3	–	–	3.7	5.1
21 Côte-d'Or	13.9	40	38	38.7	21.9 (13.7)	34
22 Côtes-du-Nord	–	28.6	30	20	8.5 (1.6)	10.1
23 Creuse	21.9	35	47.8	31.8	16.8 (5.3)	28.8
24 Dordogne	11.1	14.3	19.5	25	19	36.2
25 Doubs	25	29.4	20	23.3	11.3 (3.6)	14.6
26 Drôme	6.1	35.6	29.6	30.8	19	28.2
27 Eure	30.4	25	31.2	20.8	16.3 (2.9)	12
28 Eure-et-Loir	4.6	7.7	7.7	20	12.5	24
29 Finistère	–	30.8	26.5	28.1	14.1 (4.7)	13.8
30 Gard	–	14.6	13.7	15.9	9.6 (0.6)	10.8
31 Hte.-Garonne	5.2	8	17.8	17.4	8.1 (1)	16
32 Gers	–	9.7	15.7	21.3	15.5 (1.6)	18.7
33 Gironde	9.2	23.5	24.4	19.3	10.4 (1.7)	17.4
34 Hérault	6.3	20.3	17.6	16.3	16.2 (0.3)	21.1
35 Ille-et-Vilaine	71.1	66.7	53.3	17.2[d]	17.4 (18.7)	10.9
36 Indre	–	25	21.4	23.5	15.3	17.1
37 Indre-et-Loire	–	6.7	12.9	14.7	11.6	15
38 Isère	1.2	17.8	24.7	19.3	9.6	13.1
39 Jura	–	45.5	5.3	12	8	15.8
40 Landes	–	27	22.5	17.9	16.5	21.1
41 Loire-et-Cher	–	47	32	33.3	14.9 (4.8)	30.1
42 Loire	–	25	52.2	56.1	32.1 (14.2)	26
43 Hte.-Loire	6	40	33	33.3	3.4 (12.6)	20
44 Loire-Atlantique	2.1	28.6	42.6	39	32	32.3
45 Loiret	–	30	23.8	20.7	13.6 (1.1)	16
46 Lot	–	30	13.6	11.5	13.2	16.9
47 Lot-et-Garonne	5.5	38.5	22.2	20	14.8	19
48 Lozère	–	33	40	14.3	8 (3.6)	32
49 Maine-et-Loire	–	50	22.7	25	15.4 (0.2)	18.6
50 Manche	26.2	30	33.3	27.6	11	12.1
51 Marne	51.3	90	60.9	63	44.5 (4)	35.6

TABLE 4.1   CERES STRENGTH PER CONGRESS, 1971–83 (%) (CONT)

Department	Épinay 1971 (8.5)[a]	Grenoble 1973 (21)	Pau 1975 (25.4)[b]	Nantes 1977 (24.2)	Metz 1979 (14.4)	Bourg-en Bresse 1983 (18.2)
52 Hte.-Marne	–	66.7	63.6	58.8	42.8 (4.8)	51
53 Mayenne	–	27.2	42.9	46.7	30.6	37
54 Meurthe-et-Moselle	4.5	42.9	59.3	57.1	21.3 (13.6)	33.1
55 Meuse	79.3	77.8	69.2	70.6	23.8	34
56 Morbihan	5	22	38.4	27	15.7 (0.3)	16.2
57 Moselle	–	44.4	51.6	46.7	24.3 (3.1)	23
58 Nièvre	–	6.1	9.2	6.3	6.5	13.9
59 Nord	8.6	23.6	18.4	23.6	7.3 (9.4)	16.2
60 Oise	12.9	31.5	37.5	31.7	19 (0.3)	26.5
61 Orne	–	25	22.2	26.7	18.9 (0.5)	30
62 Pas-de-Calais	1	11.3	16	15.5	8.4 (0.9)	13
63 Puy-de-Dome	33.8	25	29.7	29.1	17 (3)	29.1
64 Pyrénées Atlantiques	18.9	11	26.3	25	14.3 (1.1)	19
65 Htes.-Pyrénées	4.4	30	29.6	32.3	13.8 (2)	17.5
66 Pyrénées-Orientales	–	4.8	23.9	29.8	17.1 (1.3)	16.1
67 Bas-Rhin	13.7	25	47.3	38.9	15	26.1
68 Ht.-Rhin	–	16.7	38.5	57.9	57	64
69 Rhône	–	26.5	28.8	25	11.3 (1.4)	10.8
70 Hte.-Saône	–	100	73.7	56	44.8	56
71 Saône-et-Loire	–	10.3	29.4	23.6	13.3 (3.5)	20.3
72 Sarthe	3.6	7.1	16	9.1	7	4.4
73 Savoie	70	63.4	56	51.5	34.6	35.7
74 Hte.-Savoie	–	20	28.6	31	17.4 (5.8)	21.1
75 Paris	40	57.3	59.6	51.6	31.5 (13)	40.1
76 Seine-Maritime	5.4	39.3	16.2	21.2	12.5 (3.5)	10
77 Seine-et-Marne	18.8	30	34.1	25.5	21.1 (5.6)	27.1
78 Yvelines	5.4	23.5	33.3	31.9	19 (11.3)	17.8
79 Deux-Sèvres	2.3	20	5	26.9	22 (4)	20
80 Somme	–	21.7	12.5	27	9.1 (6.9)	17.3
81 Tarn	20	25.6	24	20.7	22.5	20.8
82 Tarn-et-Garonne	28.7	45.8	41.6	36	20	19
83 Var	26.8	26	27.5	27	23.6	28.1
84 Vaucluse	7.5	14.3	17.4	16.7	10.1 (5.3)	16.4
85 Vendée	–	14.3	25	31.6	18.6 (1.5)	15.6
86 Vienne	9.5	44.4	33	20.7	17.6	21.9
87 Hte.-Vienne	–	21.3	22.1	19.8	15.8 (0.2)	13.8
88 Vosges	–	46.7	40	30	20.1 (25)	20
89 Yonne	1.8	33	55.5	31.6	3.8 (1)	13
90 Belfort	61.9	88	81.4	84.6	72	82.4
91 Essonne	36.8	63	59.6	55.9	31.5 (18.2)	23.1
92 Hauts-de-Seine	11.5	24	31	28.3	13.5 (6)	20
93 Seine-St.-Denis	2.7	19.4	25	35.6	21.8 (5.3)	17.4
94 Val-de-Marne	7	32.4	41.4	35.8	15.5 (9.9)	20.1
95 Val d'Oise	–	40	46.2	32.7	25.5 (6.9)	2.18

a   National average for Ceres
b   All figures in this column are final, not indicative votes (i.e. taken after failure to agree *synthèse*)
c   Figures in brackets are scores for Motion F
d   72% of the federation abstained

Source: *Le Poing et la Rose*

the advantage of a long time-run (compared with the scores of other groups who only emerged with absolute clarity at Metz) and they do allow us to make some modest initial hypotheses.

The map suggests five real zones of Ceres strength. First is the East, where in the two Franche Comté departments of Belfort and Haute-Saône Ceres has always excelled, as it had to a lesser extent across Lorraine and even Alsace. Its influence spreads then across Champagne and down through Côte-d'Or into Burgundy. But Ceres is more than an Easterners' movement. A second bastion is Rhône-Alpes, especially Savoie and the eccentric Loire department. Paris and its suburbs are an obvious third area, and we may identify an inner ring of Western departments, especially Ille-et-Vilaine and Loire-Atlantique. Finally we may note growth of late in the South-West (Dordogne, Tarn, Gers), though these areas are still less strong than the above. The consecration of this strength came in 1981 when of the thirty-six Ceres deputies elected, twenty-six came from the best areas and three more from slow-growth areas.[27]

Ceres' weaknesses are equally blatant. Apart from Var, the Mediterranean coast has been stony ground, even Aude of late, though that is a special case in some ways. So too has Corsica, whose politics are again *sui generis*. There is little improvement up the Rhône valley or through the departments that straddle the Massif Central – Lozère, Puy-de-Dôme, Aveyron; the small Cantal is a (rather minor) exception. Moving north, it is clear that the outer Breton departments have never yielded much, nor have what we might call the Mid-West ones (in a line from Sarthe southwards through the Charentes). And looking across France from this Mid-West towards the Alps stretches a line of Ceres mediocrity. Finally Nord/Pas-de-Calais is again weak, though the Nord department itself has proved more hopeful.

On a macro-political level, one can suggest some global explanations for these features. Thus one *a priori* explanation of Ceres success might be historical, namely that certain federations had always been on the left and that Ceres simply pocketed an ongoing tradition. This idea is sometimes aired with regard to Paris, the suggestion being that Ceres is simply the political grandson of Pivert and Zyromski. This simple hypothesis does not resist empirical examination. For the 1946 period, Graham identified a number of left and right federations according to congress votes.[28] Of his thirty-two left federations Ceres has only done well in nine (four in the East, two in the Paris region); four others have been distinctly poor and three more show gradual decline. Of Graham's thirty-three right federations, ten have been very good for Ceres, with gains in three more. Only five have been positively bad (usually big ones) and five more show a slow loss. We would hold that such figures do not allow us to compare the 1946 left meaningfully with Ceres.

Similar conclusions emerge from Roland Cayrol's study of the sixties.[29] Admittedly the left–right polarity was less sharp, the division being more a quantitative-cum-geographical one between the big battalions of Pas-de-Calais and Bouches-du-Rhône, with Nord gravitating towards the latter. But even if we assume the Mollet-based majority to be the left (a highly dangerous speculation), the picture is far from clear. Cayrol finds some twenty-three Mollettist federations. Ceres did consistently well in eight of these and was growing in one more (all ones where the PS was weak overall); but it also did very badly in five and has been receding in four others (nearly all ones of PS stength). In the anti-Mollet areas, Ceres did well in three, none of them its best results. What this proves, if anything, is that PS electoral strength is likely to be a more significant variable than any hypothetical 'immanent left' tradition.

Another relevant variable might be size. PS federations at Metz broke down as follows: very large (100 mandates or above) 13; very small (25 mandates or less) 19; intermediary 63 (each mandate representing 25 members). Ceres only rates well in two of the big thirteen, indeed two of the smallest of these, Paris and Var. It did poorly or lost ground in six, including Pas-de-Calais and the departments containing Marseille, Bordeaux, Montpellier and Grenoble. Against this, among the small nineteen it does very well in six and badly in only two. These figures suggest that the older SFIO apparatuses (for the big were usually big before Épinay), based in industrial cities were able to resist the newcomers. But in the less developed socialist areas without a strong tradition there were pickings to be had. And probably one of the fraction's main achievements is to have raised some initially very weak federations (Savoie, Belfort, Ille-et-Vilaine) comfortably into the middle ranks; it may be that this less visible but meritorious effort will prove one of its more lasting contributions.

Still on the level of general explanations, we might now direct our attention to areas of Ceres weakness. Thus along the Mediterranean and the Rhône, we might suggest that these were areas where SFIO was best dug in, still controlling town halls and conseils généraux in the sixties and electing deputies. In other words, there was a party machine which Ceres never broke. Yet this was true of Var where Ceres has done well enough to have a senator elected! Equally in Vaucluse a poor department for the fraction and a by-word for SFIO notabilism,[30] Jean Gatel took a deputy's seat in 1981. And Ceres growth in the South-West, well populated by ex-SFIO caciques, as Charzat likes to call them, shows that Ceres can progress in such zones. Finally the Nord, with its very sophisticated party machine and long Guesdist tradition has seen some impressive Ceres gains, particularly at municipal level. So although the theory might have some validity at national level, federal and especially subfederal evidence suggests considerable exceptions.

If we turn to another weak area, outer Brittany, the tempting explanation is religion: socialism never did well in catholic subcultures which looked to conservatives or christian democrats. While this thesis, like the above one, undoubtedly contains some truth, it does suffer from exceptions. Ille-de-Vilaine has a similar history, yet was long a jewel in the Ceres crown and even today boasts a minister and two deputies (all admittedly ex-Ceres).[31] Loire-Atlantique is in some ways similar.

Again one might explain poor Ceres performances in Eastern departments like Jura or Doubs by a catholic subculture. Yet neighbouring Alsace-Lorraine is even more catholic and a Ceres heartland. And to complicate things further, Ceres does well in areas like Belfort and Haute-Saône, where there is a strong tradition of anti-clerical Radicalism. Even if we accept the seemingly obvious explanation of Ceres dominance in Paris (the traditional leftism of Paris because of the high weight of intellectuals in that federation), this begs the question of why the suburban departments (which are not short on intellectuals) are so uneven in their support for Ceres.

In short every obvious macro-explanation of strength or weakness at once invites qualification. It is clear that only regional, federal and arguably subfederal case studies can really explain the reasons for fractional performance. Suffice it to say that these are usually complex and that the case studies in the next chapter will attempt in, it is hoped, an initiatory way to demonstrate the hidden logic of hegemony (or lack of it). In any federal study there are, however, some *a priori* variables of a general nature that need to be considered; we shall list them here.

First we must ask if there is an SFIO tradition in the department prior to 1971, or failing that, if Radicalism was strong. In either case we might expect to find notables with municipal or parliamentary mandates and, if these were SFIO, a party apparatus of varying efficiency. If the party or the left was weak, we would need to ask what were the prospects of this changing in the short to mid-term. We then need to look at other left forces, notably the PCF. According to whether it was well established or secularly weak, or whether it was growing or not (NB, this refers to 1970) the prospects of the PS and Ceres would be different. In addition to the PCF we must be aware of significant PSU presence, where relevant, and, in catholic areas, of a persistent MRP presence. And in the background might figure trade union strength, given the close relationship of CGT and PCF, as well as the contorted one between the CFDT and emergent PS.

We could then need to consider other elements of the party in 1971. What would be the strength of Mitterrandism for instance, or indeed of Poperenism, which at that time had as strong a claim as Ceres to be the left spearhead? Above all we would need to know about the emerging Ceres. Who were they, sociologically and in terms of past political experience? How did they understand the role of Ceres, ideologically and politically? How did they see the position in their department in relation to the rest of the party and to the wider left? In consequence of this, what strategy did they adopt? And how did this fit into national or even regional Ceres strategy: in other words, what degree of relative autonomy from Paris did the local Ceres enjoy?

This list is intended as a bare minimum and could surely be extended. And the variables would need to be taken diachronically as well as synchronically for *rapports de force* change over time and with them the evaluations of actors. Even as it stands, though, the list demonstrates the difficulty of analysing fractional operations at subnational level. Before we apply our variables to the case studies, however, we might try some of them out at macro-political level in the hope of eliciting some initial hypotheses.

TABLE 4.2   CERES AND PS STRENGTHS COMPARED

Type of department: For PS as a whole (1970)

For Ceres (n)	Very strong	Strong	Average	Weak	Very weak	Total
Strong (27)	3	3	4	16	1	27
Average (23)	2	6	6	6	3	23
Weak (16)	4	7	3	2	–	16

Two major variables which invite comparison on this level are the previous strengths of SFIO and PCF, given Ceres' chosen position of mediation between the two. We took as an aggregate measure of strength performance in legislative elections, though this may obscure particular municipal strengths. We also took socialist, CIR and Radical votes as interchangeable, given that they were allied for the period in question. Clearly as a measure of pre-1971 strengths the 1967 and 1968 polls are especially relevant, and we used Leleu's data to construct a five-point spread for evaluating party performance per department in terms of each party's own national average.[32]

Table 4.2 thus compares Ceres strength post-1971 with that of the party as a whole pre-1971. Two points seem clear. In general, the weaker the PS in 1970, the better Ceres was likely to progress (top line). Conversely (bottom line) a strong PS has usually implied difficulty for Ceres. When we look at Table 4.3 (top line) we see that a federal Ceres has an even better chance when the local PCF is weak or at best average (twenty-two cases out of twenty-seven). In other words the fraction did best in *terres de mission*, where the left was weak all round; hence its success in East and West. We can confirm this picture by looking at the relatively few cases where the left generally was quite strong, as well as

TABLE 4.3   CERES AND PCF STRENGTHS COMPARED

Type of department: For PCF

For Ceres (n)	Very strong	Strong	Average	Weak	Very weak	Total
Strong (27)	3	2	8	9	5	27
Average (23)	5	5	6	3	4	23
Weak (16)	1	4	6	4	1	16

Ceres. Two of the very strong departments in this group are Belfort and Haute-Saône, which had not so much an SFIO–Guesdist tradition as a Radical/Republican one; clearly Ceres has somehow managed to become heir to this. Of the remaining departments in this category, Loire-Atlantique is discussed separately below, and Charente-Maritime is marginal, Ceres never having had full control of this federation. The only other case is Creuse, very much in the old Southern Guesdist tradition; success here must be due to local factors. These exceptions apart we may conclude that generally Ceres does best in areas with weak socialist bases.

Looking at good Ceres departments where the PCF is strong, it is plain that these are mainly Paris and suburbs. Here the PCF was well ahead of SFIO by 1970 and thus Ceres must represent the forces of renewal that sought to make the party competitive again. Our case study confirms this. The two other departments in the same category are Var and Creuse. In both the SFIO was running neck and neck with the PCF, and it seems that in these Southern federations acute competition for a large left electorate actually benefited the most competitive wing of the party.

Ceres weakness tends, as observed, to be commensurate with party strength (eleven cases out of sixteen). The two cases where both party and fraction are weak, Jura and Ardèche, have a long right-wing tradition and carry little weight against the thesis: PS strength = Ceres weakness. What may be significant here is that Ceres weakness seems less linked to PCF performance, the latter's weight in weak Ceres areas being spread almost evenly between strong, average and weak categories (Table 4.3 bottom line). In weak Ceres departments where the PCF is strong, we may claim that these are usually old SFIO areas (Bouches-du-Rhône, Nord/Pas-de-Calais, Gard). Here the clash between a still vigorous SFIO apparatus and a rising PCF challenge has simply closed down the space available to the socialist left, whatever efforts it may have made.

Average Ceres departments are harder to categorise. In some cases the SFIO was already strong (Saône-et-Loire, Haute-Vienne or Puy-de-Dôme in the Centre, or Ardennes in the more industrial North). In some, particularly south of the Loire (Haute-Vienne or Pyrénées-Orientales) there was also a strong PCF challenge, which again was bound to squeeze the socialist left. On the other hand when a

TABLE 4.4   CERES AND THE PS/PCF RACE UP TO 1970

Type of department: In which For Ceres (n)	PCF closing	PCF ahead	Roughly equal	PS ahead	Total
Strong (27)	3	8	7	9	27
Average (23)	3	8	6	6	23
Weak (16)	3	3	3	7	16

moderately successful Ceres has had a weakish PCF to contend with, this has usually been in the catholic West (Morbihan, Vendée, Orne, Maine-et-Loire). The party in general has usually been weak here, so there seems no cause of weakness specific to intra-left dynamics. We would thus need closer investigation, concentrating perhaps more on the nature of the electorate.

Thus far we have compared Ceres with its own party and the PCF in a rather static way. But we can see the nuances of our picture by incorporating a more dynamic variable, namely the degree of PS/PCF competition.

Table 4.4 corroborates some of our findings. Returning to the equation between socialist strength and Ceres weakness (bottom line) we now see that in six of the sixteen cases the PCF had either forged ahead or was rapidly catching its rival. Most of these are old areas where the non-communist left has long done well – anti-clerical Allier and Corrèze in the Centre, Radical Alpes de Haute-Provence and Gard. In these cases the PCF had pushed ahead in the sixties, to some extent doing Ceres' task of renovating the left, much as an earlier SFIO had itself pushed out Radicalism. Hence one understands better the fraction's failure. The same is often true of average Ceres departments. In half of them the PCF was ahead by 1970, including ones like Pyrénées-Orientales and Lot-et-Garonne where SFIO was clearly in decline. Others include areas such as Loiret or Eure where the left had long been weak and such gains as it had made were due to the PCF. In other words, in the first type of average zone there seems to have been a failure by the old SFIO to renew itself, in the second the failure of *any* left to make much headway. In both these instances there seems no reason why Ceres might not have done better than it did, and here clearly closer investigations must be made.

Turning now to strong Ceres areas we see another dimension. If the fraction did well in a surprisingly high number of strong communist areas this is because the PCF had got so far ahead as to leave the PS helpless. Thus *any* proponents of dynamism and renewal were bound to get their chance, assuming that there was still some socialist potential to mobilise. Paris and its suburbs are the *locus classicus* of this, but we might also note two Eastern departments, Meuse and Marne, where the left had never been strong. The exception to this pattern of SFIO decline or absence combined with the strong communist showing would appear to be Var, where the two parties and Ceres all did well despite bitter competition. Clearly there was much potential to be mobilised.

It remains for us to categorise succinctly those areas where Ceres has experienced gains or losses over time. This covers a wide range of situations and at the risk of being selective we single out the following features. The gains would seem to be of two types, first in the South-West where in Aude and Dordogne Ceres seems to have represented a renewal of generations in what were always strong socialist areas – central to this is probably the high calibre of local leaders of national stature such as Guidoni or Suchod. In some other parts of the South-West such as Tarn or Gers, where the PCF has never been strong, but where the tradition is more Radical than socialist, the fraction has also gained; this suggests a local effort of some quality, as this situation is not necessarily favourable to a left pole. Some of the losses are understandable, such as Hérault or Hautes-Pyrénées, areas where the PCF was creeping up on the established left – a situation which does not really favour Ceres. The fraction has also missed out in central areas like Lozère and Haute-Loire, where PS and PCF were both traditionally weak but where the former did have electoral success after 1971. Clearly other fractions were quicker off the mark. Less surprising are losses in such as Gironde or Isère where the mainly suburban socialist tradition is dominated by powerful notables, well able to out-manoeuvre newcomers.[33] In other words the evidence from these more volatile cases tends to confirm that from those where Ceres performance has been more steady, whether good or bad.

We may now in fact summarise these macro-findings. Basically Ceres did best where the PS was weak and worst when it was strong. A weak PCF usually implied a strong Ceres, and a strong PCF made the

fraction's task harder. A dynamic comparison of the PS/PCF relationship deepens these patterns. A strong PCF plus a strong PS (i.e. an SFIO
apparatus) usually closed down the space available to a nascent Ceres.
The result was usually the same when the PS was in decline and the
PCF progressing. But there comes a break in this pattern when the PCF
gets so far ahead as to leave the PS at rock bottom (Paris and suburbs);
here Ceres could indeed be the means to reviving the party at large. But
the PS had to be very weak for this to happen.

All these patterns are very general and show exceptions which only
local studies could elucidate. Such studies would almost certainly
show that none of these patterns are fore-ordained and that much
depends on the quality of a federal Ceres and the effort it mobilises. As
it is these analyses do reveal the very narrow space between reformism
and leninism in which the left pole has chosen to manoeuvre and the
difficulties it faces in winning support.

Given the speculation about links between Ceres and militant
Christians, we thought it useful to consider Ceres in areas of
recognisable christian democrat tradition. Indices of this were taken to
be a significant MRP vote in the final electoral appearance of that party
in 1962, plus votes for Lecanuet in 1965. Looking at weak Ceres
departments, we see that in nearly every case the christian democrat
score is at best close to the MRP national average, and in some cases
well below it (usually Southern areas of Republican tradition). The
only above-average score is in Jura.

Good Ceres federations show a mixed pattern; if one or two are
poor for the MRP, these are again in Southern anti-clerical ones (Var,
Creuse). But otherwise there are not weak MRP zones among Ceres'
better areas, and a number of these come in very strong MRP areas
(Ille-et-Vilaine and Loire-Atlantique in the West; Moselle, Haut-Rhin in
the East; Savoie). It seems then that catholic departments are
promising for Ceres, which makes the case of Jura more puzzling.
Initially Ceres had 45% at Grenoble, but only 8% at Metz. The most
likely explanation of this decline from a very promising position is that
the 1974 *assises* saw a particularly vigorous Rocardian entry which
confiscated the new-found support. Certainly the loss of a promising
area in the midst of the Ceres heartland must have been infuriating.
Whatever the causes, though, it does not alter the fact that *a priori* at
least federations with a MRP tradition like Jura should have been easier

meat than the likes of Creuse or Var. The problem for Ceres was that in order to become hegemonic it had to win both.

A more interesting correlation might be with the Rocardians. In the twenty-one best federations of this group at Metz, Ceres did badly through the seventies in seven and lost ground in six more. Only in three did it prosper, one in the Paris suburbs and two which have been studied separately, Ille-et-Vilaine and Savoie. In both these cases local factors explain the parallel growth of two rival fractions.[34] Our own study stresses the ecumenical approach of the local, always extremely autonomous Ceres leaders; and Charvet's study of Savoie shows Rocardism there to be an alliance of a strong PSU base and local notables, led astutely by the national figure of J.-P. Cot. Within the next group of nineteen fairly good Rocardian departments, there are nine where Ceres has done well or is gaining. These include catholic areas like Mayenne and Haute-Savoie and culturally mixed ones like Loire-Atlantique, as well as old left ones like Tarn-et-Garonne. They raise the question of how far the two fractions cater for different clienteles. In what conditions does success of Ceres rule out that of Rocard? Equally, in what conditions can the two expand together? Again it would seem that local studies alone can reveal the answer.

The worst Rocardian federations, some twenty-one (all 15 per cent or more below the national average for the fraction) include some of Ceres' poorest. These are mainly old SFIO ones, confirming that *any* renovating force finds it hard to break into an established apparatus. But in two areas in this category, Belfort and Vosges, Ceres has succeeded particularly well, the implication being clearly that it took root early and strongly enough to beat off the challenge. Moreover taking the less weak Rocard areas, there are some good Ceres ones (Loire and some Eastern departments). In Rocard's worst twenty-five departments Ceres has scored well in twelve. This tends to show that Ceres can flourish where Rocard cannot and vice versa. But there are exceptions to this rule. We should certainly be wary of reducing the opposition to the straight ideological choice which both claim it is. To do this is to ignore crucial elements of the local situation, not least the calibre of fractional élites and their choices. We may conclude provisionally that the strength or weakness of Rocardism may well be a key element in the progress of Ceres but that the relationship between the two fractions might be more complex than would be expected.

It seemed advisable finally to compare Ceres performance with that of Poperenism, given the historical rivalry of these two marxist fractions. Moreover the Poperenite collapse of 1973 coincided with a Ceres upswing, leading the unwary to suppose a wholesale transfer of Poperenites to Ceres. The assumption would be that there is a type of left socialist who might vary indiscriminately between the two left poles. Such a view is always likely to underestimate the pull which fractions exert on their faithful, and an examination of the two groups' evolution in 1971–3 suggests this. Taking the forty-seven departments where Poperen achieved a significant score (over 10%) at Épinay, we found five types of relationship to Ceres. The first is the rarest (two or possibly three cases), where Ceres made no impact whatsoever; the *locus classicus* of this, Indre-et-Loire, is known as a Poperen stronghold and suggests that in these cases there was a very strong Poperenite machine before 1971.

In about half the cases (some twenty-three) Ceres does appear to have virtually cleaned out all Poperen support; but there are two patterns. In some cases (Paris and suburbs, the East) it was a springboard to further success; but more frequently it was a summit, Ceres achieving little later. Some of the latter cases are old SFIO territory (Landes, Gironde, Hérault), others are poor for the left (Orne, Haute-Loire). In both instances the failure was understandable as there was only a limited amount of support available and both left groups had to fight for it. But other areas (Ardennes, Oise, Somme) were much more promising for the left, and one wonders why Ceres then failed to progress.

More interesting are the twenty or so departments where Poperenite support seems to have been split fairly evenly, again suggesting that there was an apparatus of varying efficiency. Once more this could mean either a springboard for Ceres (Haut-Rhin, Moselle) or a brick wall (especially Brittany and Southern SFIO strongholds like Isère, Pyrénées-Orientales and Vaucluse). Again in these latter instances limited support for the left pole was available, either because the party was too weak or too strong.

Like all our generalisations, these patterns are patchy and show exceptions. At most they suggest that Ceres could win over Poperenites but that the transfer is by no means automatic. Once more we suspect that the key to such transfers can only really be found in the study of individual federations.

4.4 STRENGTHS OUTSIDE THE PARTY

The electoral arena

In addition to intra-party strength, we must consider other areas of influence. The offices of mayor and *conseiller général* have long been considered essential dimensions of party influence, providing as they do opportunities for rising into national eminence. Often a parliamentarian will be found to have kept many of his local offices as well, so valuable are these in terms of winning support. These *cumulards* have been seen as the most efficient means of linking local demands to those Parisian centres which can respond to them, and notables' power is based on this. In some ways it is one of the best measures of a party's influence and hence of a fraction's.

On this score Ceres comes off poorly, at least in aggregate terms. Of 1,013 socialist *conseillers généraux* in 1980, we were able to identify a bare 68 as Ceres;[35] even adding in the 13 Pierret supporters, this only took the total to 8 per cent, far below the fraction's national congress score. The same holds for mayors. The FNESR (Fédération nationale des élus socialistes and républicains) records mayors who are socialists or sympathetic in communes of 1,000+. Given that some are not actually party members, this is a crude guide but it does give some hints. We could not obtain sufficiently precise data on these smaller communes, but we were able to do so for the next largest group, namely those of 9,000+. Of the 442 of these which were socialist in 1980, we found 49 Ceres mayors and 13 Pierretists; again this proportion (12%) is below congress scores.[36] It may be that the scores from small communes would improve this but that is doubtful, for where Ceres does have a rural presence it tends to be in smaller departments which are in its heartland (Belfort, Haute-Saône). Another feature of Ceres *élus* is their rather thin geographical coverage. While the PS as a whole is represented in every metropolitan department, Ceres only boasts mayors (of 9,000+) in 49 and *conseillers généraux* in 37.

Ceres electoral strength at departmental level is striking mostly by its gaps. It is totally absent from the assemblies of departments with huge numbers of PS *conseillers généraux* such as Pas-de-Calais (29 PS members), Bouches-du-Rhône (22) and Gard (20). Even in areas of recent success like Finistère (17) or Côtes-du-Nord (23) the picture is the same. Older SFIO areas in the Centre are equally barren, like Nièvre (no councillors out of 19) or Saône-et-Loire (none out of 21). Where Ceres has broken through in such areas its presence is symbolic: 1 out of 25 in Aude, 1 out of 34 in Haute-Garonne, 1 out of 24 in Drôme and Gironde. The astonishing thing about these latter is that there are any Ceres at all, for they are typical of the older socialist zones where as we saw the fraction's congress scores were usually weak.

Where such isolated pockets of strength exist, they are invariably due to the success of a local personality or group. By dint of skill and hard work such figures are able to dig in and impose themselves against the rest of the party. These 'geographical compromises', if the misuse of a key Ceres concept can be forgiven, are frequent (cf. our study of Aude). Such clusters of strength as exist at this level are in the East (10 out of 10 councillors in Belfort, 4 out of 7 in Meuse, 3 out of 7 in Moselle) and the West (5 out of 10 in Ille-et-Vilaine). Essonne is noteworthy with 4 out of 8. In all these areas Ceres clearly reaped the benefit of its revival of the party.

The figures for mayors confirm these trends. Apart from strong zones in Eastern departments and Essonne (where the cluster of Ceres mayors is very much due to the hard work of Pierre Noë and his team of helpers based on the atomic research establishments in that area), the pattern is of Ceres weakness in strong PS areas, with the odd outstanding individual emerging in places, often doubling as a general councillor. Some even found themselves deputies, unexpectedly and doubtless ephemerally, after the shock of 1981. Typical examples of these dynamic, youngish mayors, usually running newish suburbs with few amenities and many problems are Roland Carraz in the Dijon suburbs, Kléber Haye in Gironde and François Geindre near Caen.

In general it is hard to avoid the feeling that Ceres is under-represented in this sphere, and the fraction's acknowledged local government specialist Pierre Noë has admitted as much.[37] 'Electoralist' as it might be, it is an invaluable training ground for party and fraction élites and a real source of influence. The fraction would need to progress further here.

The next level of election, parliament, shows some curious features. The first real contest for the fraction came in 1973. Charzat and Toutain claim some fifty Ceres contested the 474 metropolitan seats.[38] Only four were elected – Chevènement and Forni in Belfort, Bernard in Meuse and Vacant in Puy-de-Dôme, the latter a very atypical Ceres in some ways. Maurice Blanc won a by-election in Savoie in 1974, and in 1978 Ceres fielded some eighty-four candidates, seven of whom won.[39] Guidoni in Aude, Pierret in Vosges and Beix in Charente-Maritime entered the Palais Bourbon, along with Autain from the Nantes suburbs (Blanc and Bernard lost). Edwige Advice then won a re-run election in the birthplace of Ceres (the 14th *arrondissement*) but this only took the Ceres tally to a modest seven out of 101 socialists. The Pierret split saw the defection of Beix and Pierret himself, but this was compensated by the arrival of Suchod in November 1980 after inheriting a safe seat through years of local implantation. The Ceres' parliamentary élite was thus weak when the elections of 1981 gave it an unexpected boost.

We identified some fifty-six Ceres candidates, along with some twenty Motion F supporters, most of whom had by now joined other fractions. (We shall refer to Motion F supporters simply as 'Fs'.) Yet of these no less than thirty-six were elected, along with eleven Fs, giving Ceres at last a share of deputies approaching its congress strength.[40] Thus despite losing support since 1978 Ceres was still able to cash in with the rest. This is seen better when we compare 1981 candidacies with 1978 ones. Twenty-nine of the 1981 Ceres victors had already stood in 1978. Of the seven new ones, two were Parisian (here Ceres clearly carved up the seats in a deal with the Mitterrandists). Only five were thus unexpected winners.

It is also instructive to compare winnable seats with hopeless ones. Assuming any seat won by the PS in 1981 to have been within reach in 1978 (probably a generous assumption) we find that Ceres was present in 1978 in fourteen such seats, in addition to the other twenty-nine. From these fourteen bankers it was ousted between 1978 and 1981 by Fs (9 cases), Mitterrandists (4) and Rocardians (only one). Of the hopeless seats in 1981 (where the PS could not get within 2,000 votes of the right) we find that of the twenty unsuccessful candidates, *every one* was in just such a seat. This suggests a change in Ceres strategy. The symoblic struggles of earlier years were now left as far as possible to rivals, as Ceres strove to put people into winnable seats. The Metz alliance with Mitterrand which permitted this had thus paid off handsomely. With its new cohort of deputies and using the influence which a good deputy can wield Ceres was now well placed to increase its following in many departments. Its place in the majority was as useful as the voluntarism of its members.

Ceres penetration of the Senate has been slight, unsurprisingly given the rural bias which goes into the election of this body, its past record as a buffer to change and its reputation as a bolt-hole for declining politicians. But senators have resources and prestige which can be used. Ceres has thus used its control of Paris to secure the election in 1977 of Bernard Parmantier, a likeable SFIO veteran of unshakeable left convictions, and also of Dr Cécile Goldet, who left Ceres at Metz. Maurice Jannetti's election for Var was almost certainly due to a bargain between Ceres and its partners in this unusual federation, the Mauroyists (the only such instance in France). A similar deal probably took André Lejeune from Creuse into the Luxembourg Palace in 1980, but he soon became a deputy instead. In general it is safe to say that Ceres sets little store by the Senate other than in terms of the resources it can bring.

Beyond the party: Ceres and the unions

Parties and pressure groups of necessity enjoy complex relation-ships. If the former seek political power and the latter the realisation of more limited goals, then there are many areas where the two meet. Relationships can thus vary from relative equality to outright domi-nation (in both directions). In the case of the PS after 1971, advancing electorally yet structurally weak, certain groups, especially trade unions, had clear advantages. The unions represented millions of potential electors, as well as being a source of skilled and committed activists. Moreover, contact made with the unions when the party was in opposition might facilitate the work of government later.

For all these reasons, apart from any natural affinities between PS and labour movement, the decade saw attempts at a rapprocement. This was not confined to the official party, but was imitated by its left fraction. Ceres made a deliberate attempt to spread its influence in the world of labour. The results of this controversial and delicate, but little-known, operation were mixed.

Given the splits within the unions, different tactics were necessary. The CGT affords a symbolic presence to socialists (usually some six seats on its 100+ national executive), among which was usually to be found the Ceres Pierre Carassus, alongside other PS marxists such as the 'Joxist' Germon or some Poperenites. The advantage of such symbolic representation was twofold. It showed militants that collaboration with the 'real left' was possible for socialists (however nugatory the results) and thus served to emphasise the true left credentials of Ceres. But given the PCF's hegemony, the CGT was always a non-starter. The real attempt at fractional penetration was bound to concentrate on the other unions, particularly the teachers' FEN (Fédération de l'éducation nationale).

FEN is big, rich and powerful.[41] It unionises a much higher proportion of its trade than the average (90% compared with around 20%). It has considerable bargaining power and material assets, and ideologically it has always been on the left, with a strong Republican/ secularist strand. Politically this tradition, due especially to the weight of the primary teachers' SNI (Syndicat national des instituteurs) within the union, meant support for the majority wing of the socialist party. But the union is divided into professional categories and also on political lines. This has meant a vigorous internal fractional life at every level, with highly structured *tendances*. The PCF tends to dominate the secondary teachers in their SNES (Syndicat national de l'enseignement du second degré), but there are also vigorous PSU and trotskyite groups. FEN provides the PS with a great number of activists, of course, and also an unquantifiable amount of resources (including the HQ in rue Solférino). Given these facts and the inviting fractional structure of the union, Ceres was always likely to become involved. The only questions were: at what level to attack and what tactics to use.

Ceres was early concerned with FEN. An early circular ('for restricted circulation') records a decision by the national council of Ceres to create a group for sympathetic teachers in FEN;[42] its aim was to 'confirm within FEN the vitality of the *courant autogestionnaire*'. This might best be done in the short term by working to transform the majority fraction UID (Unité, indépendance, démocratie), whose recent leadership changes seemed to be pulling it to the left.[43] In particular the document warned Ceres teachers to stop working in UA (Unité et action), the pro-PCF group, even though the latter was

actually dominant in the SNES (though not in the FEN as a whole). By
1974 disenchantment with UID was acute, and criticism of its anti-
communism, preoccupation with bread-and-butter issues and bureaucratic style were frequent and it seems clear that a decision had been
taken to launch a specifically Ceres fraction in FEN. A manifesto and
candidates' slate were duly put together, much of the work being done
by two rising second-generation Ceres, Bernard Manin (who would
leave with Pierret) and Jean Exbrayat from Var (later expelled from the
PS). The list contained some prominent non-Ceres, such as Daniel
Percheron (later Mauoryist leader of Pas-de-Calais) and Mitterrandist
René Souchon (now a minister). Known as UR (Unité et rénovation –
title of the Ceres' Épinay motion) it won 5.7 per cent of the vote, giving
it four seats on the *commision administrative* and one on the bureau of
SNES.[44] The fraction was launched.

The PS majority was furious, recalling that the official line was
support for UID. Thus at the CD of May 1975 Ceres was censured for
differing in public from the party line and, amusingly, for 'interfering
with union independence'.[45] The fraction countered by pointing to
the breadth of support for its motion and to the discrepancy which it
saw between UID policy and the party's policy.

Investigation of the texts shows what Ceres meant.[46] FEN texts are at
first sight indistinguishable, with their references to socialism, trade
union unity, etc., but the UID text had elements which roused Ceres
ire. The UR text attacks it for its anti-communism, lack of enthusiasm
for *autogestion* and mistrust of the CPG. The UR text is generally much
more *basiste* and egalitarian, whereas the UID one prefers to talk about
secularism. It is clear that these two fractions mirror the situation in the
PS in 1975. On the one hand a majority confident of electoral success
and in close symbiosis (ideological and political) with the FEN
leadership; on the other an active campaigning minority, committed to
left unity and dynamic change.

The situation did not last, however. The UR fraction seems to have
functioned up to the 1977 SNES congress with a national structure of
delegate meetings, and its manifesto for that congress (which preceded
the PS congress at Nantes) was full of characteristic Ceres themes. UID
was accused of opposition to the CPG and the nationalisation
programme, being pro-EEC, pro-German and, worst of all, wishing to
be the trade-union pillar of 'a French type of social-democracy'.[47] But

in the end the UR leadership had to call on followers to vote for the pro-communist UA.[48] It was in fact unable to produce a credible list of candidates, for several reasons. Some key members had effectively been bribed by UID; other likely recruits preferred to work through the better-established UA anyway. Thirdly and crucially, the worsening PS/PCF partnership put intolerable strains on the left socialist position; thus at Toulon Exbrayat became entangled in a PS/PCF duel over the municipal elections which would see him leave the party.

The conclusion to be drawn from this bold attempt is probably that there was little room for newcomers in an organisation already so clearly polarised between communists and right socialists. Be that as it may, the failure of UR undoubtedly cost Ceres the chance of posts on the FEN executive, influence and ultimately some good recruits.

Force ouvrière (FO) is generally considered a moderate union. Splitting from the CGT in 1947, it has professed an apolitical approach, which is a polite formula for anti-communism. Hardheaded and pragmatic, it prefers to bargain for concrete benefits for its members without too many ideological flourishes; probably most of its leadership and activists incline to a moderate socialist reformism. Under its tough-talking leader André Bergeron it reminds one of a big TUC general union, were it not for one very French characteristic, its unyielding secularism; it is not unusual at congress to hear the rival CFDT derided as 'les curés'. On the face of it such a union seems unpromising terrain for Ceres, displaying as it does all the symptoms of 'social-democracy'. Except, that is, for two features: one is a strong fractionalism, albeit kept within limits,[49] and the second is the fact that much of FO's strength lies in the public sector. The postmen whom Sarre recruited and took with him into the CFDT in 1972, through disappointment at FO's lack of radicalism, are typical. Whatever the attractions, though, it seems clear that Ceres resolved to make an attempt at fractional penetration.

The 1972 congress thus saw a challenge to Bergeron led by Roland Massard and Maurice Labi (a chemical workers' official who later joined CFDT). Their attack was openly political, attacking the failure to campaign jointly with the other unions against government policy. Labi went further, asking FO to commit itself to a decentralised, council-based socialism and getting shouted down in the process.[50] Their motion got 5 per cent. At the Toulouse congress of 1974 they tried again, now scoring 8 per cent and drawing an accusation of 'fractionalism' from Bergeron. One delegate claimed that 'Ceres' take-over bid has failed'.[51] The 1977 congress saw a similar pattern with the Ceres motion, as one reporter described it,[52] defended by Paris delegates who were PS members, especially from the banks, post office and inland revenue (all areas where Ceres had big workplace branches); in geographical terms, it had particular support from Rhône-Alpes (Massard's region). It repeated the charges of the previous occasion, but in a more oblique and less polemical way; clearly it was felt that the previous offensive had been too open and too political. This marked the last attempt at a distinct presence in FO, as Ceres was soon overtaken by its own internal quarrels.

There is some doubt as to how structured this attempt to create a fraction really was. Massard nowadays denies there was such an attempt;[53] but he did leave Ceres in high dudgeon around 1977. Christian Pierret, high in the Ceres leadership at the time, has no doubt whatsoever that a knowing attempt was made to create Ceres fractions in this and other unions.[54] Ceres probably believed that there was support to be had from disgruntled FO members, but was never able to canalise it durably for several reasons. First it lacked the resources for such a campaign. Secondly, its high-profile tactics were too political and too divisive in a union which has a horror of both; Bergeron played on this. Thirdly Sarre's defection to CFDT was extremely ill-received. And finally, many oppositionists to Bergeron were already organised in the trotskyite fraction of Hébert which wanted no rivals. For all these reasons Ceres never got more than a foothold in FO. Work in unions and work in parties is not the same. It remained to be seen whether CFDT would yield better results.

The development of the Confédération française démocratique du travail is complex. Originally a catholic white-collar union, it developed an industrial base after 1945 and widened its ideology beyond social catholicism. After its 'deconfessionalisation' of 1964 it radicalised swiftly, marxist influences and the mass movement of 1968 driving it towards *autogestionnaire* positions. Its work in popularising this ideology was decisive for the PS and the left generally. The union's own line, not always entirely clear, involves commitment to workplace struggles, seen as paving the way to generalised workers' control and direct democracy; opinions vary as to how to achieve these goals, with a more revolutionary tendency confronting a more consensual, modernising one. The CFDT generally mistrusts parties, despite the strong sympathies of many members for the PSU, preferring social movements; it never signed the CPG and its support for left unity was always critical. Despite its proclaimed non-denominational stance, CFDT does best in areas of catholic culture;[55] some observers see something fundamentally catholic about its style, perhaps the rather moral tone which it likes to adopt. Certainly it is a volatile and energetic organism.

Ceres attempts to penetrate CFDT were governed by several factors. First, the early seventies saw an influx of catholic recruits, most of whom were unionised in CFDT to begin with. But the leaders did not try to build up a fraction from the base. Rather they chose to do the reverse, aiming at the 1974 *assises* to coopt the national leaders of the *gauche syndicale*, the most marxist group of CFDT and the most committed to a party-political action. A major factor here was clearly desire to counter the more numerous Maire/Rocard group of modernisers who also joined the PS now. As well as making some very useful members in the provinces, Ceres hoped thus to have a direct input into national CFDT decision-making, tying the union in better to the left union and thus reinforcing its own position. The gambit failed. Within eighteen months most of the *gauche syndicale* leaders (who were given places on the Ceres national secretariat) had left, alienated by the fractional battles of the PS, which they saw as linked mainly to careerism and political ambition. The more open style of CFDT polemics and the frankly more naïve style of the new entrants clashed with the harsher and more arcane manoeuvrings of the party. And the fundamental secularism of the PS, just as present in Ceres (to the astonishment of many) as in the other groups, was very off-putting. The limits to Ceres success were thus early set. Though it kept one or two influential regional leaders like Garnier from Loire, it never had a hope of challenging Maire's leadership.

The failure raises some questions about this impudent attempt to penetrate the labour movement. Results were slight, amounting to no more than some useful recruits; of hegemony there was no chance. Inadequate resources only partly explain the failure to do better.

At the risk of generalisation we may say that Ceres' great mistake was to appear as an external, divisive force. There is a difference between party fractions and those in unions. The latter depend absolutely on a high degree of unity in everyday action if they are to do their job of protecting their members, and all fractional tensions have to be subordinated to this. Even the apparent exception, FO, confirms this; for its congress battles are ritualistic postures which give symbolic satisfaction to the left without inconveniencing the right, while allowing both to continue normal union business. The brash intervention of Ceres disturbed this subtle balance.

Ceres also appeared too political, which means too close to the PCF. Its calls for left and union unity always gave this impression and were bound to cause problems in unions whose existence is to some extent defined by opposition to the CGT, hence PCF.

Above all, style and attitude counted. The highly formalised fractions of the PS breed a corresponding sophistication among activists. While not pretending that unions are free from conspiracy or manoeuvre, there does seem less room for the type of arcane struggle in which PS groups indulge. This is because the pressures are tighter and the stakes higher; unity and solidarity are thus more necessary. In a word, there is a qualitative difference between preparing a deal before a party congress and fighting on issues like redundancies or victimisation. It is this difference in attitude, for want of a better word, which seems to have caused most activists to whom we spoke to be put off Ceres.

All these points apply not just to Ceres but to the party as a whole. Clearly the relationship between party work and union struggles is a difficult one. Between the leninist model of party supremacy, the labourist one of union domination, and the Latin one where each goes its own way, symbiosis is difficult.[56] Ceres failure here mirrors that of the wider party.

A final curious attempt at extra-party activity concerns student unionism, an area renowned for its low representativity and high volatility.[57] Yet it is a valuable training ground for future élites, and the left drew many of its cadres from the generation that opposed the Algerian war; Ceres found in student unionism such leaders as Guidoni and Jacques Guyard, former first secretary of the Paris federation.

By the late sixties the party student movement ES which carried on the struggle in the main union UNEF (Union nationale des étudiants de France) was in a parlous state, and split between two groups, the emergent Ceres and much stronger Poperenites. After Épinay Ceres began to grow, with members in a number of big university towns and a clutch of very able young leaders – Gérard Jacot in Paris, Alain Bartoli in Marseille, and Wolf. On the ES bureau they were of equal strength to the Poperenites (with a neutral chairman), when UNEF broke up in 1971.[58]

The real interest of UNEF lies in the body it controls, the MNEF (Mutuelle nationale de l'éducation française), which looks after student medical insurance and health care. Financed both by student contributions and public money and catering for over 400,000 students in 1970, it had a budget of four thousand million francs and employed over 400 staff. Its bureau is student-elected and the president of UNEF usually runs MNEF too. The break-up of UNEF into warring groups was to bring Ceres a huge windfall. Rival groups were unwilling to run MNEF in what promised to be a period of financial stringency; thus the Poperenites and their perpetual allies in student (and sometimes adult) politics, the trotskyite AJS (Alliance des jeunes pour le socialisme), refused to stand. The communists being too weak, there remained only the Ceres and the PSU students. These two did a deal, with Jacot becoming president of MNEF. Rivals' fear, excess of principle or sheer incompetence had opened the door to Ceres, which took full advantage.

Jacot used his office to pressure government into providing more support and to campaign against privatisation of MNEF activities. ES strength rose steadily, so much so that they felt able to coopt the much weaker communist students as junior allies. Meanwhile the national Ceres had the use of MNEF resources (staff, buildings, generous travel budget) which helped it in building departmental networks. The PS majority looked on with interest (student numbers were increasing) and envy (the newcomers were mainly Ceres). This primacy petered out after Jacot's resignation, however. His successors proved less able to manage the fissiparous tendencies of the ES and indeed some of them seemed more interested in turning it into an autonomous left group than in reinforcing its Ceres character. The crash came in 1974 when Ceres' imminent departure from the majority loomed. The Finel group were driven out as a result of the Martinet split and the Mitterrandists cleverly won over some others; the remaining Ceres resigned in what looked very like reluctance to face up to managing an MNEF about to suffer sharp budgetary cuts. These splits ended Ceres control of ES and MNEF, and at Pau it was easy for Mitterrand to put the ES to sleep. Another avenue of fractional expansion was cut off.

Ceres was obviously fully behind the venture and MNEF policy was regularly discussed on its secretariat, where Jacot sat. If the ES and Ceres hegemony in it grew, then new conflicts arose. These are clearly linked to a second generation of Ceres students, more autonomous politically and more ambitious. The fraction ended up by being humiliated in public with the closing down of the ES, and Jacot sees the affair as a net loss. Certainly he and the other leaders did not carry on into national politics as they might have done; to that extent Ceres missed a chance to renew its élites. There are probably two lessons. First, the episode shows how hard it is for a fraction to supervise every aspect of its activity; it is disturbing to see how easily this big operation slipped out of Ceres' grasp. Secondly one must admire the skill of the Mitterrandists who, instead of making a bureaucratic offensive which might have proved costly, bided their time and used bribery and cooptation to achieve their ends more easily. As with the trade unions, the MNEF must have seemed an attractive option; but like them it brought its problems.

International links

Critics of Ceres sometimes hint that Ceres has mysterious international links with similar groups bent on subverting their own socialist parties. Such fantasies of a new clandestine 'Two-and-a-half' International are baseless. Ceres has various loose links with left fractions of some Socialist International parties, and some others. The PDUP has sent representatives to Ceres colloquia, for instance. There were certainly contacts with the Lopes Cardoso group in the PSP around 1975 – inevitably given the interest aroused by events in Portugal. There are strong ties of friendship between Gonzales and some Ceres leaders; indeed Ceres felt that in the mid-1970s the PSOE was developing into the kind of socialist party which it sought! In Northern Europe the German JUSO attracted early interest and *Frontières* carried material stressing the similarity of their attempt to transform the party. Chevènement and Motchane have friends on the intellectual left of the British Labour party with whom they share an economic analysis; but on defence they are poles apart. One could list other such contacts.

The point is, though, that they are unstructured; and it is hard to see how it could be otherwise. The contacts allow exchange of ideas and mutual encouragement, but little else. Most left fractions do not have the resources to give systematic aid to their fellows; moreover, visible coordination of aims and methods would inevitably lead to cries of 'conspiracy' and 'infiltration'. The task is to conquer one's own party; after that one can see about international collaboration. But in fact we believe that few Ceres leaders have much faith in international collaboration between socialists of the left, right or centre. National priorities have a logic of their own.

4.5 THE CERES ACTIVIST – A PROFILE

The eight departments on which this sample is based were selected with a view to giving as broad an idea as possible of Ceres characteristics. Given the limited time and resources of the researcher, some sharp choices had to be made. We decided thus to include no department where Cerres scores are abject (e.g. Bouches-du-Rhône or Nièvre); the reason for this is usually due in any case to monopolistic control by a local boss.[59] We did include a fairly modest one in Aude, where Ceres has fought a strong local machine with some success. Our main effort went into zones of middling-to-strong Ceres presence, and we also tried to allow for regional variations. Thus Paris and a suburban department were included. We also took in 'new' federations of the East (Meurthe-et-Moselle and the Ceres second capital of Belfort) and the West (Ille-et-Vilaine and Loire-Atlantique). Finally we included a South-Eastern department, Loire, to increase the regional spread. Loire and Loire-Atlantique have the added advantage, if such it be, of being a byword in the PS for particularly bitter fractional strife. The sample obviously overweights Ceres in relation to other groups, for its aim is to elucidate primarily the characteristics of Ceres. But it does give a good representation of the others, with the exception of the Mauroyists. To get an adequate picture of these it would really have been necessary, given their regional nature, to include either Nord or Pas-de-Calais; but as these are modest areas for Ceres their inclusion would have weakened the density of our Ceres sample. We decided then to omit the Mauroyists from our analysis rather than to use the small

Mauroyist sample which our survey yielded. Given that Ceres antagonism has been historically more towards Mitterrand and latterly
Rocard, we feel that elucidation of the characteristics of Mauroyists is
not an absolute necessity.

We are aware that this is a relatively small sample in numerical terms,
and indeed in temporal terms for it covers 1980–1 only. None the less
we feel it may support some modest hypotheses, if only because
sociologically its results are quite close to similar work done through
the seventies.[60] We also stress that these hypotheses are on a general
aggregate level. The real complexity of party life only begins below this,
at federal level (which has been little studied, as has the lower level of
party life, the branch). We have treated our data in a simple, descriptive
way, with no attempt at sophisticated statistical analysis, hence the
survey evidence needs to be seen very much as a prelude to the federal
case studies themselves which are based on interviews and archival
material. It is in these more qualitative analyses that we hope to suggest
some more fertile hypotheses about the progress (or lack of it) of the
late fraction which might, we hope, stimulate further inquiry.[61]

The general sociological characteristics of the PS have now emerged
clearly.[62] If we consider the PS as a series of concentric rings –
leadership, federal élites, ordinary members, and voters – we see a
distinct pattern. On the outside, the PS electorate is now closer than
that of any other party to covering French society at large (Table 4.5).
This is the surest sign of a party's national implantation. Moving
inwards to the ordinary members, we notice a greater specialisation.
The last really reliable survey is still probably that of Patrick Hardouin,
done in 1974. After that with the break-up of left unity and increased
fractional battles, the party became wary of outside inquiries and
probably in its published figures inflated some of the more popular
categories of membership.[63] Old as it is, the survey was none the less
done on a PS that had by then over 100,000 members; even if the figure
at the start of the eighties was around twice that, it is unlikely that these
newcomers have significantly skewed the social distribution remarked
by Hardouin. He found the party to have changed greatly from the
1951 SFIO, which had 38 per cent workers, an over-representation of
the petty-bourgeoisie (shopkeepers, self-employed tradesmen, etc.)
and a very old membership. The new PS was younger and more femi-
nine, and was losing its character as a 'popular party', becoming more

TABLE 4.5   EVOLUTION OF PS SUPPORT, 1973–81 (%)

	Voters 1973	Members 1973[b]	Voters 1978	Voters 1981[e]
Agriculture	11 (12)[a]	8.7	8 (9)[a]	11
Small business/ craftsmen	6 (9)	8.7	5 (6.6)	15
Top management/ professions	9 (6)	14.2[c]	8 (9)	
Middle management/ lower white-collars	20 (17)	30.7[d]	24 (20)	20
Manual workers	35 (32)	14.4	31 (28.5)	36
Non-working	19 (24)	23.2	23 (26.9)	18
TOTAL	100 (100)	100	100 (100)	100

a   percentage of this category in total electorate
b   P. Hardouin, Revue Française de science politique, April 1978
c   includes 7.4% secondary teachers
d   includes 5.3% primary teachers
e   J. Kergoat, Le PS, Sycomore, 1983, p. 280

an 'inter-class' one. Proof of this in Hardouin's eyes was the salience of the new, salaried middle class. Thus as one rose up through the intermediary and national élites, the lower classes (workers, low white-collars) were progressively squeezed out (as were women in general despite being more numerous at branch level). Party élites were thus much more likely to be well-educated white-collars, often public sector and very frequently teachers. Indeed the old SFIO primary teacher, that mythic standard-bearer of socialism was now more likely to be a graduate secondary teacher or, at a national level, a lecturer. Such findings lead Hardouin to call the party 'a popular rally, led by intellectual stata'.[64] These latter, radicalised, are in partnership with the 'organic intellectuals' leading the PCF ally.

The distance from electorate to ordinary membership is not all that great; obviously white-collars are somewhat over-represented and manual workers under-represented, but that is often the case in

180 Keeping left?

TABLE 4.6   PS FEDERAL ELITES, 1973–81 (%)

Congress:	Grenoble 1973[a]	Nantes 1977[b]	Metz 1979[c]	Valence 1981[d]	Our sample 1980–81
Agriculture	1.4	2	1	2	1.8
Small business/craftsmen	3.5	2	2.4	1.5	3
Professions	8.6	4	6.3	5	7.7
Top management/engineers	18.7	19	8.7	17	20.1
Secondary teachers	18.8	24	19.1	25	20.1
Primary teachers	6.1	12	11	5.5	5.9
Middle management	20.3	16	17.1	26	16.6
Lower white-collars	7.8	9	14.5	5	7.1
Manual workers	3.2	5	5.3	5	3.6
Non-working/unknown	11.6	7	15.2	8	14.2
TOTAL	100	100	100	100	100

Sources: a   R. Cayrol, Projet 88, Sept.–Oct. 1974
         b   Le Point 249, June 1977
         c   P. Pacot, L'Unité 380, 1979
         d   R. Cayrol and C. Ysmal, Projet 165, May 1982

socialist parties without a linked trade-union membership. More relevant for purposes of fractional differentiation are the intermediary élites. The federal level of activity is crucial. Within the federal committee (CEF) we will find the most dynamic elements of the mass membership. It is they who are branch officers and who have the energy and commitment to give up a lot of time to the party. They also provide congress delegates, which are a group much studied by Cayrol. Situated as they are midway between national Parisian leaderships and grass-roots members, these federal élites are as good an index as we may find of the nature of activists. Hence our survey concentrated on this level. Table 4.6 shows the socio-economic status of congress delegates for the past decade; our sample is in the right-hand column. It seems to approximate fairly well to the long-running trends of the seventies, with its under-representation of farmers, workers and low white-collars; in other words the popular classes, as French sociologists call them, are relatively absent. At the top, our sample slightly privileges the self-employed, professionals and upper management, but has less teachers: this probably reflects the slightly more industrial nature of our chosen departments. The worse discrepancy is the catch-all group of *cadres moyens* (middle management) and even here our sample compares well with pre-Metz congresses. The drop in this category since then (cf. the Valence figures) might well be due to the desire of all fractions to give their delegates a more popular appearance; fractional élites read political sociology surveys as avidly as academics (they are sometimes the same people) and are thus aware of the need to preserve appearances in a workerist party like this one. Indeed if we compare our sample with the average for all categories over the decade, we see there is no great variation in any instance. We may suppose then that our sample is fairly typical of the type of PS activist who emerged over the seventies. It remains now to consider the sample at the level of fractions.

So far as gender is concerned, party rules recommend that 20% of office holders at least should be female. Our sample has 20.7% women, with no major fraction showing great deviation from this norm. Our age-spread is close to Cayrol's, with 88% under 49 (82% for Cayrol). Of the 11% over 50, three-quarters were Mitterrandists. The great bulk of all activists lay in the 36–49 age-bracket, as previous studies suggest.

Table 4.7 suggests some variation from Cayrol. At the bottom of the scale, Ceres is the most popular fraction, with 13.7% workers and lower white-collars, but this coexists with an above-average weight of middle management (non-teaching groups). The Mitterrandists are close to the average for these middle and low categories,[65] but the Rocardians fall short here. They are above average for non-working categories, however, whereas Ceres is well below. Within the big middle group of teachers, there are variations, with a fairly high proportion of Mitterrandist primary teachers (perhaps the weight of the SFIO?) and a surplus of Rocardian secondary or university teachers.

TABLE 4.7   SOCIO-ECONOMIC CLASSIFICATION OF
ACTIVISTS, 1981 (%)

	Mitterrand	Rocard	Ceres	F	Sample average
Agriculture	4.9 (1)*	0 (1)	0 (3)	0	1.8
Small business/ craftsmen	3.3 (2)	0 (0)	2 (0)	14.2	3
Professions	11.5 (5)	3.6 (5)	5.9 (8)	0	7.7
Top management/ engineers	11.5 (15)	25 (22)	17.6 (19)	28.6	20.1
Secondary teachers	14.8 (29)	32.1 (23)	17.6 (18)	42.9	20.1
Primary teachers	13.1 (6)	3.6 (6)	2 (4)	0	5.9
Middle management	14.8 (23)	10.7 (27)	29.4 (28)	7.1	16.6
Lower white-collars	8.2 (5)	0 (5)	9.8 (6)	7.1	7.1
Manual workers	3.3 (4)	3.6 (3)	3.9 (9)	0	3.6
Students	1.2 (1)	7.1 (3)	2 (0)	0	
Non-working/ unknown	13.1 (9)	14.3 (5)	9.8 (5)	0	14.2
TOTAL	100 (100)	100 (100)	100 (100)	100	100

*Cayrol (1981)

If the technical and administrative middle classes are adequately
covered by Ceres, the Rocardians show a distinct predilection for this
category; while the Mitterrandists compensate for their shortfall here
with an excess of professionals and small employers.

Schematically thus it appears that Ceres has a solid base in the lower
classes and especially at the bottom end of the middle class; its élites
seem drawn from the intelligentsia and technical/administrative strata.
The Rocardians seem top-heavy, with a weak popular base and a high

number of non-working people; they are over-represented at the top of the scale and their top élites again are similar to Ceres. The Mitterrandists remain close to the average for most categories, especially lower down. Among their intellectual groups, the primary teacher still weighs heavily and at the top, technical or administrative expertise is held back to some extent by business and the professions.

This kind of profile would in fact delight Ceres (and the Poperen-ites), who love to portray Rocard as 'social-technocracy'; it also conforms to Cayrol's samples. But our sample does privilege Ceres at the expense of Rocardism generally, and it is probable that in the PS at large Rocardism has a more popular base. We shall simply bear these findings in mind and turn now to the social origins of activists.

Comparison of fathers' status again shows similarity to Cayrol's findings (Table 4.8). Our sample is slightly down on workers and up on farmers, but we have some 6 per cent more undeclared; it is possible that some of these are of lowly origin, which would bring the figure

TABLE 4.8   *ACTIVISTS BY SOCIAL ORIGINS, 1981 (%)*

	Mitterrand	Rocard	Ceres	F	Sample average
Agriculture	11.5	10.7	19.7	14.3	13 (10)*
Small business/ craftsmen	16.4	10.7	13.7	7.1	11.2 (12)
Professions/ top management	19.7	14.3	17.6	28.6	18.9 (18)
Middle management	13.1	17.9	15.7	21.4	16 (16)
Lower white-collars	11.5	17.9	9.8	14.3	11.8 (12)
Manual workers	9.8	17.9	13.7	7.1	14.8 (24)
Non-working/ unknown	18	10.7	9.8	7.1	14.2 (8)
TOTAL	100	100	100	100	100

*Cayrol (1981)

nearer Cayrol. All other categories are very close to Cayrol and we would agree with him that fractional differences on this score are a question of nuances, not cleavages. Our sample shows more Ceres from agricultural backgrounds, especially when we add in the ex-comrades from Motion F. Yet the fraction is slightly down for working-class backgrounds, and more so if the 'Fs' are counted in. Its share of lower white-collars is also below par. These shortfalls cancel out to some extent any claims about more popular origins that might be based on the high number of agricultural backgrounds. If the Rocardians do better in terms of lower white-collars and workers, they are below par for farming backgrounds; but their under-representation in the self-employed and top management may give them slightly more claim to popular origins. The Mitterrandists show a shortfall in terms of workers, but are otherwise unremarkable. The point about all these findings, however, is that few fractional patterns if any diverge sharply from the sample norm, and we may probably assume safely that no fraction is markedly diverse from its rivals in terms of social origins.

Educational qualifications reveal little fractional difference. Within the graduates who compose the majority of the sample, we found a slightly different weighting from Cayrol, with less arts graduates and more from science, law and social science. Mitterrandists tend to be slightly down on graduates in general but to have more than their share of scientists within this category, and less social scientists or lawyers – an image which contrasts with that of Mitterrand himself and his closest advisers. Ceres is slightly above average for social scientists and below it for arts graduates, but it does have an excess of graduates from grandes écoles; perhaps the low number of these in what is a modest sample after all should make us wary of generalisations. The Rocardians stick out most clearly, being better educated with 85% of graduates to the sample average of 64% and stronger in arts and social science (cf. Cayrol).

Previous political itinerary may be thought a pointer to fractional alignment, given that the PS is in some ways an amalgam of previous parties. 41% of our sample declared previous membership (Cayrol 42%), with an even spread between fractions; and some 40% of these named their past party. These divided as follows (Cayrol's figure in brackets): SFIO 17% (10%); CIR 5% (9%); PCF (2%); PSU 12% (14%);

other left 4% (1%). The absence of former Radicals or rightists is striking, as is the low number of ex-communists. The two sets of findings are very close, especially if we sum totals for SFIO and CIR – a legitimate move in that both are part of a Republican, Jacobin and secularist left, much nearer to each other than they are to the PSU or far left (or indeed the PCF). Our Mitterrandists are thus very low on PSU and far-left membership, whereas 36% of the Rocardians are ex-PSU (Cayrol had 39%). Conversely, Rocardians are low in terms of a CIR or SFIO past. Ceres is the most interesting, because it is the most eclectic, especially if the Fs are added in; this gives some 12% SFIO and 6% CIR (below average) but some 14.5% ex-PSU, which is above average.

We next examined the political culture of activists' homes.[66] Some 56% had been raised in a left or even far-left environment; even those few who declared no fractional loyalty were more likely to come from a left home than any other. Less than 20% came from right-wing homes and only 15% from centrist ones. Some slight nuances emerged from this pattern, with Mitterrandists coming more from left homes (66%) and less from the right; Rocardians were less likely to come from left homes (46%) and some 25% came from the right. Ceres were close to the norm for left-wing homes and slightly above it for rightwingers (27.5%); in general they were the least likely to be from apolitical backgrounds.

Turning to the more precise question of father's party, we found that 27% of our sample (28% for Cayrol) had fathers who had been in a party. 28% of Mitterrandists were in this category (Cayrol 32), 11% Rocardians (19), and 33% Ceres (Cayrol had only 20% but our very low percentage of Fs, 14%, in this category revises our figure downwards). Within these parameters, most Mitterrandist fathers tended to be SFIO; Ceres fathers of SFIO sympathies were about average, but some 12.8% had been communists, a high rate in a sample whose average is only 3%. Of Ceres' fathers, 4% had been on the right (average 2%). In general, far-left and centre fathers hardly figured here. It seems that Mitterrandists were more likely to come from left, indeed SFIO backgrounds, whereas Rocardian background might be more varied. Ceres were more likely to come from a political background than not; if it were left, then it was slightly more likely to be communist. This suggests that what counts for Ceres is perhaps less the precise nature of the politics at home than the fact that

TABLE 4.9   ACTIVISTS BY UNION AFFILIATION, 1981 (%)

	Mitterrand	Rocard	Ceres	F	Sample average
Non-union/ unknown	21 (20)*	11 (16)	15 (8)	14	18 (20)
CGT	11 (11)	4 (8)	12 (14)	–	8 (10)
CFDT	7 (19)	54 (46)	53 (47)	43	34 (28)
FO	16 (8)	3 (2)	2 (1)	–	9 (6)
FEN/students	30 (33)	21 (16)	12 (15)	36	21 (26)
Others	15 (10)	7 (12)	6 (15)	7	10 (10)
TOTAL	100	100	100	100	100

*Cayrol (1981)

there were politics at all and that they got used to it early in life.

This examination of political background in the widest sense suggests that Mitterrandism is heir to a certain Republican/secularist tradition of socialism, whereas Rocardians are more eclectic and thus more open to a 'new left' mode of political existence. Ceres appears some way between the two, visibly appealing to people from both traditions, and this suggests some tension within the fraction. We may expect attitude tests to shed further light on this.

Length of party membership is also relevant here. Of our sample, 29% had joined by 1971, including 28% Ceres and 36% Mitterrandists. Each fraction thus had a core of militants even at Épinay. After that our respondents joined in regular waves, with some 30% coming in by the presidential campaign of 1974 and a similar amount by the break-up of September 1977. Less than 10% came after that. The arrivals of Rocardians are not as tightly bunched as one might expect, with 12% in by 1971 and a further 29% by the *assises*; although 43% came then it is surprising to find so many pre-dating them. This suggests that

Rocardism has deeper roots than the hard core of PSU support that he took with him in 1974.

Turning to union affiliations, Cayrol found three features in his profile of Valence delegates: the high density of teachers (FEN) within the Mitterrand camp, and the relative strength of CGT here and in Ceres (in the party at large it is a minority interest, cf. Table 4.9). Finally he stressed the high salience of CFDT among Rocardians and Ceres. Our sample maximises these trends if anything, even if, on an aggregate level, it is slightly down on FEN and slightly up on CFDT (the catholic bias of our selection no doubt exerting an influence here). In fact our sample is more interesting for its negative indications than its positive ones. The Mitterrandists have very little interest in CFDT (much less than Cayrol's), compensated by the extra weight of FEN within their number and what is nowadays a high rate of membership, by PS standards, of FO. There is also quite a high rate for miscellaneous unions (farmers, self-employed, etc.), yet the fraction is above average for CGT. All this suggests heterogenous views about the role of unions, with activists prepared to work with the PCF cohabiting with staunch anti-communists and the ring between the two held by teachers. Three very classical approaches to unionism are thus combined, but what is absent is interest in the one which seeks to extend union involvement to most areas of society, CFDT.

The Rocardians are predictably low on CGT membership and equally high for CFDT. Like Ceres they have few non-members of unions; the two most militant fractions clearly thus follow up their rhetoric about the importance of workplace activism. But although many Ceres are in CFDT, there is also a high rate of support for CGT. Again this suggests coexistence of two styles – a classically marxist approach alongside a more experimental one. As with other aspects of the Ceres profile, one wonders about potential contradictions between the two.

Religion was an unavoidable variable and was examined both from the angle of membership of and socialisation into religion. Table 4.10 shows our survey to confirm known trends. We had a similar rate of practising catholics to Cayrol (a tenth) and a slightly higher one of non-practising (28% to 25%). This latter term is elastic, but we take it to mean that respondents feel their world-view to be influenced in some way, however vague, by catholicism; certainly they are not ready to

TABLE 4.10   ACTIVISTS BY RELIGIOUS ALIGNMENT, 1981 (%)

	Mitterrand	Rocard	Ceres	F	Sample average
Practising catholic	8	18	10	7	10 (10)*
Non-practising catholic	36	32	21	21	28 (25)
Other religious	8	11	4	–	6 (4)
Areligious	48	32	62	71	54 (59)
No answer	–	7	3	–	2 (2)
TOTAL	100	100	100	100	100

*Cayrol (1981)

declare themselves atheists or agnostics. We had 54% of the latter to Cayrol's 59%. For the Mitterrandists, practising catholics were below the norm, but compensated by a higher incidence of non-practising. The areligious (close to the norm in Cayrol's sample) were less frequent in ours; perhaps like their master, some Mitterrandists prefer to retain a loose, sentimental link with the religion of their upbringing. Rocardism revealed, predictably, a high rate of practising catholics (18%); it was also above average for other religions and non-practising catholics and hence remarkably low for the areligious (32% compared with our sample average of 54% and Cayrol's 51%). Although the Eastern and Western preponderance of the departments sampled explains some of this, it is still striking, especially when we consider that some of the non-answers (higher among Rocardians than elsewhere) may well come from activists wary enough to smell an attempt to identify them as 'les cathos'. By contrast Ceres emerged as the most areligious (65% if the Fs are added). Yet like the Mitterrandists it has a catholic core; again two distinct traditions must cohabit. We cannot thus postulate a straight religious/secularist split between the Rocardians on the one hand and the Metz allies on the other (although the religious variable does thus tend to some extent to differentiate the two) simply because of the internal differentiation within the Ceres and Mitterrand ranks. Certainly we can agree with Cayrol that Ceres has by now lost much of the catholic aura with which the media surrounded it earlier in that decade.

Analysis of religious socialisation confirms this, with fathers' religion showing a high proportion of practising catholics to areligious (52% to 28%);[67] very few respondents failed to answer this. Mitterrandists tended to be close to the average, especially when non-practising fathers were included. Rocardian homes showed much less irreligiosity (21%) and more evidence of practising catholics (61%). Ceres and Fs came from homes with above-average practice (57%), yet seemed to have had mothers who veered more towards areligiosity (20% compared with an average of 16%). This suggests that Mitterrandists and Ceres have emancipated themselves more from their backgrounds, for whatever reasons and by whatever process, than have Rocardians. Even given the nature of our departments this suggests a trend worth further investigation.

We next tested attitudes on a number of issues that were very sensitive, politically, by 1980. Choice was difficult and we attempted to select issues which touched on the characteristic preoccupations of fractions; respondents were asked to rate the issues on a 5-point scale, from very important to totally unimportant; crude as the method is, it seems to us no worse than asking respondents to give marks out of 10 to an issue. In general answers showed a high degree of orthodoxy, few wishing to step outside the party line – understandably perhaps at this period of great intra-party tension. But examination of the nuances of answers, particularly the differences between *qualified* and complete approval/disapproval does allow some hypotheses to emerge.

The first issues were decentralisation and *autogestion*, which we hoped would drive a wedge between the Jacobins (Poperen, Joxe, etc.) who have never believed in these theories, and the *deuxième gauche*. In fact on decentralisation, only 5% found it unimportant and only 6% refused to answer. 95% of Mitterrandists found it important, with a minute amount of disapproval and an above-average number answering 'very important'. The Rocardians were just as enthusiastic, with no disapproval and the highest amount of 'very important'. Ceres had 10% against and 8% who refused to answer – a small, but significant core of opposition. If this means that 82% thought decentralisation to be important, only 31% of them thought it very important. This is a good example of the nuanced answer referred to above. Clearly many Ceres are less than enthusiastic about decentralisation (if only because it is now perceived as a Rocardian theme *par excellence*). But after years of endorsing the idea they cannot reject it outright, hence the qualified approval. The Fs showed, for what it is worth, similar propensities.

Autogestion drew a similar response, with 90% approval (72% very important). No one dared to say it was not important at all. But the Mitterrandists showed the lowest number of 'very importants' and an above-average density of qualified disapproval (probably the weight of Poperenism in the sample). Predictably, the Rocardians found *autogestion* very important to the tune of 97%. So however did 76% of Ceres (above average for the sample), while a further 20% saw it as important. The Fs were similar. It seems overall that the older left is more mistrustful of *autogestion* (though not so much of decentralisation). Among the two militant poles, Ceres still shows a remarkably high commitment to *autogestion*, though its reservations on decentralisation suggest that these impulses have to struggle against old Jacobin demons in some cases.

On international relations, we chose two issues guaranteed to arouse passions: the question of European unity and the autonomous French deterrent. The former aroused less enthusiasm than most issues (39% very important, 35% important), with a solid opposition of 16%. Mitterrandist approval was above average, and opposition lower. No Rocardians were opposed and 89% were in favour (64% very much so). Ceres showed only 14% very important and 37% important; 39% very hostile. Equally significant was the fact that 86% of the Fs were enthusiastic; clearly this is an issue which cuts them off from their ex-comrades more than most.

Nuclear weapons elicited the sharpest internal divisions, with 11% of non-responses and 37% disapproval. Of the 51% supporters, only 19% see it as very important. Generally, responses were grouped in the middle, with less outright approval or condemnation; clearly this is a delicate issue. Mitterrandists showed, surprisingly, an above-average opposition of 54%; of the 33% who approved, only 8% did so strongly. Doubtless the humanitarian traditions which have influenced the past of this fraction are still strong, despite its leader's conversion to the nuclear status quo. The Rocardians were closest to the sample norm, with some 50% approving. Clearly growing fear about Soviet intentions since 1978 has eroded the strong anti-nuclear reflexes of this group. Ceres is surest on this issue, with 72% support (33% very important) and only 17% opposition. The Fs were badly split on this, with an above-average support, but also a level of opposition close to the sample norm. Possibly again this was a factor in the split with Ceres.

We next took a domestic political issue: should the PS seek a new common programme (CPG) with the PCF? Our hope here was that the question would separate those who really seek to anchor their party on the left from those mere electoralists who want communist votes at the second ballot. The results disappointed us. An astonishing 86% claimed to want a new CPG and only 8% did not. Of Mitterrandists 90% did and only 3% did not. What would they have answered after May 1981 when their leader showed that the *absence* of a CPG was the key to left victory? Only 60% of Rocardians desired a CPG, and only a third thought it very important (probably a high proportion, given the circumstances?); 29% found the issue unimportant. Again Ceres had few doubts, with 96% in favour (88% strongly), and all the Fs were in favour; perhaps their desire for wider left unity was fuelled by the lack of it inside their own ex-fraction! While the Rocard and Ceres results here were fairly predictable, the Mitterrandist one was less so.

Our final test involved two ideological issues which have divided the party much – workplace branches (SE) and the idea of 'struggle against the dominant ideology' which of course characterised the anti-Rocard campaigns. We expected Mitterrandists to be relatively uninterested in these abstract issues. The party as a whole showed great interest in the ideology question, 87% finding it important and only 6% dissenting. Mitterrandists were above average in fact with 94% and Ceres hit a similar level, including the highest tally of 'very important'. The Rocardians showed only 68% interest and 22% disinterest, having doubtless had their fill of accusations of 'American left', etc. The Fs showed 93% of 'very important', illustrating the salience which this issue must have assumed in their battle within Ceres. One would be tempted to wonder in their case if the dominant ideology was perhaps less that of the Giscardian bourgeoisie than that of Ceres. Answers on

SE showed similar patterns, except that the Rocardians were up to the 93% norm of approval (albeit with less 'very important'). As there are relatively few SE with a real existence, this question is as ideological as its predecessor; both concern a certain view of the party and its image. It is not a surprise that few wish to dissent from this image (a 'real worker's party', just as much as the PCF). Hence the orthodoxy of the answers, especially from Ceres and only slightly less so from Mitter-randists. The nuanced Rocardian replies suggest that there are limits to how far that fraction is ready to play such ideological games for their own sake.

Part of the activists' outlook is made up by their view of other parties; respondents were asked to list these on a 5-point scale, ranging from strong sympathy to strong antipathy. The PCF attracted 48% antipathy and 30% neutrality, only 22% seeing it positively. Mitterrandists saw it very negatively (64%), whatever their feelings about a new CPG, and Rocardians even more so (79%), only 7% finding anything positive about it. With only 20% antipathy and 42% positive feelings, Ceres was on its own. The Fs were split almost evenly between sympathy, hostility and neutrality, suggesting that this issue had again been a delicate one in the Ceres split.

If the older left was ill received, this was not true of the new one, as the PSU drew 46% positive responses and only 17% negative. Mitterrandists showed some wariness, though, with 41% expressing no opinion and 34% a negative response. If the Rocardians showed an expectedly high rate of approval (68%) with not a single expression of disapproval, then Ceres rated astonishingly highly with 55% sympathy and a bare 8% disapproval. Despite the Ceres leaders' contempt for this modernising left, then, it seems that the followers are much more ecumenical towards new and old lefts alike.

Trotskyism in the shape of the LCR (Ligue communiste révolution-naire) drew only 21% of sympathy (like the PCF) and a high 42% of non-answers (polite refusal to kick a marxist when he is down?). Mitterrandists do not hesitate to express 48% disapproval (only 8% approval), and Rocardians 43%. With its 39% approval and only 23% disapproval, Ceres again takes the side of fellow marxists more readily than its fellow socialists do, and once more despite its own leaders.

The moderate centre–left MRG (Mouvement des radicaux de gauche) whose proclaimed ambition was to moderate the 'collectivist' follies of its CPG partners, came out badly with 29% approval and 41% hostility. Mitterrandists are closest to the sample norm, but the Rocardians, with their 43% approval and only 21% disapproval, invert this ratio. Ceres diverges sharply with 18% approval and 59% disapproval, being clearly the most mistrustful of the centre–left, with the Rocardians closest to this and the Mitterrandists in between.

In the bipolarised Fifth Republic, two groups occupy what remains of the centre, being in reality allies of the right. The secularist pole is Radicalism, and the remains of the christian democrats, the CDS (Centre des démocrates sociaux), provide the other. Neither appeals to the PS, Radicalism attracting a 75% hostility rate, higher in Ceres than elsewhere. With only 1% approval and 85% hostility, the CDS notables associated with Jean Lecanuet come off even worse. If Ceres is again most hostile, even Rocardian disapproval reaches 82%. In short, everyone in the PS believes that these parties are simply part of the right.

Within the right proper, there is little differentiation. Giscard's allegedly more liberal PR (Parti républicain) rates 88% disapproval and 1% positive opinions, with an even spread of dislike across the board. No Rocardians are thus willing to identify their 'American left' with the 'American right', as Ceres would have it. But neither are there any 'national leninists' from Ceres seduced by the nationalist themes of Chirac's RPR (Rassemblement pour la République). It draws 85% disapproval, with 89% from the Rocardians and 94% from Ceres; only a bare 5% of Mitterrandists give it any positive rating at all. Chevènement may theorise about links between the left and the patriotic elements of the right, but none of the PS, including his own followers, sees it thus.

We also attempted to ascertain views on fractions as such. More than even the general political questions aired above, this is a delicate matter. Activists are aware that what the researcher really wants to know is the extent of their loyalty towards their own fraction, compared with that towards the party, the sole legitimate object of their affection. Discretion is to be expected, then. And some questions are not worth asking. No intelligent activist will say openly that his or her prime loyalty is to fractional comrades, or that the fractional line is divergent from the party one, even if either or both of those propositions seems to be supported to some extent by argument. We thus included at various points in the questionnaire a number of fairly modest enquiries about fractions; as it was, many sidestepped them. We are therefore left with a mini-sample, on which we may found some cautious hypotheses, which would need to be tested further (though by what means it is frankly hard to see).

On the role of *courants* in general (this was the word used), half the respondents wanted their activity to be cut down or stopped outright (42% and 9% respectively); but 43% were satisfied with the status quo and an embattled 1% wanted to increase fractional confrontation. Very few refused to answer (4%). Coming as it did at a high point of party strife and with a presidential election looming up, we might be astonished that more people did not want the confrontation to be reduced or stopped.

Those keenest to reduce fractionalism came from different places; 68% of Mitterrandists wanted to do so and 74% of the Fs. Clearly there are opposing reasons for this; the Fs had just been the losers of a particularly hard fractional battle and were clearly disenchanted about the whole fractional structure, whereas the Mitterrandists, having won just such a battle, now found it easier to stress unity. The Rocardians, with a similar proportion worried about fractions, probably had similar feelings to the Fs. But if these three fractions all show a roughly similar profile, with only a quarter in favour of fractions and the rest doubtful, Ceres again stands out: 81% are happy with the status quo and only 12% seek a reduction of fractional activity. And yet Ceres had lost nearly half its support at Metz after fractional battles (though it was of course now back in the leadership). This suggests two things. First, Ceres supporters value power and influence above mere numerical weight and secondly they see fractionalism as a means to that end (even and especially if the fraction has to be purged). In other words Ceres seems to have a more purposeful and tighter-knit identity.

We may at this point consider motivation for joining the party in the first place. Activists were asked to tick as appropriate a number of such motivations, one of which was attraction towards a particular fraction. Some 21% of the sample admitted to this and only 21% actually denied it; those who gave no answer were evenly distributed between all fractions. This delicate balance, which illustrates perfectly the methodological problems involved in asking such questions, suggests that we must nuance slightly Hardouin's claim that by and large people do not join the PS on a fractional basis.[68] Mitterrandists and Rocardians, at 10% and 11% respectively, show a low rate of fractional motivation for joining the party, but both Ceres and the Fs, with 43%, show a much clearer approach. The Rocardian score is in our view artificially low, due to the tactical consideration of not wishing to appear as an organised minority now that they were in opposition within the party. Hence their attempts to play down this question and indeed to argue (see below) that their fraction is not really one like the others.

Durability is a further criterion of fractional behaviour and we asked if supporters of Metz motions still considered themselves as close to a fraction: 77% still did so and 15% did not; a significant part of the missing 8% came from those unclassifiables who had not indicated their Metz vote and whose views on most topics showed them to be indecisive, to put it mildly. If 70% of Mitterrandists still affirmed fractional feelings, 86% of Rocardians did and 94% of Ceres; only 3% and 2% respectively of the latter now denied fractional loyalty. The Fs had split badly, reflecting the fate of their unfortunate motion. This suggests that Ceres and Rocardians do have a somewhat stronger commitment to their groups than the supporters of the then First Secretary.

We then asked respondents to identify the fractions to which they felt close, hoping thereby to trace patterns of movement between fractions. This was taken ambiguously (and deliberately, we think) by some activists to refer to *courants* beyond the PS; thus some Rocardians talked of a *courant autogestionnaire* ranging far over the French left. Interesting perspective though this raises (in terms of the perception of the nature of fractions by activists) its main motive is probably tactical, stemming from the discomfort and vulnerability felt by the Rocardians in their minority position. But in general the fit between Metz votes and continuing identification with fractions is a good one. In particular, 92% of Ceres continue to identify with their fraction, the only loss being an apparent 2% to Mitterrand. The Rocardians seem *a priori* to be slipping away, with only 61% continuity; but when we see the 18% of non-responses and the 21% who refuse to equate a Metz vote with fractional membership, we may suspect a much higher figure. No Rocardian at Metz declares support for any other fraction, at any rate; clearly their tactic is to play down the notion of fraction as such. The

Mitterrandists show similar but looser patterns: 56% continue in the fraction, but 34% refuse to answer and the other 8% refuse to assimilate their Metz vote to fractional membership. Only 2% admit deserting to Rocard. So even here there is some consistency; the fact that Mitterrandist respondents are less positive suggests that they do not live out their fractional involvement in quite so committed a way as Ceres or so subtle a way as the Rocardians. As for the Fs, of the half who answered they are scattered now among all the other groups – a eloquent testimony to the power of party rules. What would have happened had they beaten the 5% barrier?

We finally tried to assess previous fractional membership. Some 49% denied any, and a quarter refused to answer, leaving us with a quarter who had changed fraction at some time past. This percentage is boosted however by a high response-rate from the Fs who almost by definition must have changed. Corrected for this, the figure for changes reads 19% only. Within this parameter, Ceres and Mitterrandists come out below par (14% and 16%) and Rocardians some way above at 32%. This suggests some mobility between fractions, in particular movement towards Rocardism as its image became clearer through 1978–80.

We left it to respondents to indicate why they had changed and from which fraction. This resulted in a further contraction of the response-rate and a multiplicity of explanations from those who did answer. We are thus working with a very small data base and need to treat findings with maximum caution. What this suggests is that a small amount of inter-fractional movement goes on between the fringes of fractions in all directions (Mitterrand to Mauroy, Ceres to Rocard, Mitterrand to Ceres, and so on). The main reason for leaving Mitterrand seems to be dislike of the personal, authoritarian way in which he was said to run the party, plus apprehension about his Metz alliance with Ceres. Ceres had been abandoned for several reasons, including nationalism, Jacobinism, leninism, lack of internal democracy and uncritical attitudes to the PCF. We stress again that these trends emerge from a very small subsample and would need to be tested by a large-scale inquiry. The overall picture which they suggest conforms generally with our idea of the fractions as fairly stable communities, however, for it combines a fundamental stability with just a hint of movement at the edges. Certainly on this empirical evidence our perception of Ceres as a distinct entity is confirmed. Sociologically it is not sharply distinct from the others, but begins to be so in terms of political background. It seems to feel its identity as belonging very much to the traditional left (cf. union affiliation, and attitudes to the CPG or PCF); yet this coexists with a new left element from the PSU and strong sympathy for this party. Ceres attitudes on *autogestion* suggest a similar tension between new and old lefts. As for religious background, Ceres seems to be more areligious or secularist, but there is evidence of a considerable catholic dimension. The surest parts of Ceres identity have to do with questions of national sovereignty and defence, and also with the positive identification with the concept of fraction, seen as politically essential. We might summarise these findings by saying that although there is a certain tension within the fraction, its overall sense of identity and purpose are high, probably more so than the Mitterrandists and at least as much as the Rocardians.

We have seen then in this chapter how Ceres is organised, what are its strengths both inside and outside the party and what its activists are like. It is now time to go beneath this general level of analysis and see some examples of Ceres political practice.

NOTES TO CHAPTER 4

1   M. Charzet *et al.*, *Le Ceres – un combat pour le socialisme*, Paris, Calmann-Lévy, 1975, p. 43.

2   Interview with Georges Sarre, Assemblée Nationale, Paris, July 1981.

3   G. Toutain, *Le Ceres – tentative de renouveau du PS*, Paris, Faculté de droit (mémoire de DES), 1972, p. 13.

4   J.-P. Chevènement, *Le vieux, la crise, le neuf*, Paris, Flammarion, 1974, pp. 259–63.

5   X. Charvat, *Le Ceres en Savoie, 1968–79*, Grenoble IEP (thèse de doctorat), 1980.

6   M. Charzat, op. cit., p. 93. It seems surprising in retrospect to find Ceres and Poperenites on opposite sides, given their broad ideological similarity. The reason is the latters' hesitation over the alliance with the PCF, which they wanted to defer until sufficient guarantees were given. The more voluntaristic Ceres was confident, as was Mitterrand, of PS ability to beat the PCF regardless and has always resented this hesitancy, which does characterise Poperenism despite its verbal leftism (interview with Didier Motchane, Paris, July 1981).

7   Ibid., p. 101.

8   The most interesting portraits of regional PS élites are in J.-F. Bizot *et al.*, *Au Parti des socialistes*, Paris, Grasset, 1975.

9   Although Ceres did receive a number of provincial activists from the *assises*, few stayed long (see Sections 5.2 and 5.4).

10   Interview with Gilles Martinet, Paris, October 1980.

11 Le Poing et la rose 78, February 1975.
12 M. Charzat, op. cit., p. 131.
13 Parti socialiste, Projet socialiste – pour la France des années 80, Paris, Flammarion, 1980.
14 Y. Roucaute, Le Parti socialiste, Paris, Huisman, 1983, p. 132.
15 For a partial autobiography see J.-P. Chevènement, Etre socialiste aujourd'hui, Paris, Cana, 1980. There is an interesting interview in Le Monde 31 July 1984.
16 There seem to have been also assemblées générales with a more open admission and bigger numbers; the difference with the collectif is not fully clear.
17 Internal circular, n.d., (c. late October 1974).
18 Basic Marx and Lenin texts figure prominently, as do Ceres ones. Study of Gramsci is encouraged, but there is also considerable material on trotskyism, austro-marxism and even libertarian theory. The overall impression is of some eclecticism, albeit with a clear marxist core.
19 This account is derived from an internal circular, Information sur le MJS, n.d., (clearly December 1974). A former Ceres leader told us that the secretariat had entrusted Guidoni with the task of expelling the dissidents. He was apparently unable to utter the word 'exclu', so much so that Chevènement, watching at the back of the room, walked out in disgust. Formalities apart, the desired result was in the end achieved.
20 Symbolic of the need for 'real' as opposed to 'formal' cohesion is the fact that at national Ceres meetings applause is supposed to be forbidden and votes not taken.
21 L. Laignel, Les exclusions du PS depuis juin 1971, Paris I (DES), 1976. Details of disciplinary procedures are given in the statutory report of the CNC, published in the special congress numbers of Le poing et la rose.
22 Internal circular 5 April 1976.
23 La Voix du Nord 9 June 1977.
24 Parti socialiste, Statuts, Paris, 1982, pp. 37 ff.
25 Internal document n.d. (c. May 1977).
26 These figures apply to ninety-five metropolitan departments, Corsica being considered as one despite its being split in 1976.
27 D. Hanley, 'Les députés socialistes', Pouvoirs 20, 1982, pp. 55–66.
28 B. Graham, The French Socialists and Tripartism, 1944–7, London, Weidenfeld and Nicolson, 1964, pp. 160–1.
29 R. Cayrol, 'Les votes des fédérations dans les congrès et conseils nationaux du parti socialiste, 1958–70', Revue française de science politique, XXI, 1971, pp. 51–75.
30 Rouge 23 June 1976.
31 D. Hanley, 'The Ceres in two départements' in D. Bell (ed.), Contemporary French Political Parties, London, Croom Helm, 1982, pp. 123–37.
32 C. Leleu, Géographie des élections françaises depuis 1936, Paris, PUF, 1971. This text has the advantage of numerous particularly clear diagrams. The spread used ran thus: very good, 7.5% or more above; good, 2.5% to 7.5% above; average, within 2.5% of national average either way; poor, 2.5% to 7.5% below; very poor, more than 7.5% below.
33 J. Derville, 'Les militants socialistes de l'Isère', Revue française de science politique, XXVI, June 1976, pp. 568–99.
34 X. Charvet, op. cit.
35 Fédération nationale des élus socialistes et républicains, Annuaire des conseillers

généraux socialistes, Paris, 1980. I am greatly indebted to Georges Mingotaud for his help in identifying Ceres office holders.

36 Ceres itself seems to regard some eighty-one mayors as significant in this context; but some of these are probably from communes below the 9,000 threshold.

37 Interview with Pierre Noë, Senate, Paris, December 1980.

38 M. Charzat, op. cit., p. 105.

39 *Le Monde* 11 November 1977.

40 D. Hanley, 'Les députés socialistes', op. cit.

41 D. Granet, *Nouvel Économiste* 302, 14 September 1981. The clearest recognition of FEN's weight within the PS was the appointment of its then General Secretary A. Henry as minister of Leisure upon Mitterrand's victory.

42 Undated – probably late January 1973.

43 'L'avenir de la FEN', *Frontières* 6, May 1973, pp. 38–42.

44 *Unité Syndicale* (official SNES magazine) 16, 23 June 1975.

45 *Le Monde* 6 May 1975.

46 *Unité syndicale* 12, 7 May 1975.

47 Ibid. 26, 20 April 1977.

48 Ibid. 33, 15 June 1977 and 28, 4 May 1977.
A similar operation seems to have been conducted in the SNESup for university teachers, where the fraction *Socialisme et éducation* managed to take 6–7% of the vote. It still existed in 1981. Although it seems to have outlived its SNES equivalent, it is much less important, given the low degree of influence exerted by SNESup, thanks in part to its small membership (only 6,000 according to *Le Monde* of 22 March 1981).

49 Bergeron's group usually commands 85% of congress votes, the remainder dividing between abstentionists, anarchists and trotskyites (invariably the most vocal anti-clericals), whose antics are tolerated with benign amusement by the leadership. This would not be the case in the CGT from which many are refugees.

50 *Force Ouvrière, Congrès de Paris, 1972: compte rendu*, Paris, 1972.

51 *Le Monde* 14–17 June 1974.

52 J. Roy, *Le Monde* 12–15 June 1977.

53 Interview with Roland Massard, Villeurbanne, December 1980.

54 Interview with Christian Pierret, Assemblée Nationale, Paris, November 1980.

55 P. Martin, 'Les élections prudhomales de décembre 1982', *Pouvoirs* 26, 1983, pp. 125–32.

56 A. Bergounioux, 'Typologie des rapports syndicats-partis en Europe occidentale', ibid., pp. 17–30.

57 For a recent survey see A. Blainrue, 'Le syndicalisme étudiant', ibid., pp. 117–24.

58 I am grateful to Gérard Jacot (now chief executive at Épinay town hall) and to Alain Bartoli (former Ceres student leader in Marseille) for their recollections of this little-known topic.

59 On Marseille see G. Rochu, *Marseille – les années Defferre*, Paris, Alain Moreau, 1983; D. Bell and B. Criddle, *The French Socialist Party: Resurgence and Victory*, Oxford University Press, 1984, pp. 224–7; D. Bleitrach, J. Lojkine et al., *Classe ouvrière et social-démocratie: Lille et Marseille*, Paris, Editions Sociales, 1981, pp. 123–58.

60 R. Cayrol, 'Les militants du PS: contribution à une sociologie', *Projet* 88, September–October 1974, pp. 929–40 and 'L'univers politique des militants socialistes', *Revue française de science politique*, XXV, January 1975, pp. 23–52; P. Bacot, *L'Unité* 380, 1980; P. Hardouin, 'Les caractéristiques sociologiques du PS', *RFSP* XXVIII, April

1978, pp. 220–56; R. Cayrol and C. Ysmal, 'Les militants du PS: originalité et diversités', *Projet* 165, May 1982, pp. 572–86.

Our sample showed a response rate of 51% (total number 325) and broke down as follows: Mitterrandists 36%, Mauroyists 4%, Rocardians 17%, Ceres 30%, Fs 8%, unknown 5%. Each fraction's own rate of response (actual number of responses over potential number) was close to the sample average, with Mitterrandists slightly above it and Ceres and Rocardians slightly below. Obviously the sample overweights Ceres in strict comparison to its Metz score, but it should be able to bring out the specificity of the fraction in regard to its rivals (Mauroyists excepted).

61   There is still relatively little in the way of federal studies on the PS. In addition to Charvet and Derville op. cit., we found the following useful: J.-P. Chagnollaud, 'La federation socialiste de Meurthe-et-Moselle, 1944–77', *Annales de l'Est*, 1978, pp. 137–66; R. Ferretti, 'Les militants de la fédération du Bas-Rhin du PS: éléments pour une sociologie', *Nouvelle revue socialiste* 14–15, 1975, pp. 8–16; C. Marjolin, *Une fédération du nouveau parti socialiste: étude structurale de la fédération de Paris, 1969–73*, Université de Paris I (DES), 1973; H. Portelli and T. Dumias', Les militants socialistes à Paris', *Projet* 101, January 1976, pp. 35–43.

62   On the PS electorate see J. Capdevielle (ed.), *France de gauche, vote à droite*, Paris, FNSP, 1981; J. Jaffré, 'De V. Giscard d'Estaing à F. Mitterrand: France de gauche, vote à gauche', *Pouvoirs* 20, 1982, pp. 5–28; *Nouvel Observateur* 4 July 1981. On party élites see, in addition to work listed under note 60, P. Bacot, *Les Dirigeants du PS: histoire et sociologie*, Lyon, Presses Universitaires de Lyon, 1979 (a very detailed study of the early seventies which tries to maximise the presence of the lower classes in the party and presents it as being more revolutionary than reformist) and H. Portelli, 'Nouvelles classes moyennes et nouveau parti socialiste', in G. Lavau (ed.), *L'Univers politique des classes moyennes*, Paris, FNSP, 1983, pp. 258–73.

63   Interview with Patrick Hardouin, Paris, December 1980.

64   P. Hardouin, op. cit., p. 254.

65   The high weight of Mitterrandist farmers is almost certainly due to Aude, this largely wine-growing department being renowned within the PS for its loyalty to the Paris leadership.

We used in this survey the standard classifications of INSEE (*catégories socio-professionelles*) as used in most French surveys. Converting them into terms of social class is a controversial process; but on a descriptive level they help show up the sociological differences between fractions.

66   The question referred to the general political attitudes of fathers. At the risk of seeming sexist we supposed these to be dominant in most homes.

67   We also asked about the religious beliefs of mother, which in most cases corresponded to those of fathers.

68   P. Hardouin, op. cit., p. 243.

CHAPTER 5

Ceres on the ground – fractionalism and federal politics

Dans le parti, personne ne fait de cadeaux; on n'obtient quelquechose que sur la base d'un rapport de forces. Encore faut-il le créer.

Ceres federal leader

This chapter presents our case studies which should be read in conjunction with others available (cf. Chapter 4, note 61). Lack of space excludes the presentation of all our findings from the departments sampled and necessitates a choice. The following factors governed the choice of the four studies which follow.

Given the geographical strengths of Ceres, East and West had clearly to be treated in some depth. In the East, Belfort seemed natural as the 'Ceres capital', an area where the fraction took over swiftly and totally. Nearby Meurthe-et-Moselle suggests a different profile, being an area where Ceres had to struggle long and hard for a hegemony which was never easy and has since been lost. In the West our study of Loire-Atlantique needs to be seen alongside our previous study of Ille-et-Vilaine; if in many ways this department is, like Ille-et-Vilaine, typical of the catholic West, it is also significantly different in that its urban centres have shown a continuing old left presence of the type which Ceres set out to conquer. Here again the conquest of hegemony has been a complex and perhaps inconclusive process.

To counterpose these regional strengths we also include a South-Eastern department, Loire, from the Rhône-Alpes region which was generally kind to Ceres. Here again the department is an interesting mixture of catholic and working-class socialist traditions whose compatibility is not obvious and which should *a priori* require some varied tactical approaches. Although Paris may seem an important omission, we would argue that it has been the object of a certain amount of attention already and that more importantly the patterns of fractional antagonism observed there can effectively be subsumed into the findings from our other examples.

In short our hope is that these examples incorporate a certain number of regional variables, as well as political ones in the shape of the clash between 'new' and 'old' lefts and cultural ones (the secularist–catholic polarity). *A priori* these situations should require a number of varied strategies and tactical responses from a would-be successful left fraction. We are aware of the limitations both in number and in depth of these samples – limits which it seems difficult to avoid given the limited resources available for the research. None the less we believe that these studies may well suggest a number of hypotheses about the hidden laws of fractional logic within the PS, on which later research may be able to build.

5.1   BELFORT – THE TEMPTATIONS OF ABSOLUTE POWER?

France's smallest department is in some ways its most unusual. The territoire de Belfort shares with its neighbours in Alsace and Franche-Comté much of the nationalist traditions of Eastern France. In 1870 the troops of Denfert-Rochereau held out there for months against the invading Prussians; their feat is commemorated in a monument in the shape of a lion which the mayor, J.-P. Chevènement takes a particular pride in showing to visitors. Before 1939 the area was represented in parliament by André Tardieu, a patriotic rightwinger and, prophetically, a convinced *dirigiste* and industrial moderniser. In 1945 Leleu's index put the territory firmly on the right, with a large MRP vote; but as manufacturing and tertiary activities developed rapidly through the fifties and sixties, it moved markedly to the left, first towards the PCF and later towards the non-communist left. In 1966 at the peak of Gaullism the left got a deputy elected.

Such is the rich political history of one of the first departments to fall to Ceres. The fraction's vote for the Épinay congress of 1971 was bettered only in Savoie and Ille-et-Vilaine. Ceres' control of the federation was swift, brutal and never faltering. In 1973 Chevènement won the deputy's seat for the city, and Forni for the rural area. A Ceres mayor won Belfort city in 1977 and the *conseil général* fell in 1976 (in 1980 eight PS councillors out of ten were Ceres, as were at least eight of the department's 24 socialist mayors). The only jewel missing from the crown was the senator's seat which went after a protracted battle to Ceres' historic opponent, the Mitterrandist Michel Dreyfus-Schmidt. In the public eye this 'bastion de l'Est', as the nationalist politician Barrès might have put it, seemed the archetype of a Ceres federation.

Belfort socialist party in 1970 was a depressed institution. Its hundred or so members were ageing SFIO faithfuls in the Guesdist mould; many apart from the core in the city were rural primary teachers. The party was in any case overshadowed as a vehicle for the renewal of the left by the following of Dreyfus-Schmidt, a young and dynamic lawyer in the Radical tradition. Son of the former deputy-mayor Pierre, a *progressiste* (fellow-traveller), he was elected as an FGDS deputy in a 1966 by-election, losing out in 1968 to a Gaullist. As mayor of Belfort his father had governed on a left-unity platform which included socialists, communists and MRP, as well as Radicals who in Belfort had always regarded themselves as being further to the left than most of their like; broad-left unity was thus no stranger to Belfort city at least. Although the Dreyfus-Schmidt group did join the PS before Épinay, relations between them and the old SFIO were poor. Among the latter were, however, some dynamic elements who would form the backbone of the new party. One was Michel Plomb, first secretary for much of the seventies. He and his comrades were mostly CFDT shop stewards in the big Belfort factories (Bull computers and Alsthom engineering) or the car plants at nearby Sochaux-Montbeliard.[1] Some were FEN teachers. The events of 1968 had fuelled their radicalism (j'ai dansé dans les usines', as one of them had it) but left them looking for a political vehicle to canalise it. Wary of the PCF (whose strength in the unions and factories in Belfort was much greater than its electoral clout) they saw the need for a renovated socialist party dedicated to left unity and *autogestion*. The old SFIO had failed (Plomb himself had not bothered to renew his card). But just before Épinay the activists discovered the writings – and soon the personalities – of a group whose project was precisely to transform the moribund SFIO. 'Here were people who thought exactly like us'. This link between Paris theorists and provincial activists who were 'Ceres without realising it' would be repeated elsewhere. Now equipped with ideas and a programme the Plomb group were able to secure a 62% vote for Ceres at Épinay.

We should not acribe this entirely to the merits of Ceres arguments, however. For a key role was played by the municipal elections of spring 1971 in Belfort city which the united left list lost by a mere 92 votes. The left's campaign had been poisoned by rivalry about the headship of the list between Dreyfus-Schmidt and Émile Géhant. The latter led the old SFIO and was a lawyer respected for his record as a wartime resister and survivor of the concentration camps. A private opinion poll commissioned by Dreyfus-Schmidt suggested that the left had most chance of winning if he himself were head of the list. He and Géhant thus arranged for this to happen, so that the left would win the town hall.[2] But Dreyfus-Schmidt would also contest the deputy's seat in 1973, which was almost bound to revert to the left; once elected he would concentrate on this and hand over the mayoralty to Géhant. The deal broke down, however, with Géhant getting himself nominated head of the list by the party and duly being beaten. Clearly the rift between the old SFIO and the newer FGDS supporters was wide. Fearing the latter, the old SFIO apparently chose to throw in its lot with the emergent Ceres.

Subsequent events confirm this hypothesis. When the federation had to choose parliamentary candidates in 1973, Dreyfus-Schmidt put his name down. But the federal majority put up against him not Géhant, but Chevènement, summoned from Paris for an opportunity too good to miss (and thereby rescued from a career as a politics lecturer). Dreyfus-Schmidt believes that the Géhant group had tried and failed to bring in the late Georges Dayan, the veteran Mitterrandist whose political itinerary through the waters of Radicalism towards the PS was ironically similar to his own. A Homeric battle for the nomination ensued, both sides trying desperately to make members before voting day (candidates were selected by a straight vote of the members). There were abundant complaints and counter-accusations (Dreyfus-Schmidt had a 30-page dossier printed and circulated within the PS to no avail), but after a second vote (in deference to Dreyfus-Schmidt's protests) it was clear Chevènement had won. He and Forni duly entered parliament and from then on the new resources, prestige and Paris connections of the deputy, allied to his undoubted ability, boosted the federation no end. Members and election wins mounted up (even Géhant became major in 1977) and the ripples of the Pierret split and Metz congress stopped well short of Belfort; only the 20% vote for Mitterrand showed the continuing presence of Dreyfus-Schmidt, and even he had his *conseil général* seat taken from him in 1979. Despite the disappointments of Mitterrand's presidency, Chevène-ment could still win the town hall again in 1983 (albeit with little to spare), and the Bourg congress showed a Ceres score of 82%. The iron grip had not slackened. How are we to explain Ceres' success?

First there was a general move to the left in the department, as by the late sixties the Territory was rediscovering some of its left past while Gaullism became exhausted. With the PCF visibly unable to take advantage, any fraction which dominated the new PS clearly had big prospects. This is a huge incentive, especially for young activists.

But this must be seen in conjunction with another factor, the swiftness of the Ceres take-over, which depended on the alliance of the new activists with the old SFIO. In theory these are two groups which should fight each other to death. But they were thrown together here by outside pressure in the form of Dreyfus-Schmidt and the threat he posed. He represented a different tradition, certainly (Radical-socialist rather than Guesdist), though many of his policy stances were virtually indistinguishable from the latter. He might be seen as a notable, given his family connections. But he also represented a personal and even a professional challenge to Géhant, in the closed world of the Belfort bar where the political class was long recruited. Clearly old and new had an interest in joining against such a rival.

The tactical urgency of the alliance was such that it seems to have overridden what might have been an awkward point, namely the opposition between activist catholics (which many of the new Ceres were) and the secularist SFIO. Possibly the arrival of Chevènement reinforced the latter, but even in 1979 most of the original Ceres seem to have stuck with their colleagues from the rival culture rather than split off towards Rocard or Pierret. Perhaps in some cases the advantages of a share in power can blur deep antagonisms; or perhaps these latter only emerge fully when power is out of reach or likely to become so.

In order to marginalise its rivals Ceres used other weapons besides the tactical skill and commitment of its militants. One was the setting up of workplace branches at Bull and Alsthom; these branches which Sarre helped organise were decisive in getting Chevènement his nomination and keeping control afterwards. Bernard Py, in charge of workplace branches in the federation, confirmed this.[3] The choice of a Parisian figure with a growing reputation and wide connections was also a shrewd move, for he could hope to put the territory on the map inside the party and outside.

Once the initial breakthrough was made (and here the small size of the Territory doubtless helped) we see easily how Ceres became institutionalised. As electoral success accrued, the fraction placed its people in key posts (mayor, *conseiller général*, etc.) across the department, gaining a monopoly of political life there. The French system gives wide opportunities for patronage and job-creation of various sorts to such officials. In addition, Chevènement set up a Belfort Development Agency, aimed at bringing public and private investment into the department.[4] It is hard to estimate the agency's success in terms of job – or wealth – creation, but it has certainly done no harm to party or Ceres standing in the department. Clearly once a group is in this relatively powerful position, incentives to join it are multiplied, both for the career-minded and those who want to see concrete action. Thus Ceres had little problem in building an élite (Plomb estimated about 100, which is very high for such a department), which could not only run Belfort but was able to spread over and help neighbouring areas in a kind of regional multiplier-effect, with gains in one department strengthening the next, and so on.

A final feature of Ceres control is its ruthlessness. At the start the group was clever enough to conciliate the old SFIO, but was always very hard on the opposition. Dreyfus-Schmidt's eviction from the *conseil général* has been mentioned, and even his win in the senatorial election was snatched almost from under Ceres' nose by some very shrewd lobbying at a moment when nationally and even to some extent locally the party was in some uncertainty. The few Rocardian surivivors of the 1979 Metz congress debates recall how hard it was to defend Motion C in public, given the very hostile and envenomed atmosphere created and maintained by Ceres.[5] This very exclusive winner-take-all style of politics contrasts sharply with the compromises or ecumenicism practised elsewhere, but it worked. In 1979 only one branch out of 22 failed to show a majority for Ceres; such opposition as there was voted

Mitterrand with Dreyfus-Schmidt.[6] Possibly the relatively high absten-
tion rate concealed a few frightened Rocardians; but overall, Ceres
hegemony was indisputable.

What is the record of Belfort Ceres then? By a swift tactical ploy it
took over a promising federation, which it ruled single-mindedly and
exclusively, making wide electoral gains. It has recruited a high
membership, which shares largely its view of socialism. In terms of
political practice outside the party, it is hard to see much that is
specifically Ceres about town or departmental management; most
measures taken seem broadly similar to those used in many towns
which the left won in 1977. Such practices include raising taxes to pay
for better housing and infrastructure, schemes to attract industry and
jobs, greater readiness for dialogue with interest groups (though not
necessarily to comply with their demands) and of course the perpetual
arm-twisting that goes on between local *élus* and central bureaucracy
'pour obtenir quelque chose de Paris'. If procedures are perhaps more
open, it is far from being generalised *autogestion*. In Belfort city the main
difference might be the cultural policy of the town hall, which is less
willing to sponsor light entertainment at the expense of more thought-
provoking material. The battle for hegemony goes on here as
elsewhere, as Chevènement reminds us frequently. It would be hard to
agree with the claim of the subprefect who claimed that Ceres wanted
to turn the area into a laboratory; or if they did, it is as much a PS one as
a Ceres one. We may conclude that Belfort Ceres shows that a tough
group of activists can take over party machinery, keep it and use it to
win office. But there are limits to what it can do with that office.

5.2   MEURTHE-ET-MOSELLE – SOCIALISING THE MISSION
LANDS?

Socialists have long regarded the East as a 'terre de mission' and their
pessimism seems justified in the case of Lorraine. Bonnet's classic
study brings out the weakness of reformist socialism in the area,
especially when compared to its successes across the nearby frontiers.[7]
Before 1914 SFIO never captured what was then an important
working-clas vote in this major iron and steel area. Later, via hard graft
through the CGT, the PCF made the breakthrough, being clearly

hegemonic on the left by 1945. Against it were the dominant forces of
the right, mainly notables at first and then Gaullism, which as Bonnet
argues, owed much of its success to its strong nationalist profile.
Despite the strong catholic culture of the region and the readiness of
the clergy to give a political lead, there never emerged a strong
christian democrat current. Writing in 1970 Bonnet could even
speculate on the disappearance of reformist socialism, its support
crumbling partly to the PCF and partly to some new poujadism. If the
non-communist left had any future, the best bet seemed to be the PSU.

Meurthe-et-Moselle is typical of this grim picture. It was 1936 when it
first elected a socialist deputy and 1937 for a *conseiller général*; at this time
the SFIO federation numbered, ephemerally in the surge of enthusiasm for the Popular Front, some 5,000 members.[8] The Liberation saw
a similar surge with the party winning numerous town halls, entering
the *conseil général* and with two deputies coming ahead of the PCF in the
election of October 1945. It seems to have polled well in industrial
zones and indeed to have had a large working-class membership.[9]
Descent from there on was quick and relentless, as a militant PCF
squeezed the party out of its best zones. No deputy was elected
between 1951 and 1978 and no *conseiller général* till 1973. Members
dwindled to 241 by 1967, in only ten branches compared with thirty
odd in 1945. The crowning blow was Defferre's 2.9% in the 1969
presidential election, below the score of the PSU's Rocard, now
making an impact in the department. Épinay thus found a virtually
moribund party which had fallen a long way from a position not of
domination but of relative influence at least. Épinay seems to have
produced a revival, with the 1973 election seeing the party catch up
with the FGDS score of 1967 and in the same year elect 3 members to
the *conseil général*. Mitterrand topped 50% in the 1974 election and the
party's strength increased through the decade, despite a hiccup after
the 1978 election. Three out of the seven deputies' seats were won in
1981, confirming the renaissance. This story was of course repeated
across much of France, but this federation was a Ceres one *par excellence*;
an analysis of the decade reveals much about the relationship of Ceres
to the rest and also about the fraction itself.

If we begin with the former, it is fair to say that by the mid-seventies
fractional strife had become symbolised by the clash between Gérard
Cureau and Daniel Groscolas, the Ceres leader.[10] Cureau was first

secretary and leader of the rump of SFIO which survived in Nancy and one or two other towns. Politically exhausted, their main activity was by now minority membership of the Nancy town council, run by the centrist senator Martin. Here they strove to increase social spending and prevent the ravages of property speculators as best they could. This type of PS/centrist arrangement remained frequent of course in many towns after 1971, despite the national pact with the PCF, and it roused the ire of many besides Ceres. It would become the major bone of contention in the department and matters were worsened by the presence of the centre–left deputy J.-J. Servan-Schreiber, a symbol of the sort of compromise-politics against which the PS was supposed to have set its face.

There had long existed in Nancy elements like Groscolas who denounced the deal with the notables, which they saw as typical of 'social-democracy'. It is they who, together with the big influx of new members after Épinay, led the drive to win the federation from Cureau and force his group off the town council. It was a prolonged and dirty battle. The Cureau group were said to have refused membership to newcomers so as to keep their majority, while at one moment in 1972 Groscolas actually set up a rival federation, claiming it to be the legitimate one. Cureau's delaying tactics, plus discreet conciliation from Paris, meant that his group served out its time in the town hall but also that as from 1973 the federation passed under the control of Ceres, for whom Groscolas was now beginning to be known nationally. It seemed like a copybook demonstration of Ceres' *raison d'être*: a clique of social-democratic bosses, colluding with bourgeois politicians in the town hall, running down the party (some branches only met once a year) and mainly interested in their own careers had been given a deserved come-uppance thanks to a newly militant party stiffened by the principled Ceres. And yet during all this the party progressed electorally, showing that what was good for Ceres was also good for the voters at large.

This is grossly simplified, for in fact the conflict was on several levels and Ceres itself was far from homogeneous.

Certainly the Cureau group drew opposition. Their anti-communism stood out in this period of the CPG and PS electoral progress. Their belief that modest changes could be won in partner-ship with the progressive centre seemed a return to Fourth Republic

Molletism. But the political conflict was also generational, with Cureau's supporters being older and owing their formative experiences to the Cold War, whereas their challengers had learned more from 1968. Chagnollaud states that by 1975 some two-thirds of the party was new to politics.[11] This implies another differentiation, this time sociological. The membership had shifted from the worker-dominated one of 1945 to one closer to that of the PS nationally; in short it was dominated by the salaried intellectual middle class. (In 1975 22% alone were teachers.)

Nor is it simply the case that social and generational differences explained the political differences and that the matter ends there. It was not the case of two lines clashing with the right one winning. Other pressures were at work.

Thus although the conflict was often portrayed in very acrimonious terms, it seems on inspection that it was kept within certain bounds. Partly this is due to the national leadership, whose reaction to the 'two federations' crisis of 1972 is classic. When attempts to resolve the dispute via the *commission des conflits* had failed, the CD sent a three-man team to Nancy to mediate. As ever it was supposed to reflect the interests of the aggrieved parties and so contained a Poperenite, Chevènement and the amiable, rotund and expert conciliator *par excellence*, Roger Fajardie – a sort of one-man ACAS.[12] The team soon hammered out a deal, whereby Groscolas though technically in the wrong was not expelled and Cureau kept control of the federation till the next congress. He was then duly supported by the local Ceres in his unsuccessful parliamentary candidacy in 1973. Thus far it would seem that Paris alone had imposed order.

But this is only half true. After 1973 Cureau was offered a place on the secretariat, subject admittedly to his leaving the town council (a ploy which he deftly sidestepped). Thereafter he was always the party's front-runner for the mayoral lists in Nancy, actually being asked by Ceres to lead the list in 1977. This made sense in that Nancy is tertiary, well-off and right-wing, hence a moderate socialist might win a few more votes than a Ceres. But it is also possible that there was to some extent an *ad hoc* division of labour, with the old SFIO being left the electorally difficult parts of the department while the newcomers tried their hand at winning back some of the more promising areas in the suburbs and other industrial zones. The distribution of fractional strengths across the federation confirms this. The point is that limits to fractional strife were set less by Paris than by local leaders aware of the real advantages of cohabitation that might lie beneath visible political and rhetorical oppositions.

The challengers' nature was also ambiguous. In 1971 there were hardly any Ceres in Meurthe-et-Moselle, the national leaders were unknown and people voted simply on the texts of the Épinay motions.[13] Thus the Poperen text scored 31%, and Groscolas had to be 'loaned' a few votes so as to secure admission to the CEF. Yet in 1973 Ceres scored 43%, and Poperen only 7%. Clearly the challengers were not convinced Poperenites (or else they would have preserved some sort of federal machine), but rather they were simply opposed to a type of 'social-democracy' incarnated by Cureau: as a later first secretary put it, the Cureau group meant to him 'the Fourth Republic, bossism (*notabilisme*) and sloppy electoralism'.[14] Nor were the challengers newly convinced Ceres, for in many cases their opposition dated back to the sixties. This was true of Groscolas but also of the other Ceres leader in embryo, Job Durupt. He was mayor of Tomblaine, a suburban commune with a long tradition of left unity and a reputation for being on the far left of SFIO (the branch had sent a telegram of condemnation to Mollet over the Suez expedition, for instance). This type of activist clearly welcomed Épinay and *any* left group with open arms.

But their opposition needed to be given ideological and organisational coherence, and here Ceres came in. After Épinay, in a pattern typical of the period, contacts between the Paris Ceres and the Meurthe-et-Moselle leftwingers were multiplied, with the locals campaigning and recruiting while Paris provided speakers, ideology and organisational help. Crucial here was the network of contacts between the élites of the numerous other Eastern federations where Ceres was rising or taking control, particularly the political and organisational training seminars that seem to have figured prominently. This effort was a key factor in Ceres' progress throughout the East. Yet it could still be asked how coherent the new Ceres was and how far it was held together only by its success in the party and outside it and the presence of a reassuring anti-model in the shape of Cureau.

External pressures would in the late seventies expose the relative fragility of the local Ceres, though the extent of the pre-Metz schisms took most people by surprise according to one experienced observer.[15] The federation divided thus: Mitterrand 25%, Mauroy 14%, Rocard 25%, Ceres 21%, Pierret 14%. Yet in 1977 Ceres had 57%. Even deducting the dissident Pierretists, it is clear that much Ceres support had gone to Rocard, and there are several factors involved.

To take the Pierret split first, it was one of the biggest in France and was led by Groscolas. Many of Pierret's policy differences with the *historiques* clearly found an echo in the Nancy Ceres, especially doubts about *suivisme* of the PCF (mainly on international issues), the ideological overkill used against Rocard and the oligarchical nature of Ceres (perhaps discovered late in the day?). In the case of Groscolas can be added defence policy, for he was a species that was common in SFIO but rare or at any rate mute nowadays, that is a convinced unilateralist. These discontents had of course long simmered, but needed a catalyst to make them explicit. This may well have been the rivalry between Durupt and Groscolas for the mayor's seat in Tomblaine and also for the more winnable of the two deputies' seats in Nancy, both of which Durupt eventually won. It is not the intention to suggest that this was a problem of careerism, for there were political differences between the two men (on defence and also on town management for instance). Rather both were powerful and energetic figures, with followings that were to some extent personal – a practice which Chagnollaud sees as very typical of this department.[16] This also means that if a leader did split he could expect to bring many of his supporters with him.

One cause which does not seem to have been significant is again the secular question. The problem certainly existed in this area and we were told of branch meetings where tempers were lost and accusations of 'being in league with the freemasons' were exchanged against charges of 'taking orders from the bishops'. But it seems less significant than the generational gap between the old SFIO and the newcomers as a whole. The latter included convinced secularists like Durupt and Groscolas (a full-time official with the Fédération des Oeuvres laïques) and also catholic activists, often with a union background in the CFDT beginning to emerge as a serious force alongside the CGT down the industrial Moselle valley. Many more of these came with the 1974 *assises* but they went straight to the non-Ceres majority. Of those who were already in Ceres by no means all left in 1979. The real cause of the split was a complex mix of political differences, mediated through personal antagonisms and based on groups of followers.

The 1979 indicative votes showed clear zones of influence in fact. Ceres did best in the ring of Nancy suburbs, especially Tomblaine. Control of the Northern branches round Longwy and in the Moselle valley had been slipping since 1975, and these could now be seen to be Rocardian (this was the weight of CFDT activists).[17] Chagnollaud points out that in this part of the department the struggle is very much against the PCF, not the right, and hence Ceres' alleged *suivisme* may have lost support. Motion B (Mauroy) was heavily concentrated in Nancy and Lunéville (an old SFIO town) – clearly the bases of the Cureau group. The Fs were strong both in Nancy and its suburbs, exactly the area where Groscolas was active in the party and as a councillor; many of these branches were split up the middle, showing how influential he had been within Ceres.

By 1980 the federation appeared split politically and geographically. The victories from the 1981 landslide must have helped heal wounds, but as the Mitterrand presidency ran into difficulties, Ceres could still muster 33% for the Bourg congress, and this with Groscolas now supporting the Mitterrandist majority. Clearly the fraction in Meurthe-et-Moselle is particularly tenacious.

The experience of Meurthe-et-Moselle Ceres suggests that it responded intitially to demand for a new socialist politics, more aggressive and less prone to compromise. On this basis it attacked the 'social-democrats'. But it soon learned to use this older group, apprehending that it represented a real social base inside and outside the party. At the same time this Ceres was not very homogeneous, but the differences could be suppressed so long as it was the opposition; once in control there was nothing to stop differences emerging.

One might reflect similarly that it was the prospect of office through the 1981 campaign that dragged the fraction away from internal feuding. In 1983 Meurthe-et-Moselle Ceres showed a big recovery from 1979, scoring well above national average with 33%. Without detailed knowledge of the indicative vote it is hard to be definite about the provenance of this Ceres vote, but the suspicion must be that it represents above all a protest vote in a declining industrial area which Mitterrandist policies of rationalisation have hit more than most. If that were true it would confirm what seems to have held for earlier years,

namely that the local Ceres certainly helped to build up the party but it
did so more on negative bases than positive ones.

5.3   LOIRE – UN CERES PAS COMME LES AUTRES?

Activists of all shades of opinion like to tell you that politics in Loire
is different from anywhere else. Indeed history confirms the para-
doxical patterns of its political life. The Gier valley running from Lyon
through to Saint-Étienne has housed heavy industry for over a century,
in grim towns lodged at the base of sparse hills, reminiscent of the
manufacturing towns of East Lancashire. But apart from the old SFIO
town of Roanne, the rest of the department consists of agricultural
upland and the rich Forez plain. Even within the towns the left has
never dominated. The industrial town of Saint-Chamond was represented for half a century by Antoine Pinay, a byword for financial and
conservative orthodoxy. For most of the postwar period Leleu's index
would class Loire as firmly on the right, a proclivity not unconnected
with its high rate of religious observance. Well entrenched notables
have kept power, shifting their labels in accordance with the prevailing
wind from Paris (MRP in 1945, Gaullist in 1958). Loire had a certain
Radical tradition based, it is said, on small employers seeking to defend
regional interests against Paris and outside competition;[18] the Dura-
fours are typical of this. Within the working class the PCF had been
strong but was slipping by the sixties. So too was reformist socialism,
however, for if socialists and Radicals in 1945 had taken 17% of the
vote, the 1968 FGDS was down to 11%.

The PS at Épinay had some 150 members, mainly ageing SFIO.
Secularist and Republican they were not opposed to united action with
the PCF, but their activity was now purely electoral. Renewal and
challenge came not from Ceres, non-existent at Épinay, but from
Poperenism. A distinct group of Poperenites, mainly in the CGT and
mainly catholic (odd elsewhere, but not in this area) joined the party
and challenged the old men.[19] But as new members came in, such as
the future deputies Auroux and Badet, Ceres did begin to recruit,
pushing its vote up to 25% by 1973 and forging ahead of the
Poperenites as the spearhead of renovation. Relations between all
fractions seemed healthily competitive until the *assises* of 1974, when

there occurred an event which marked the federation durably. This was the arrival of a mass of members largely from a PSU and CFDT background who unlike Rocard joined not the majority (which they saw as typical of the worst of social-democracy) but Courant II – Ceres. This took place after much local debate and contrary to the national agreement (only Loire-Atlantique did the same). The newcomers made a bargain with the existing majority shortly before Pau, allowing the old SFIO and the Mitterrandists to keep the posts of treasurer and first secretary despite their numerical superiority – a naïve error, as they were to admit. Soon grave friction set in.[20] In summer 1975 Jean Vincent, first secretary, took advantage of an ultra-left press statement on Portugal at variance with the official line made by a Ceres leader. Refusing to work with the newcomers he asked the national CD to discipline the federation – a move blocked by Ceres supporters on the CD. Mediation having failed and the federation being now paralysed, its executive organs were dissolved and it was run by a three-man committee, chaired by a delegate appointed from Paris.[21] This was the case till the next federal congress prior to the Nantes one of 1977, and during this time Loire became a byword in party and media for sectarian squabbling. At Nantes Ceres duly took over. Meanwhile the party made steady electoral gains, with a left list (PCF-led) winning Saint-Étienne town hall in 1977, and Auroux and Badet achieving a similar feat at Roanne and Saint-Chamond. The following year Auroux became a deputy and Badet failed to do so by a whisker. But the 'crisis', as activists refer to it, had left its mark, revealing fissures between Ceres and the rest but also fissures within both camps. The Metz congress showed a divided party with votes thus: Mitterrand 34%, Mauroy 5%, Rocard 14%, Ceres 32%, Pierret 14%. In 1977, Ceres had had 56%. Now divided, it was forced to relinquish control of the federation to the Mitterrandists. But in 1981 the pink wave washed over Loire, with Mitterrand scoring 51% and deputies' seats being snatched from the notables by Badet, Bruno Vennin (the leader of the Fs) and even in Saint-Étienne by a communist.

The Bourg congress of 1983, following the loss of Saint-Étienne town hall, showed Ceres could still muster 26% of the vote, but it now seemed clearly second to the block of its adversaries. *A priori* it looked as if the fraction had provoked a sectarian battle in which it had ended up as a loser.

Closer examination suggests a more complex picture. First, it makes sense to speak not of one Ceres but of two. The pre-1974 group consisted mainly of new members, who seem not to have had a strong ideological profile, other than opposition to the old SFIO; they were in Ceres because it was young and dynamic, while at the same time acceptable electorally. Indeed in so far as there was a characteristic profile it was characterised – according to Ceres and non-Ceres alike – by an above-average degree of secularism and indeed masonic connections. Thus future federal leaders like Badet and Auroux would begin in Ceres but later slip away as they became figures with a power base of their own. In fact this first Ceres seems to have had little difficulty in accommodation with the old members, but the post-1974 variety was very different, and one of its effects was to scatter the original Ceres members to all points of the party spectrum by 1979.

The new Ceres was formed above all of CFDT activists, often in the PSU, which was then arguably better implanted in the Loire working class than the PS. Most of them belonged to the *gauche syndicale*, particularly strong in Rhône-Alpes and which sought a more offensive political role for the unions (cf. Section 4.1).[22]

As May 1968 receded, CFDT activists sought a political vehicle to express the demands of the social movements they saw emerging from a working class now undergoing extensive change. Whether nearer to orthodox marxism (as with men like Michel Coffineau) or to the less class-based analysis associated with Touraine or Rocardian theorists (such was the case for Maire and the CFDT leadership), they all felt the PSU to be inadequate. Given their mistrust for democratic centralism, the new PS had to be looked at seriously, despite its past. The question was whether to follow Rocard, Maire and the modernisers into the Mitterrand camp or join Ceres. In most of France the former option prevailed, but the weight of the *gauche syndicale* in Loire, evidenced by the presence of its national leaders like Coffineau, Héritier or André Garnier, meant that Ceres was preferred.

There were pressing reasons. The Paris Ceres was very interested and offered a place on the party's BE from its quota (which eventually went to Garnier). Also on the level of theory the two groups seemed close; both were committed to left unity, workers' control and the importance of mass movements, an economic policy based on nationalisations and most of all a dynamic conception of the party. Here the

newcomers admired Ceres' support for workplace branches and its
resolve to create a campaigning party in factory and neighbourhood. A
familiar reference of the period was the Chilean PS of the late Salvador
Allende, admired as a real socialist party despite its grim end. All these
factors made it logical to join Ceres, and indeed many newcomers
thought less of adding their weight to Ceres than of using it as
springboard for their ideas inside the party, trying to do to the fraction
what it was trying to do to the wider party.

Conflict between such newcomers and the older men was inevitable, but there was also a less foreseeable conflict within Ceres' own
ranks. Let us first consider the clash with these 'ex-SFIO men with a
great destructive capacity', as one newcomer put it.[23]

The older generation pulled no punches in its determination to
outface 'les PSU', as they still call them. The antagonism has less to do
with policy than we might expect. The old SFIO were unitary (Vincent
is even in the CGT) and practised joint lists, not centrist alliances. Fear
of a challenge to their prospects, municipal and legislative, is certainly a
factor, and the generation gap is also crucial. Generally the old SFIO
men were over 60, the newcomers nearer 30, with all the different
formative experiences that this implies. But more important is the
newcomers' style. They arrived as a group with their own habits,
loyalties and even language. Though they were quite open about this, it
was none the less perceived as a kind of invasion. Their political
practice was very different. Using a more aggressive, argumentative and
workerist discourse, more interested in strikes and community politics
than municipal elections, they clashed sharply with a party where
arguments were few, certainties shared and activism infrequent.[24]
Above all, though, the dispute had cultural foundations in the shape of
the catholic–secularist polarity, which in Loire surfaced rapidly and
explosively.

For all CFDT's attempts at 'deconfessionalisation', for all its activists'
self-descriptions as 'ex-catholics', it seems that convinced secularists
never believe them. As Vincent said, they do not have 'the same spirit,
method or view of things'; in his eyes, their politics springs fundamentally from religious urges (as opposed to rational or humanistic
motives for true socialists).[25] The fact that both Ceres leaders Garnier
('le pape du Ceres') and Vennin had been in Vie Nouvelle, an élite
organisation for socially committed catholics, was widely cited.[26] The

Ceres reacted similarly denouncing the 'combisme' of their adversaries.[27] Ex-Ceres when interviewed would readily speak of the masonic connections of their opponents and cite Mitterrand's and Chevènement's alleged remarks that 'les cathos' were trying to take over the party.

These reactions are cited not for their amusement value but because they show how hard it is to break a cultural mould two centuries old. Although economic modernisation is said to have broken down the historic antagonism between catholicism and Republicanism and socialism, it is clear that the antagonism lies skin deep and will easily emerge on the slightest pretext especially in the absence of powerful counter-incentives, such as large amounts of power to share (cf. Belfort). This is not surprising when we recall that several generations have now been socialised into these opposing sets of values and that this is an ideological process which goes on to some extent independently of socio-economic modernisation. The situation in Loire is simply a very explicit version of antagonisms which were more discreet or better mastered in many other federations. Certainly this antagonism, in conjunction with the other factors mentioned, prevented the link-up between Ceres and the old party. Many of the latter left and joined the left Radicals (MRG).

But within Ceres there were also contradictions, both within the federation and more significantly between this latter and the national leaders.

First some Ceres had a different strategy from the start: supporters of Rocard and Maire in the PSU, theirs was a modernising, non-marxist variant of autogestion. But they saw this as quite compatible with membership of Ceres – a vision perhaps not entirely implausible in 1974, whatever subsequent events proved. Their main spokesman was Bruno Vennin, an associate of Martinet who aimed precisely to bring together Rocardians and Ceres in a sort of broad left. With the emergence of the basic incompatibility between the two styles of politics, fuelled by the Rocard–Mitterrand rivalry, this group was eventually forced to make the choice which it should have made in 1975. Hence many followed Vennin into support for Motion F, as a prelude to joining up openly with Rocardism. They were influenced obviously by general political and ideological criteria here, but also by experiences with the national Ceres leadership. Here their reactions were like those of the mainstream *gauche syndicale*, with whom they had obvious political differences; but in many cases the result was the same – departure from Ceres, if not from the party itself.

The experiences of Rhône-Alpes CFDT under Ceres were depressing. Héritier found a gulf between Ceres discourse and practice.[28] The latter was like that of other fractions, with a centralised leadership that discouraged debate and seemed mainly interested in power within the party. Workerist though Ceres discourse was, workers had no more influence in this fraction than any other; the sociology of its élites was no different. As one rueful survivor put it, no one asked you what the party should be doing, but rather 'whose side are you on . . . which leader are you backing?'[29] By 1976 these conflicts were eroding the faith of many of the newcomers. A few such as Garnier and Coffineau, more orthodox marxists to begin with, found a niche in the national Ceres structures, but many were voting with their feet and leaving the party. Political and cultural differences which it had seemed possible to overlook in a period of party upswing now came to the fore as the style of Ceres' operation emerged. The CFDT men had never liked Ceres' nationalism or its support for a French deterrent; thus events like Chevènement's appeal to Gaullists in 1976 or the party's moves away from unilateralism in 1977–8 did nothing to hold their affection. Worsening relations with the PCF and the electoral fiasco of 1978 were the last straw. Most *assises* entrants were ready either to join Rocard or, more likely, leave the party. They were heading back towards that abiding mistrust of political parties that has characterised CFDT, and their assertion of the need to replace existing parties by 'a mass working-class party' sounded suspiciously syndicalist.

Some Ceres in Loire believe that the federal 'crisis' was decisive in defining Ceres' identity.[30] It seems that the encounter with the national Ceres leadership needs also to be taken into account. At the end of the process the fraction remained with a slimmed-down membership (but still a viable one) and a leadership (Garnier especially) which had successfully integrated with the national Ceres. Loire Ceres had a certain power base in Saint-Étienne town hall, thanks to the PCF alliance. On the right it had largely forced the old SFIO out of the party, leaving the field to the remaining Mitterrandists and their Poperenite allies, who had largely been spectators in all this. Ceres had also purged its ranks of Rocardian modernisers and also of a different kind of left, the syndicalists of the CFDT. By 1983 when fractional life re-emerged at the Bourg congress, the federation looked almost normal, with a majority of Mitterrandists, Poperenites, Rocardians and Mauroy supporters[31] confronting a by-now orthodox Ceres which could still claim a quarter of the votes.

The essential lessons of the Loire Ceres are not so much tactical, for socialist politics seems to have been conducted on both sides with a highly sectarian logic, regardless of cost to self, adversary or party. Rather they have to do with the identity of Ceres. The first Ceres seems to have had few problems with the older generation. Doubtless it was more active and theoretical, but it was aware of the importance of elections and seems to have known that there were limits not to be transgressed. This is doubtless because culturally its members were of classic Republican secularist tradition. The new Ceres in both its forms, modernising and syndicalist, transgressed those limits, despite apparent ideological and political similarities, and did so because fundamentally the culture which sustained its politics was different from that of the Guesdist one which predominated. This much is unsurprising. What is really striking is, however, the incompatibility which emerged between this culture and political style, and that of the mainstream Ceres. Any Ceres in Loire who wished to remain in the fraction did so on the latter's terms – an adjustment which must have been particularly painful in some cases, at the summit as well as at the base. On these terms Ceres did indeed establish a respectable foothold in Loire. But clearly much potential support went begging, and this must clearly be true of other departments also. This support was lost because of fundamental cultural incompatibilities. The lesson of Loire Ceres is thus that there are deep and hidden limits to what socialist voluntarism can achieve: 'Chassez le culturel: il revient au galop'.

5.4 LOIRE-ATLANTIQUE – THE LONG MARCH OF CERES

In 1971 Loire-Atlantique looked promising for a left fraction. Like most of the West, its traditions were catholic, finding expression less through the MRP (which never got more than an eighth of the poll) than through the classical right or Gaullism. But there was also in the towns a strong working-class tradition, and around Nantes a trade-unionism renowned for its combativity and syndicalist leanings. There was also reformist socialism, particularly of the municipal variety practised in the shipbuilding town of Saint-Nazaire, held by SFIO for half a century. The deputy for Saint-Nazaire was usually a socialist and in a good year the party might hope for another seat in Nantes. By 1971 the Nantes SFIO survived mainly thanks to its place in a centrist municipal alliance led by mayor André Morice, symbol of the Radical tradition which the city had long sustained. The ideological cement of this alliance was anti-clericalism and the political cement the desire to conserve positions. Disaffection with this rather limp variety of socialism was canalised less by the PCF, which never seemed able to rise above 10% of the vote, than by a vigorous PSU, the eleventh biggest federation in France according to Cayrol.[32] Thus if ever the PS were to revive there seemed a certain amount of support to be won.

Initially the left wing was incarnated not by Ceres but by Poperenism, the few early Ceres being left-wing catholics radicalised by 1968 and having links with Objectif 72, the small catholic group which fused with Ceres at Épinay. The federal majority was careful to keep them at arm's length until the 1974 *assises* when, in a gambit similar to Loire, a new wave of militants joined not the majority but Ceres. These numbered some 300 PSU members, plus a core of CFDT activists from Nantes and Saint-Nazaire. As an added bonus they brought the town hall of the working-class suburb of Boguenais and its mayor since 1971, François Autain.[33] The latter's power base was the CFDT branch at the SNIAS aircraft factory in his commune who joined *en masse*. Many of these would of course in time turn out to have Rocardian sympathies, but that was in the future as the federation now embarked on two years of fractional battles.

The federal apparatus which the newcomers took on was above all located in Nantes. Ceres thus attacked its weak point, the centrist alliance which was against party policy. In 1975 the CD responded to pressure and ordered the PS councillors to form an opposition group on the council. All refused save Alain Chenard (who would become mayor in 1977) and thus in effect expelled themselves from the party. But this was no struggle of virtue against vice or principles against careerism, as an analysis of the contending forces shows.

To take the dissidents first, if we can describe the ex-SFIO councillors as such, there seem to have been two attitudes. In the case of the older ones, Routier-Preuvost and the deputy Chauvel, there was a straight refusal to admit any wrong; the more subtle elements, especially J.-C. Routier-Leroy, the son of the chief dissident, played for time, condemning the municipal alliance in principle but doing nothing until the last minute and then playing the Chenard card, attempting to suggest that the federation was being renewed. In this way the ex-SFIO members kept control in Nantes. But compared with Nancy the federal apparatus seems inept. It should have been easy to strike a compromise, such as the setting up of an opposition group, which would largely have defused the critiques of the rising Ceres. This was all the more true as Ceres itself contained quite diverse elements which a cleverer adversary could have exploited. The alternative policy of a vigorous offensive against Ceres (as in Loire), with threats to dissolve the federation was never canvassed either, the federal apparatus never going further than the dissolution of two or three (Rocardian) branches. In short the federal apparatus lacked skill and resolution; these inadequacies need to be explained by more than the fact that it was technically in the wrong over the municipal question.

Leaving aside explanations in terms of the personal inadequacies of federal leaders, one is struck by the fact that these latter always referred to their challengers as 'les cathos'.[34] In the clerical West where the SFIO had long been an embittered minority, such a reaction was probably overdetermined. Certainly many newcomers were of catholic background and often practising, but men like Autain were of classically secularist background,[35] and many Ceres like Jean Natiez were heavily involved in secularist organisations. Perhaps the political weakness of the apparatus led it to reduce a political challenge to ideological terms, but this flabby response certainly made the challengers' task easier.

The latter had, of course, their allies, notably the Poperenites. This fraction has always retained a certain strength in Nantes, thanks to a hard core of union activists; some believe that it has strong links with so-called Lambertist branch of Trotskyism (the Parti communiste internationaliste) which is particularly vigorous in the armaments industry around Nantes and whose leader, Hebert, is prominent in the FO. Be this as it may, the fraction has a recognisable presence in the area and a municipal base in Saint-Herblain, whose mayor is J.-M. Ayrault. Until 1973 Poperenism stood for renewal against the SFIO much more than Ceres. But with the arrival of the new type of Ceres in 1974, the position changed. Fundamentally hostile to *assises*-type politics, Popernism would find itself among the worst enemies of the new Ceres, even if this meant moving closer to its previous enemies. At the peak of Rocard–Mitterrand rivalry in 1980, it would force the Rocardians to resign from the secretariat, thus wrecking a carefully built synthesis.

Within Ceres there was little friction between Rocard supporters and pure Ceres as yet, despite the emergent conflict at national level. This worried the party leadership, anxious to normalise fractional alignments in the federation in view of the coming Nantes congress and various elections. This was achieved by the visit of another Fajardie committee in 1976 ending in the so-called Borel agreement (it took place in one of the motels belonging to that group).[36] As a result some two-thirds of the *assises* intake left Ceres and went into the majority. They thus admitted to being Rocardians and would duly vote as such at Metz. At the same time Fajardie sorted out the problem of parliamentary candidacies among the fractions, the losers being the Poperenites with the winnable seats being allotted (unofficially of course) to the Rocardian Évin at Saint-Nazaire and to Autain, who remained with Ceres. This Paris-induced split did not envenom relations or reduce collaboration, however. In 1977 Rocardians and Ceres combined at Saint-Nazaire to deselect the old deputy Carpentier in favour of Évin and to remove Routier-Leroy in Nantes-Sud in favour of Autain. When after Metz Ceres took over federal leadership in its own right, the first act of Natiez was to offer Rocardians places on the secretariat[37] – a gesture which speaks volumes in the poisoned atmosphere of the period.

This unitary feeling could be explained by the need to preserve allies in the face of an aggressive party right; but we have seen that this latter was non-existent. We need thus to seek deeper explanations, and in so doing we come across a distinct concept of conquering hegemony. Loire-Atlantique Ceres was aware that such a conquest would be long and hard, very much a 'war of position'; Nantes was not Belfort or Paris. As a result a long-term strategy was embarked upon. It began with a sustained effort to set up new, rural branches for the Nantes city branches were deemed to be irretrievably in the hands of the ex-SFIO members. Indicative votes for the Metz congress showed Ceres strengths to be, apart from Boguenais, especially in the agricultural South of the department, along the Loire valley with its villages and in the Brière (the Western agricultural area). Now when we see that the weight of the big six branches in the federation (Nantes and suburbs, plus Saint-Nazaire) has declined steadily,[38] and when we see the narrowness of the Ceres lead in 1979 (32.2%, compared with 30% for Rocard and 26% for Mitterrand), it is clear how intelligent was this Mao-like tactic of 'encircling the towns'.

The long-march strategy was also associated with great tactical subtlety however. For as well as the Rocardian alliance, Ceres could also use other ploys. At Saint-Nazaire it allied with the Rocardians to oust the old SFIO deputy, but it then concluded a tacit alliance with that very SFIO against the Rocardians in an attempt to capture the town hall. With only two Ceres on the town council, which was dominated by the old SFIO mayor Caux, and only one-third of the branch members, Ceres was none the less able to get its man Batteux designated as heir to Caux. The price to pay for this was acquiescence in a classic style of town-management, especially refusing to liaise with the voluntary associations beloved of Rocardians. But the tactic paid off when Batteux became mayor in 1983. Certainly Ceres did not repeat its error of 1975 when its intransigent insistence on getting the post of assistant mayor on the Nantes list meant that it ended up with no seats at all on Chenard's council.

Both the long-haul strategy and the ecumenical style of federal management stem from Ceres analysis of the political culture of Loire-Atlantique. Logically, as Natiez remarked, it should with its catholic, syndicalist and *basiste* traditions and its mistrust of Paris, be the most Rocardian federation in France.[39] Certainly the local Ceres is probably more catholic, more *basiste* and more attached to *autogestion* than elsewhere. To avoid their absorption into Rocardism, the best tactic was to avoid polarisation between the two fractions. This involved playing down ideology as much as possible and working together on the ground in campaigns with concrete aims, such as the municipal and legislative ventures described. Opening up the secretariat fits into the same logic, as it invites militants to sublimate ideological differ-ences to hard graft and campaigning on real issues. One may call this pragmatic or cynical but it certainly produced positive results – directly in that Ceres ended up with two deputies in 1981 and not one, and indirectly in the sense that there was virtually no support for Motion F in 1979, surely the ultimate vindication of Ceres' ecumenical style. A respectable 32% in 1983 showed that Ceres had put down firm roots.

The Loire-Atlantique Ceres suggests some interesting hypotheses as to the success of left fractions. Adversaries and allies were crucial here. The poor quality of the old federal élite gave Ceres a head start which it should arguably never have had. Ceres was also aided initially by the Poperenite presence, but as time went on the latter moved ever closer to the old élite (in conformity with the national attitude of the fraction); this suggests that the Poperenite commitment to the left is of a more limited variety and that it could only ever go part of the way with Ceres. Crucial also was Ceres' strategy, both the patient build-up or 'long march' and also the tactical flexibility as shown in the practice of contradictory alliances. The object of these was to secure power; but once this was achieved, Ceres chose to adopt an ecumenical style of management, trying to sublimate ideological differences by dint of vigorous campaigning. This meant that the fraction's own ideological profile was deliberately blurred; but in a department with the political culture of Loire-Atlantique that was deemed to be the price to pay if *any* progress were to be made. To have persisted with a 'pur et dur' approach would have meant ending up in a sectarian impasse.

The main reason why this strategy was able to be implemented lies in the quality of the local Ceres leadership, which seems to have been particularly aware of its possibilities and limitations. It was thus able to avoid two problems. First was excessive subordination to Paris (all interviewees stressed that the Loire-Atlantique Ceres leaders' language and style was very different in Paris from what it was in Nantes). Second was the danger of internal rivalry, which as we saw was decisive in Meurthe-et-Moselle. Here it seems to have been ruled out thanks to a systematic division of labour, with Natiez devoting himself exclusively to party affairs and Autain assuming responsibility for electoral matters (mayor, deputy, and eventually senator). This factor of leadership was probably decisive, for if it was true that at the beginning there were good chances for a left pole, there was nothing fore-ordained about its success.

5.5 CONCLUSION – PATTERNS OF FRACTIONAL PROGRESS

Many observers had a standard view of Ceres federations. Young groups of activists, radicalised by 1968, were believed to have swept aside an old or moribund SFIO, usually in areas where the latter had been weak. Often they were thought to be educated white-collars, predominantly of catholic background and with CFDT experience. Having swiftly taken over the local party and revived it by sheer effort they would then reap the electoral rewards which proved that this version of socialism was what the voters had been waiting for. Our studies show, especially when read in conjunction with the other federal studies available, that this version needs so much qualification as to be confined to the realm of myth.

To take the nature of Ceres first, it is clear that often it recruited elements which had been oppositional long before 1968 or even 1966 when Ceres was founded. Although white-collars were important (Chevènement and his associates who took over the Paris federation would be good examples), we should not forget that there were crucial inputs from the lower classes. Sarre's postmen were vital in winning Paris, and the mass entries in Loire and Loire-Atlantique had many working-class militants. The initial Belfort group were mainly shop stewards. It is clear also that in many cases Ceres was anything but homogeneous in political terms, as well as sociological, and we shall return to this point.

The adversary was also varied. If the federal apparatus was non-existent in Ille-et-Vilaine or weak as in Loire, those of Belfort and Meurthe-et-Moselle were more serious. But the adequacy of the riposte was in any case not always proportional to federal strength, as Loire proved. It is in fact possible, we believe, to construct a threefold typology of Ceres/federal relationships which subsumes existing studies. Each type has subvariants.

First is the case when Ceres takes a federation immediately. This may happen through absence of a federal apparatus (Ille-et-Vilaine), its weakness (Paris), or its readiness to ally (Belfort, where the enemy was neo-Radicalism). Subsequent progress depends less on the style of federal management, which may be exclusive (Paris and Belfort) or open (Ille-et-Vilaine), than on the internal cohesion of the fraction. If this is high and if there are reasonable electoral rewards to be had, then progress should be steady. Belfort is a *locus classicus*.

At the other end of the scale comes a type not treated here, but which our study of Aude highlights.[40] Here Ceres confronts a strong federal machine, usually with a base in electoral politics. But rather than provoke a head-on clash, it opts for a 'geographical compromise', trading any pretensions to overall hegemony in the federation for predominance (intra-party and electoral) in one specific area. Departments where, despite modest congress scores, Ceres has made electoral gains almost certainly fit into this scheme – Vaucluse, Gironde and Mermaz's Isère, which Derville analysed.[41] An extreme version of this is the few departments where Ceres presence is nugatory, despite considerable potential. We refer to cases like Nièvre and Bouches-du-Rhône, where a powerful local machine run by a national figure (Mitterrand, Defferre) has practically forbidden opposition. So rather than conduct a hopeless but principled fight, Ceres has accepted its fate here in return for non-interference in other areas. The geographical compromise works here in national terms, not local. This explains perhaps why Defferre has often been an ally of the fraction in CD wrangles, and possibly may be one additional reason why Mitterrand has never conducted a total offensive. A variant of this position is the rare principled battles conducted by a Ceres against a very powerful federal apparatus, refusing any compromises it might offer; the classic case is Marc Wolf's group in Nord. Here party and electoral progress was sacrificed in the name of ideological consistency, but in the end that Ceres crumbled anyway through internal divisions.

Less clearcut is the third type, which emerges from our last three cases. Here a vigorous Ceres took on federal machines of varying quality with mixed success. The major determinant here seems to have been not so much the quality of the adversary as the internal consistency of Ceres itself. The two cases of Loire and Loire-Atlantique show what can happen if a Ceres is vulnerable to internal tension, especially cultural. The withering of left unity in the mid-seventies, the failure of the party to win expected national office and the tensions which ensued, symbolised in the Rocard–Mitterrand clash were always likely to release centrifugal forces which could previously be controlled. To limit the damage needed leadership skills of high quality, especially if there were few electoral rewards available to help mitigate friction; the achievement of Loire-Atlantique stands out as remark-able here.

Unity is indeed the key criterion. A united Ceres could beat off all comers, as in Belfort. But an initially strong Ceres which failed to master its contradictions as in Ille-et-Vilaine could soon collapse from hegemony to minority status.[42] Retrospectively it seems that many Ceres in 1971 contained the seeds of discord on a number of issues. In policy terms, defence and foreign affairs were always strong con-tenders, as was the tension between *dirigisme* and *autogestion* in economic policy; so were the way in which the fraction was structured and, underneath, the secularist–catholic tension. In many cases CFDT members came in alongside CGT or FEN stalwarts, practising catholics joined with fervent *laïcs*, often freemasons to boot; nationalists rubbed shoulders with convinced Europeans and unilateralists or pacifists with admirers of de Gaulle. What they had in common was hatred of 'social-democracy' and the belief that change was possible through a PS renewed on its left. They would learn that the left is to be found on many different points of the compass. The question was how far these divergences were fundamental and how far they could be reconciled. In our view more reconciliation seems to have taken place in some areas than others; the reason for this is the quality of the local leadership.

Parisian leadership is less important than local. At the start the Paris Ceres could with its expertise help provincial Ceres to achieve viability or in some cases dominance, specially in the East. Once the network of correspondents was set up, it could give rapid logistical help. But it could never *create* a Ceres. For this to happen there had to be local militants willing to do the fighting on a terrain that they knew and largely with tactics of their choosing. The fact is that the department (and its sublevels) is the real level of day-to-day struggle and that for most fractions the federal troops are left to get on with it in the assumption that they know best. The only exception to this rule is Paris itself, where the Mitterrandists eventually unseated Ceres after a prolonged and centrally-directed effort; this is so because of the vital position of the capital. But this exception confirms the rule.

For the rest, we may conclude that what emerges above all from our typology is that the key variables are two dialectically interdependent ones – internal unity of Ceres and the quality of its federal élites. The best proof of this is one *a contrario*. In his study of the Savoie Ceres, Charvet portrays a fraction which put in years of hard work to build a genuinely militant PS.[43] It then had the electoral – and ultimately the intra-party – fruits of its labour confiscated by a politician, J.-P. Cot, who understood better than it the electoral sociology of the area, and above all the nature and needs of local élites (mayors and *conseillers généraux*). The moral could be applied to every Ceres. In politics naïvety brings its own reward and in the end there is no substitute for class.

NOTES TO CHAPTER 5

1 Interview with author, Belfort, September 1980.
2 Interview with M. Dreyfus-Schmidt, Senate, Paris, October 1980. See also *Le Monde* 2 September 1980.
3 Interview with author, Belfort, October 1980. The role of the SE is always delicate as there is a constant temptation to overlap with the unions. One of their most effective roles is to help publicise disputes, such as the big strike at Alsthom in 1979–80, where the PS branch seems to have won a lot of publicity and support for the strikers.
4 J.-P. Chevènement, *Etre socialiste aujourd'hui*, Paris, Cana, 1980, pp. 47 ff.
5 Interview with J. Morel, Belfort, September 1980.
6 Dreyfus-Schmidt's own political line was an additional reason for his being a natural focus for opposition to Ceres. Very independent (in the best tradition of the old Radicals) he is as firmly committed to left unity and state-led economic expansion as any Mitterrandist or Ceres. But he opposes what he sees as the party's excessive nationalism and its belief in a French nuclear deterrent. He is thus able to reach newer types of anti-Ceres socialist as well as the older Republican secularists.
7 S. Bonnet, *Sociologie politique et réligieuse de la Lorraine*, Paris, Colin, 1972, pp. 463 ff. For a recent more limited study of the Nancy region see R. De Angelis, *Blue Collar Workers and Politics – A French Paradox*, London, Croom Helm, 1982.
8 S. Bonnet, op. cit., p. 340.
9 J.-P. Chagnollaud, 'La fédération socialiste de Meurthe-et-Moselle', *Annales de l'Est*, 1978, pp. 137–66.
10 For an interesting if racy account see J.-F. Bizot *et al.*, *Au Parti des socialistes*, Paris, Grasset, 1975, pp. 224 ff.
11 J.-P. Chagnollaud, op. cit., p. 150.
12 Interviews with D. Groscolas, Nancy, November 1980 and R. Fajardie, Paris, July 1981.
13 Interviews with Jeanine and Job Durupt and Wilfrid Roux-Marchand, Tomblaine, November 1980.
14 Interview with J.-J. Guyot, Nancy, November 1980.
15 Interview with F. Borella, professor of politics and leader of the Rocard fraction in the federation, Nancy, November 1980.
16 J.-P. Chagnollaud, op. cit., p. 164.

17   Typical of this is the fact that CFDT official Yvon Tondon could be elected as deputy for the Moselle valley in 1978 and 1981.

18   P. Héritier, R. Bonnevialle, J. Ion and C. Saint-Sernin, *150 Ans de luttes ouvrières dans le bassin stéphanois*, Saint-Étienne, Le Champ du Possible, 1979, p. 344. Michel Durafour was deputy-mayor of Saint-Étienne and successively Labour minister and minister of Regional Planning under Giscard d'Estaing. His father was a Third Republic Labour minister.

19   Interview with Paul Faye, full-time federal official, Saint-Étienne, December 1980.

20   'Les Frères ennemis de la Loire', *Rouge*, 25 June 1976.

21   Interview with J. Vincent, Saint-Chamond, December 1980. The committee comprised one Ceres, Vincent and Badet.

22   The phenomenon of the *gauche syndicale* has been little studied, given its importance for the politics of the seventies. I am grateful to Michel Coffineau, deputy for Val d'Oise, and Pierre Héritier, CFDT regional secretary for Rhône-Alpes for their memories and analyses of the period. See also Héritier *et al.*, op. cit. and an interview by Coffineau in *Que faire aujourd'hui* 5, 1980, pp. 48–9.

23   R. Bonnevialle, *Que faire*, p. 52.

24   Loire had seen strong and sometimes violent industrial militancy in the early seventies, as the older industries contracted and modernised under the weight of recession. Battles like the 1973 Peugeot lock-out or the strike for union recognition in the *Nouvelles Galeries* chain store were the sort of meat on which the younger CFDT activists had been raised.

25   Interview with J. Vincent.

26   Vie Nouvelle has provided the PS with some leaders, including Jacques Delors and Christian Pierret. The journalist Philippe Warnier, long a Ceres sympathiser, of *Témoignage chrétien* is also a member (interview with author, Paris, July 1981). It would be interesting to measure in detail its (sometimes much resented) contribution to the socialist revival. See M.-A. Poisson, *La Vie nouvelle et la politique*, 1968–71, Paris, IEP mémoire, 1972.

27   Interview with B. Vennin, Saint-Étienne, December 1980. The allusion is to Émile Combes, Radical prime minister of 1902–5 who prepared the ground for the separation of church and state. His name is a byword for a crude anti-clericalism based on unflinching faith in the inseparable couple science-and-progress.

28   Interview with author, Saint-Étienne, December 1980. See also interview with J. Ducos in *Que faire*, op. cit.

29   R. Bonnevialle, ibid., p. 51.

30   Interview with Martine Souvignet and Jacques Ion, Saint-Étienne, December 1980.

31   The latter are mainly Badet supporters, Courant B (the letter of Mauroy's motion at Metz) being known sarcastically as Courant Badet.

32   M. Rocard *et al.*, *Le PSU et l'avenir de la France*, Paris, Seuil, 1969, pp. 34–5.

33   Interview with Daniel Mathieu (Rocardian leader), Saint-Nazaire, November 1980. Mathieu believes that after the *assises* the only remaining activists in the PSU were students.

34   Interview with Jean Natiez, Nantes, November 1980.

35   Interview with François Autain, Assemblée Nationale, Paris, October 1980.

36   Interview with Roger Fajardie, Paris, July 1981.

37   The posts were: workplace branches, associations, liaison with branches, the

federal bulletin and buildings and equipment. None of these are trivial and they prove how serious was Ceres' offer.

38 In 1979 they represented 41.3% of the federal membership, compared with 64.3% in 1973.

39 Interview, November 1980.

40 D. Hanley, 'The Ceres in two départements – political compromise on Aude and Vilaine' in D. Bell (ed.), *Contemporary French Political Parties*, London, Croom Helm, 1982, pp. 123–37.

41 J. Derville, 'La Fédération socialiste de l'Isère', *Revue française de science politique*, XXVI, June 1976, pp. 568–99.

42 Ille-et-Vilaine Ceres had 67% in 1973, 17% in 1979 and 11% in 1983.

43 X. Charvet, *Le Ceres en Savoie, 1968–79*, Grenoble IEP, thèse de doctorat, 1980.

CHAPTER 6

Ceres in government

Lorsqu'on sait ce qu'on veut et que l'on sait commander, on se fait obéir.

J. Mandrin, 1983

The victories of May–June 1981 put Ceres into a new position. With the PS leader now president of France and his party enjoying an absolute majority in the National Assembly, all the fractions which had supported him could now expect their reward. It would come with unexpected precision. Mitterrand swiftly appointed Mauroy, who had headed his campaign team, as prime minister; he would head a series of governments that would govern until July 1984. Although these contained a small number of communists, left Radicals and non-party members, they were composed essentially of socialists and these held all key posts. Ceres was thus involved from the start and its leaders knew the stakes. What posts could Ceres secure for itself in government and other parts of the state apparatus? How far would these enable it to influence policy? And how would these factors react on the fraction and its place within the party? After four years of the Mitterrand presidency we have some answers to these questions.

As Roucaute shows, government posts were shared out among fractions in proportions not very different (Rocardians apart) from their Metz scores[1] (see Table 6.1). If the underlying trend was towards consolidation of Mitterrandist support at the expense of Rocardians, Ceres did quite well in percentage terms. But there was also qualitative progress. From the start Chevènement was a *ministre d'État* (senior minister) alongside the other fraction bosses; beginning at Research and Technology he would from June 1982 combine these responsibilities in a superministry which also included Industry until his resignation (given in February 1983 but only effective after the March

TABLE 6.1 FRACTIONAL WEIGHT IN GOVERNMENT SINCE 1981

	Mauroy I		Mauroy II		Mauroy III		Fabius		
	Abs. no. of members	% of PS posts only	Abs. no. of members	% of PS posts only	Abs. no. of members	% of PS posts only	Abs. no. of members	% of PS posts only	Metz (%) score
Mitterrand and Defferre*	26	66.6	23	63.8	25	71.4	27	75	47.9
Mauroy	6	15.4	6	16.6	6	17.1	3	8.3	13.6
Rocard	3	7.7	3	8.3	1	2.8	1	2.8	20.4
CERES	4	10.2	4	11.1	3	8.5	5	13.9	14.5
MRG	3		2		2		3		(plus 3.6
PCF	–		4		4		–		for smaller
Others	1		2		2		4		motions)
TOTAL	43	100	44	100	43	100	43	100	100

*includes E. Hervé (motion F)

Source: adapted from Y. Roucaute Le PS (Paris, 1983) p. 132 and Le Monde 24 July 1984

TABLE 6.2 CERES IN GOVERNMENT, 1981–5

	Post	Tenure	
J.-P. Chevènement	Minister of State* (Research and Technology)	May 1981	– June 1982
	plus Minister of Industry	June 1982	– March 1983
	Minister of Education	July 1984	–
N. Questiaux	Minister of State** (National Solidarity)	May 1981	– June 1982
E. Avice	Minister of Leisure, Youth and Sport	May 1981	– July 1984
	Under-Secretary of State (Defence)	July 1984	–
F. Autain	Under-Secretary of State (Social Security)	May 1981	– June 1981
	Under-Secretary of State (Immigration)	June 1981	– March 1983
	Under-Secretary of State (Defence)	March 1983	– November 1983
R. Carraz	Under Secretary of State (Tourism)	March 1983	– July 1984
	Under-Secretary of State (Technical Education)	July 1984	–
J. Gatel	Under-Secretary of State (Defence)	November 1983	– July 1984
	Under-Secretary of State (Social Economy)	July 1984	–
J.-M. Bockel	Under-Secretary of State (Tourism)	July 1984	–

* Till July 1982 only
** Till June 1981 only

municipal elections). Another senior ministry was given to Nicole Questiaux in her specialist area of Social Affairs, renamed Solidarity in a declaration of intent. The other Ceres ministers were all junior (see Table 6.2). In office Ceres followed the practice of all fractions, packing ministerial *cabinets* with fractional loyalists where possible.[2] Chevènement thus found places for the Treasury economist Louis Gallois (*chef de cabinet*) who had long advised him on economic matters, and other faithful such as the all-purpose ideologist Bondoux, or Bruno Gazeau who looks after his constituency in Belfort. In general he drew on the expertise of the PS research commission (where Ceres had been prominent); sectarianism did not extend to the refusal of posts to two Rocardians, presumably posts Ceres could not fill. Other Ceres ministers did similarly and so the fraction entered government well-advised and relatively well-placed. Before assessing how it used its strength, we should mention other spheres.

One was the National Assembly where the 36 deputies (most of whose offices seemed to be in close proximity) might hope to act as a pressure group within the socialist group as a whole. Another was the new public sector (NPS). When the banks were nationalised in 1982, senior posts again seem to have been distributed in the form of a fractional share-out.[3] Thus merchant banker Jacques Schorr (who writes under the pseudonym of Sandeau) found himself at the head of a minor nationalised bank and Ceres treasurer Escande at the head of a similar institution. In the legislative process of nationalisation a key role was played by the *rapporteur* of the parliamentary committee, Michel Charzat, who then became head of the high authority set up to monitor the new public sector.[4] It is probable that these positions are of little immediate consequence in influencing government, but they might provide foci for longer-term influences, being places where supporters or clients can be won over.

To assess Ceres influence overall on government performance since 1981 would require a book on its own, so we shall limit ourselves deliberately to the two most sensitive areas – the economy and foreign and defence policy. In all these areas it seems that the pattern was one of initial Ceres influence, but soon policy drifted away from the Ceres line and beyond its control.

The attempt at 'reflation in one country' by the Mitterrand presidency is now history.[5] Faithful to the schema that had sustained Ceres and much of the party through the seventies, the government dashed for growth as the major solution to the considerable economic problems left by the recession and the Giscardians. In Beaud's words 're-flation, social progress and the struggle against unemployment and inflation are all part of the same movement'.[6] But as he also remarks, the attendant difficulties were foreseeable; and as for the spirit in which it was undertaken, 'it was hard to tell where the frontier lay between scientific analysis, ideology . . . voluntarism and commitment'.

The strategy sought growth by a mix of keynesian and *dirigiste* means, much as outlined in Chapter 3. The latter means involved nationalisation of the banks and two major finance houses, 100% purchase (made more expensive after a lengthy wrangle with the Constitutional Council) of six major groups and majority shareholding in what remained of the steel industry as well as major parts of the arms and aerospace industry and pharmaceuticals. After reorganisation and recapitalisation this NPS was to serve as the spearhead of a drive to recapture home and export markets, hopefully acting as a 'tow-rope' for the rest of the economy and stimulating smaller firms by its purchasing, subcontracting, etc.

The 'redistributive keynesianism', to use Hall's phrase, aimed at reflation via increased demand. This was provided for by wage and benefit increases and extra holidays and shorter hours without loss of pay. The creation of some 200,000 new public sector jobs can be seen as part of the same strategy, as can the 'solidarity contracts' with firms which encouraged early retirement, with the proviso that the jobs thus vacated were passed on to younger workers. All these changes benefited the lower-paid especially, Hall calculating that the purchasing power of these social transfers went up by 12% in 1981–2.[7] The hope was that firms would respond to the potential market by extra investment and by taking on more labour. The extra receipts generated would enable both investment and job-creation to be maintained, as well as increasing the capacity of firms and individuals to pay taxes; this would enable government to recoup its initial outlay. Thus a virtuous cycle of production and growth would restart, with a return to full employment and rising living standards. In the mid-term some new form of indicative planning might emerge.

There had been warnings, including from Rocard, of the dangers inherent in such a strategy, especially in terms of inflation, balance-of-payments problems and related difficulties for the currency. These problems soon materialised. The absence of a prices-and-incomes policy meant that employers and retailers simply passed on higher costs to the customer, with clear inflationary consequences. The large budget deficit was always potentially inflationary, and firms' costs rose further thanks to the movement of another key variable, the franc. As the dollar rose mercilessly and the franc slipped, key imports – especially energy – had to be paid for in dollars, vastly increasing costs and inflationary pressures.

But the real problems stemmed from the insertion of the French economy into the international system and its consequent vulnerability. An immediate consequence of increased spending power was rising import penetration. It was not just that the French bought German goods as their own manufacturers were unable or unwilling to satisfy demand; for as Beaud shows, the absolute amount of imports did not increase that much.[8] What made the difference was the relationship of the franc to the DM, which was such that the strategy if it was to work needed a sharp initial devaluation of the franc against the DM – but one greater than that permitted by the EMS. The three eventual devaluations that did take place were arguably too little too late, and could in any case do little against the remorseless rise of the dollar and the effects on the balance of payments, given that so many imports had to be paid for in dollars.

At the same time domestic investment did not progress fast enough, despite heroic efforts by the state sector, so unemployment continued to creep up, albeit slower than elsewhere. Government income suffered from the shortfall in anticipated growth, meaning a higher debt, more borrowing and increased debt servicing. By mid-1982 the strategy had been, to quote a well-known social-democratic leader, 'blown off course'.

Under the adverse pressure of balance-of-payments and currency problems plus high inflation, policy began to move from mid-1982 towards deflationary means. Eschewing ideas of withdrawal from the EMS or import controls, the Mauroy–Delors team sought to shrink the deficit by classical means, namely pressure on consumers. Thus after a snap 4-month price and wage freeze, taxes and public service charges began to rise and benefits to be reduced. Efforts were made to lighten the fiscal burden on firms while increasing it on wage-earners, so as to free greater profit margins. Social and even defence spending were cut in an attempt to find greater direct investment for industry. Under its new watchword of rigorousness (sometimes interpreted as austerity) the government strove generally to direct resources away from consumption to investment, from households to firms. Official discourse increasingly stressed the values of the entrepreneur; there was less talk of socialism and more of modernisation (the PS would hold a mini-congress on this at the end of 1984). The hope seemed to be that as inflation shrank and the trade deficit narrowed, enough new investment might come through out of rising profits to start creating jobs (many of which had begun to disappear because of the deflation) in time for the 1986 elections.

All in all the record was a mixed one. If growth was higher than in neighbouring states and if a real redistribution of purchasing power had been achieved, the rate of inflation still remained above competitors and the large trade deficit still had some way to shrink at the end of 1984. Despite the efforts of the NPS and government incentives in general, industrial investment had still not caught up to 1970 levels.[9] The initial stemming of unemployment had faltered as deflation began. Nothing resembling a form of 'democratic planning' could be remotely discerned; and so far as *autogestion* went, it was limited to the law democratising the public sector and the 1982 Auroux laws. These provided for worker representation on the councils of the new public industries and reinforced the position and bargaining rights of unions as well as health and safety regulations. But in no way could they be described as workers' control. This record could be seen as an honourable one compared with that of neighbouring governments, but obviously one falling well short of Ceres demands. How did the fraction react?

Ceres was both participant in and critic of the above strategy. We can usefully distinguish several phases of its attitude to these policies and indeed policy in general. The first phase lasted till mid-1982 and elicited little criticism, unsurprisingly given Ceres presence in government. We should recall that Ceres had long argued in favour of the very bold reflationary policy implemented and it may well be that its voice was decisive in opposing those (Delors and Rocard) who favoured a slower approach on this and on nationalisation. A second phase of muted discontent then began as Questiaux was sacked for protesting at spending cuts, but anger only really surfaced with Chevènement's departure in March 1983. From then till the Bourg congress in October Ceres went on the offensive, arguing for an alternative economic strategy (AES). At the convention in May Chevènement savaged Delors's policy, claiming it was deflationary, unsocialist and doomed to fail anyway; he foresaw a further devaluation. Shortly after this, the fraction published Le Socialisme et la France[10] in the same vein, while preparing a congress text largely based on that book. This was the moment of peak tension between Ceres and the government. At Bourg a synthèse was duly reached, showing the limits of Ceres opposition; the fraction had made its point and the government, through its support in the party majority, seemed willing to take some notice – how much remains to be seen. This compromise prepared the way for Chevène-ment's return to government in July 1984, which meant a toning down of the vehemence if not the substance of Ceres critiques. This was likely to remain the position as the party faced the crucial 1986 election.

The burden of Ceres' critiques is stated in Le Socialisme et la France. This polemical and at times strangely emotional work admits that the 1981 victories were not the sort of Ceres had dreamt of and that socialism was not on the agenda immediately. Credit is given for the attempts at growth and redistribution but their inadequacy is criticised.[11] In terms of explaining this, much is made of the harsh external environment where the dominant economic mechanism is that which transfers surplus value from industry towards finance capital and where the dollar is so powerful. Giscard and Barre's passivity in the face of these trends is also singled out. But there are socialist mistakes. The 1981 devaluation was too weak, mainly because key ministers (translate as Rocard and Delors) never believed in the reflationary strategy anyway and constantly talked it down. We are told that foreign constraints were overestimated (a judgement contradicted by much of what follows);[12] that the nationalisations were too long delayed (Rocard's fault again); that too few changes were made in key positions in the state – presumably in the economic apparatus. France should have left the EMS if need be. All this meant that an industrial policy took too long to emerge. Above all the state lacked authority and conviction.

Be this as it may, the fraction recognised clearly the problems which have been outlined and the need to counter them. The first priority is to fight rising unemployment which alone will suffice to defeat the left in 1986. Ceres suggests that growth should be given priority even at the risk – though it does not spell it out exactly – of inflationary and balance-of-payments side-effects. The tailpiece of the fraction's motion to the Bourg congress thus argues that it is possible to create an extra 1.5% growth and 100,000 jobs.[13] But if the extra investment is to come forward, visible and sustained support for demand, that is increased purchasing power is vital. In the hope of pegging any inflationary effects from such a policy Ceres advocates something like prices-and-incomes policy, with 3-monthly adjustments to be achieved by what it calls, in language reminiscent of Bob Hawke, 'a major national negotiation'. To reduce the trade deficit, Ceres wants 'an offensive exchange-rate policy, with sharp adjustment vis-à-vis mark and florin'; if EMS rules will not allow this then a 'temporary departure' is called for. It is further claimed that import deposits and selective quotas could lop a further 20 thousand million francs off the deficit, giving French industry also the chance to modernise behind the barriers so as eventually to be able to substitute many imports. These defensive proposals are supplemented with more positive ones, involving highly selective aid (from both government and banks) to small firms and the strengthening of the Industry ministry to work alongside a revived planning commission. These could identify better the areas which need funding and divert to them the increased revenues available from savings schemes (which are to be made more attractive) and from the higher taxation which Ceres also recommends.

Ceres thus sees a statist and voluntarist way out of the crisis.[14] Its main objection to the Mauroy governments seems to be their lack of firmness towards economic actors; it seems as if the style and sense of purpose exhibited by the state is almost as important as the content of policy.[15] Logically Ceres streses the links between this AES and the ideological struggles which must underpin it; hence the campaigns against the 'American left' or 'deuxième gauche' go on.[16] But there has emerged another ideological strand, previously dormant, namely Republicanism. When, in the sixties or later, socialists spoke of a 'République moderne' they were usually Rocardians who thought in terms of modernising the economy, institutions and above all beliefs and mentalities which they saw as archaic. Often the pragmatism of Pierre Mendès-France was taken as paradigm (his major work was called *La République moderne*) and the 1966 Grenoble colloqium where he and Rocard figured is generally seen as a landmark in the development of a modernising left. But since 1981 most of the PS has been seeking to lay claim to the Republican heritage. This matter was probably put on the agenda by two different sources. First the right, going into the unfamiliar situation of opposition, chose to describe itself as 'l'opposition républicaine' suggesting somehow that socialism was not Republican, hence was illegitimate. Within the PS, the Rocardians also began a debate on the Republic. A clever article by Jacques Julliard asked whether Mitterrand's win was not, in the psyche of the average voter, more a triumph for traditional Republican values than those of the marxist type of socialism incarnated in, say, the *Projet socialiste*.[17] Later *Interventions* would devote a whole number to the theme.[18] The question of what Republicanism meant was thus posed unavoidably and Ceres could not simply write off such preoccupations as part of the problematic of its neo-liberal enemies.

Republicanism has in fact provided a useful adjunct to Ceres' doctrine. We suggested that the 1979 Pierret split led the fraction to rediscover some of the Republican heritage; the crisis of socialist economic management has taken it further down the road. Today Chevènement claims to speak for *la République moderne* (and has even founded a club of that name). In Ceres discourse the Republic is now conflated with the national interest which only the left, by its policies of social justice and national independence can realise. The AES outlined above can easily be fitted into such a cultural framework and in fact this Republicanism reinforces the centralist and voluntarist features of Ceres ideology. The Republic is a focus of discipline, effort and loyalty, a goal as well as a means, in pursuance of which the French are asked to mobilise.[19]

If these are the Ceres criticisms of government performance, we must still assess the specific Ceres contribution, in particular the ministerial role of Chevènement. We would first repeat that without Ceres presence in government it is unlikely that the reflationary strategy would have been so boldly pursued; indeed it would never have been so strongly inscribed in the party's collective unconscious, as it were, without the years of Ceres effort before 1981. On the question of ministerial roles, Chevènement certainly seems to have pushed the growth strategy as far as possible. As Research minister he secured a 29% increase in the research budget for 1982 with 17% annual increase programmed through to 1985. Obtaining the tutelage of the various research councils, previously scattered among different ministries, he changed their directors and set up a series of regional colloquia, culminating in a national *assises* of researchers, where some 3,000 met in Paris to create guidelines for future research policy. Observers were struck by the similarity with the organisation of Ceres' own colloquia. But the aim was to make France the third power in research terms after the USA and Japan. Research was to be linked more than ever before to industrial development. His brief tenure of Industry showed similar traits.[20] What he wanted was a superministry like the Japanese MITI combining technology, industry and trade. Ceres texts of the period enthused over Japanese productivity, which was seen as relating to the organisation of strong state/industry links and also to the disciplined culture which enabled the workforce to achieve its objectives (whether such a culture was easily transposable to France is another question). At any rate Chevènement sponsored several planning contracts between government and the NPS groups (offering finance in return for production and employment commitments). He began to organise filières to reduce import-dependence in sectors such as chemicals and electronics and started an inquiry into the feasibility of making the capital goods sector more autonomous. He continued with the series of rescue plans for some eight major sectors of industry begun by his predecessors.[21] And before he left office he had set in motion plans for another series of colloquia which thus became redundant.

J.-M. Quatrepoint believes lack of time prevented Chevènement from tackling two other projects;[22] one was to improve the flow of private investment into industry and the other was to vocationalise the school system in line with industry's needs. His return as Education minister in 1984 would give him another chance to grasp that nettle. Quatrepoint sees him as an 'industrialist' and his successor Fabius as a 'financier'. He suggests that Chevènement's visible willingness to champion industry was beginning to win him friends among manufacturers. Certainly after resignation the Ceres chief still called for 'a productivist consensus ... a sort of Saint-Simonian Holy Alliance

among producers in the interest of the whole nation'.[23] With the cheap
success under his belt of French defiance of the USA over the Siberian
gas supply (a splendid example of how cultural anti-Americanism can
coincide with national self-interest), he was even being talked of as a
future prime minister. Certainly Ceres dissent was kept well muzzled
during this time and it was thus a shock to hear of his resignation.

It was in fact more of a sacking. But it was less for opposition to
policy than for other political reasons. It seems that Chevènement
made enemies within the state. The Finance ministry disliked his
investment demands with their budgetary implications. Technical
ministries like Telecommunications resented attempts to confiscate
some of their activities under the umbrella of a technical superministry. The heads of the NPS (including presumably Ceres' founder-
member Alain Gomez) appear to have resented both his abruptness
over certain restructuring problems within the NPS and also excessive
interference in their day-to-day operations. This doubtless explains the
sarcasm in Mandrin's polemic directed at heads of nationalised
industries who take the idea of managerial autonomy too far. These
combined pressures resulted in Chevènement's departure; but it is
significant that critiques of policy only gained momentum afterwards.

The experience of other Ceres ministers tends also to prove
Quatrepoint's claim that there are limits to what voluntarism can
achieve; but they also show that for Ceres limited success is felt to be
better than nothing. Thus Autain at Immigration would probably have
liked the government to proceed with its stated aim of giving
immigrants the vote in local elections; but when the government
backed down he did not resign. The junior ministers remained in post
throughout the period. The exception was the sacking of Questiaux in
1982 for her clear disagreement at what was obviously the beginning of
a more austere policy. But even then Chevènement stayed, and once
dismissed strove successfully to return. We may thus conclude that
Ceres' criticisms of policy took a long time to emerge and that they
were limited in how far the fraction was prepared to go (certainly not
to the point of resignation *en bloc*). We believe these patterns to be true
of foreign affairs and defence also.

We may consider Mitterrand's foreign and defence policy under
three heads: East–West relations, Europe, and the Third World.[24]
Relations with the Soviet bloc were dominated by the aftermath of

the invasion of Afghanistan, the Solidarnosc movement and the growing tension over the intermediate nuclear forces (INF). Mitterrand's long mistrust of the USSR was boosted by this chain of events and within weeks of election he was proclaiming support for the NATO two-track decision, whereby Cruise and Pershing II missiles would be installed in Western Europe, though not in France, as a bargaining counter to obtain the withdrawal of the already positioned Soviet SS-20s. Cheysson, the Foreign minister, spoke of the impossibility of normal relations with the USSR so long as it remained in Afghanistan, and Time magazine saw his views on East–West relations as not too far from Reagan's. Although Mitterrand would later visit Moscow, his general hardening of tone and thus far unswerving position on the Euromissiles could be read, if not as outright Atlanticism, then at least as a considerable rapprochement with the USA, compared with, say, the era of high Gaullism. We might expect Ceres to be vexed.

Criticism was muted. On the one hand Ceres was tempted to explain such gestures tactically; Mitterrand was hoping to bargain diplomatic support for the US against a benevolent attitude on its part towards the French attempts at economic reconstruction.[25] As such the trade-off could be justified in the long-term interests of socialism. But Ceres knew that such explanations would not satisfy its supporters and offered a fuller view in Le socialisme et la France.[26] Recognising grudgingly but more clearly than before the need for France to remain in the Atlantic Alliance for the foreseeable future, if only because of sheer Soviet strength (the authors refuse to enter guessing games about Soviet intentions) and indeed paying lip-service to certain American values (enterprise, dynamism), Ceres none the less seeks to keep French involvement to a minimum. Its acceptance of the Alliance is reluctant and conditional, for it still sees it as a means of US overlordship of ally and adversary alike. Mitterrandist support over the Euromissiles has thus been an embarrassment and Ceres has tried to avoid the subject as far as possible. But what it has said is clear. First it does not accept the idea of an *overall* strategic imbalance in favour of the USSR, which the INF (intermediate-range nuclear forces) are said to remedy.[27] It does not see the Pershings as bargaining counters for the SS-20s, for it believes that the USA does not care about these since they cannot reach US territory. What Pershing gives the USA is enhanced deterrence. Potential first-strike weapons as they are, they can probably take out not just the first-strike capacity of the USSR, but also most of its second-strike.[28] Thus the USSR, well aware of this, is globally inhibited from acting, even at lower levels of conflict. It is not that the USA seeks a first strike, simply that the possibility cannot be ruled out, especially as the resultant 'limited war' would take place in Europe. Thus the net effect of the INF is to sanctuarise the USA even more while offering Europe nothing except higher risk. If one accepts this theory it must be hard to swallow the Mitterrand line. All Ceres could do was insist on strengthening French deterrence in any case, as the US ally was now less reliable than ever. As the government was prepared to do this, albeit for different reasons, conflict remained muted. Certainly the fraction shared Mitterrandist contempt for peace movements and advocates of non-nuclear defence in general.

By hammering away at the global structures of power as opposed to regional questions like the INF and by deploying familiar critiques (the USA as dominant imperialism, recollections of Franco-Russian solidarity against the German threat), Ceres sought to wean Mitterrand from excessive anti-Sovietism.[29] It is this concern which partly explains its general soft-pedalling of support for Solidarnosc, a movement which a priori corresponds well to previous ideas of self-governing mass-movements.[30] Part of the explanation may also lie in fractional patterns. As the Rocardians invested heavily in this crusade, linking it to a wider critique of the 'totalitarian' nature of the Eastern regimes, the Solidarnosc issue was to some extent ruled out as a potential campaigning ground. But this factor probably takes second place to the main concern, which was to try and decrease Franco-Russian tension. Perhaps Mitterrand's 1984 visit to the USSR, followed by Cheysson's departure from office at the year's end, may have led the fraction to believe that its efforts were not totally in vain. In his press conference of December 1984 the president certainly used some characteristically Ceres phrases.[31]

On Europe, Mitterrand strove in accord with the PS line to inflect the EEC in a more reflationary, interventionist and welfare-orientated direction. He and Delors thus pressed for goals such as the development of common trade and industry policy to improve employment; the levelling up of social and welfare provisions, including regional spending, and firmer attitudes to US and Japanese competition. In a recession-hit Europe where liberal and monetarist government's prevailed, such a strategy was never likely to get far; thus by 1984 few of the hopes in the 1981 election manifesto had even begun to be realised.[32] Ceres contempt for the EEC meant that the fraction was not surprised by this; but withdrawal was not an option and there was no point in attacking the president for trying to implement party policy. Ceres' Bourg text repeated previous demands for reform of the EMS and the Common Agricultural Policy[33] and a firmer stance against Japan and the USA. But really France had little room for manoeuvre in Europe and Ceres knew it. It hinted that a variable-geometry Europe might emerge, with different structures for transnational cooperation emerging for different issues.[34]

African and Third World policy was again little criticised. Ceres approved early symbolic gestures such as the supplying of some arms to the Sandinistas, the call for negotiations with the rebel left in El Salvador and the Cancun declaration on development. But though it cited the government's disinterested desire to aid the Third World and the necessity for autonomous development, the fraction was hard put to find examples.[35] This is doubtless because development policy since 1981 continues on the same lines as that of the earlier Fifth Republic. Cheysson expressed this logic when he called for increased financing from European governments or international agencies so as to expand consumer demand in the South, thus stimulating European exports and employment. Such a strategy has arguably more to do with increasing Southern dependence on Europe than with promoting autonomous development. In its heart Ceres probably agrees with this approach, hence there was little sympathy for the resignation of the Development minister, Cot, partly on issues like this one. What Ceres did appreciate were the diplomatic and commercial deals with the bigger Third World states – Algeria, India, Mexico – which it saw as helping, however hesitantly, to create a multipolar world, outside the two-bloc system. In this context of 'grand-design' policy the fraction could feel at home.

Generally then Ceres seems to have given Mitterrand the benefit of the doubt on foreign affairs, seeing him as sticking reasonably close to an independent line. But there was another way of looking at it. In an article published three months after le 10 mai when the general shape of policy was already fairly visible, a Ceres typical of the 1970s recruits launched a slashing attack on it.[36] Claiming that the policy was contrary not only to the *Projet* but also to the PS/PCF declaration which preceded the formation of the second Mauroy government, Séguillon found that underneath its anti-American gestures policy was 'moving very sharply towards overall alignment behind American capitalism and its centre the USA' or even that it was like 'reciting an Atlanticist credo'. The pro-Cruise line and Cheysson's declarations were cited as proof and compared unfavourably with the views of Willi Brandt or even the British Labour party. African policy was no better than Giscard's and even the gestures in Latin America were more than nullified by the rigid anti-Ghadafi stance in Africa and the excessive enthusiasm for Camp David, which merely aligned France with America's regional ally, Israel. Even the rapprochement with Algeria was compromised by similar overtures towards Hassan's Morocco. Not believing these moves to be merely tactical, Séguillon related them to the Cold War spasms of the old SFIO.

The Ceres leadership promptly disowned this of course, but it is highly significant in that here speaks the voice of the real Ceres grass roots of the seventies, principled to the point of idealism and especially so on foreign matters. Why did the leadership echo these critiques so little? The answer is that Séguillon's enthusiasm went further than was wanted, especially on nuclear matters (he is a member of the Mouvement de la paix, close to the PCF). Ceres had decided to swallow minor inconveniences, such as the Moroccan connection or even major ones like the INF provided that the essential were maintained. One essential was an insistence on French autonomy in the military field, and here the Mitterrand/Hernu tandem had few concrete differences with Ceres when it came to modernising the deterrent (even if their strategic conceptions may have varied). Once this *sine qua non* of military and hence of any other kind of independence was secure, it was worth supporting the government on other foreign issues or at least muting criticism. Ceres knew where its priorities lay and it has certainly never let principle get in the way of problems of power.

Parallel to its attempt to influence government, Ceres kept up its struggle for hegemony inside the party. If the Valence congress of 1981 could only be unanimous in the flush of victory, Ceres was quite happy to join its name to the single motion, and also to profit from the few extra points which the majority awarded it and all the non-Rocardian fractions at the expense of the Rocardians. This was illegal but *rapports de force* prevailed over legal niceties and the Rocardians knew there was a price to be paid for relegitimation.

Two years on, with the strains of economic policy showing, it was harder for Ceres and the Rocardians to keep quiet. If Rocard chose to repeat his Valence gambit and stay silent while remaining in government, some of his supporters did not. Motion III sponsored by Alain Richard, deputy and *énarque*, urged the government to regard the period of austerity not as a parenthesis but as a chance to experiment with a new mode of production, stressing quality rather than quantity.[37] Rocard disowned his supporters but Ceres was acutely uncomfortable. To put up no motion was to be seen as endorsing current policy which, as we saw, fell well short of Ceres' aims. It might also demoralise Ceres militants and their organisation, which was still recovering from the traumas of 1979. Yet frontal opposition would be seen as divisive. It would also make it hard to leave Ceres ministers in office, and in intra-party terms the fraction would lose its posts in the apparatus – all this with the 1986 elections on the horizons. What was needed was a spirited campaign to wean the government away from deflation, culminating in a motion that would still leave the door open for a *synthèse* at Bourg.[38]

The text duly contained the economic package outlined above, plus a foreign affairs section that sought a less anti-Soviet line; France was said to be 'equidistant from Washington and Moscow'.[39] After an 11-hour marathon in the resolutions committee the *synthèse* was duly achieved, to the joy and surprise of the militants (journalists were less amazed). The agreed text incorporated notably some lines on the need for the government to boost domestic demand.[40] Ceres could then claim that government had taken some notice of its views, though it must have doubted if policy would really be affected. It thus remained on the leadership with strength as follows: CD, 23 out of 131; BE, 5 out of 27. Full posts on the secretariat went to Motchane (education), Charzat (public sector) and Sarre (local government); half-posts to Carassus (workplace branches) and Natiez (elections).[41] Strength in the federations had gone up from 14% to 18% but unevenly, with a tendance to do better in areas the fraction did not control. Two types of gain seemed noticeable: first in areas with Ceres deputies (e.g.

Suchod in Dordogne and Lejeune in Creuse) and second in previously barren areas like Aube and Orne which seem ascribable only to sheer militant effort plus perhaps a swing from disgruntled Mitterrandists. But Ceres had lost in some of its heartlands, especially Paris, control of which was one of the prices paid for *la synthèse*. Now Ceres had sole control of only four federations (all Eastern bastions), and joint control of two more (Savoie and Mayenne).[42] But elsewhere there were encouraging signs of strength, and the fraction did seem to be building a more even base across the country. Although these gains did not yet add up to federal control they could prove very useful after 1986. Certainly Ceres had confounded those who prophesied its disappearance; but those who did were ignorant of the fundamental dynamics of left fractions.

It is too early to say where this new support came from, but a strong probability is that some of it came from the Mitterrandist left. It is no secret that Ceres was trying to win over some of its leaders, notably Joxe, Goux and Laignel. These men are close to Ceres in their marxist analysis of capitalism, their commitment to left unity, their statist approach to economic management, and – less visibly but equally potently – their militant secularism.[43] Given the debt, human and political, which such men owe their mentor Mitterrand, there was never a strong hope of winning them over. But in some departments their supporters were clearly dissatisfied and voted with their feet. In Joxe's Saône-et-Loire Ceres went from insignificance to over 20%. Thus the fraction might believe that it is beginning to attract some of the mainstream of the party and that there might be more to come in the *après-Mitterrand*.

Thus in party terms Ceres was recovering from the setbacks of 1979. But party is not government and one of the lessons of the Mitterrand presidency is that even a socialist party cannot significantly inflect the logic of the Fifth Republic whereby decision-making has become increasingly presidential.[44] Having accepted the new institutions before most of the rest of the PS Ceres was less surprised at this. Thus, while it values the party for its educative and campaigning functions and also as an essential means of winning office (especially presidential, for its role here is crucial), Ceres knew that it must be in government to have any real influence on president and policy. The Bourg *synthèse* can thus be seen retrospectively as a negotiation of

Chevènement's re-entry into government, which duly occurred in July 1984 when he took the Education portfolio in Fabius's government. This denoted no burning desire to grasp the nettle of education but rather the wish to be in cabinet, so as to argue for growth and spending (outside, Ceres kept up its reflationary demands albeit less stridently than during his resignation).[45]

In fact Chevènement seized the chance left to him. Three years of negotiations between his predecessor Savary and the catholic schools, aimed at incorporating the latter into the state system, had broken down and Savary was forced to withdraw his bill after Mauroy inserted clauses designed to placate the secularist majority of deputies (many of whom are teachers and who believed that the catholic schools were being funded with too few strings attached). Finding both sides exhausted Chevènement did the simple thing and prepared not a new law but simply a ruling which left most of the existing situation intact, while awaiting a more definitive legal text.[46] Having thus emerged as a fortuitous face-saver for both sides, he used his advantage to launch a plan for republicanising education (by rehabilitating history, geography and civics courses) and also vocationalising it more. Linking schooling very specifically to industry as in Japan, the minister declared his aim of improving basic skills in the lower school and of introducing more technology. His lack of enthusiasm for innovative pedagogy and regard for the three Rs, his stressing of the need to instil knowledge as an end in itself and his implicit criticism of the level of some teachers drew fire from various quarters.[47] Socialist deputies challenged his 'élitism', as did Edmond Maire; but Chevènement remained unrepentant.[48] Both these features of his policy have a characteristically Ceres basis, the Republican element relating to the nationalist values of the fraction and the vocational bias to its commitment to industry and productivism.

Ceres was thus back in government and well visible within the party. But Chevènement had also launched a club, République moderne.[49] Modelled on the 1960s clubs or think-tanks that had brought many people to socialism (and which Ceres had long despised), it aimed to recruit on a non-party basis various activists and professionals. It would aim to spread the solidarity values of Republicanism but in an updated way, relevant to the 'economic war' which France was forced to fight. It would stress technological education and reward for effort and hard

work. It would further national independence and European cooperation, aiming at creating a multipolar world. It appealed specifically to
the young and the dynamic. Much of this is old Ceres ideology, and
some of it newer. But the club's real meaning lies deeper than its
propaganda function. It is in reality the nucleus of an eventual
presidential campaign for 1988, and the above catalogue is tantamount
to a Ceres presidential programme in its broad outlines. Even now the
postulant must begin to create an extra-party base and discover,
particularly in business and media, the kind of support that will help
him get his party's nomination in the first place and then diffuse his
message through and beyond the PS electorate.

Only time will tell how successful this gambit will prove. But at the
beginning of 1985, Ceres was prominent and had recovered well inside
its party. It clearly sensed that further prizes might be in reach.
Certainly there seemed everything to play for, and this is as good a
moment as any to try and assess the fraction's achievement and put it
into perspective.

NOTES TO CHAPTER 6

1 Y. Roucaute, Le Parti socialiste, Paris, Huisman, 1983, p. 132.
2 M. Dagnaud and D. Mehl, L'Elite rose, Paris, Ramsay, 1982, p. 322 ff.
3 Le Monde, 2 July 1982.
4 Assemblée Nationale, Rapport fait au nom de la commission spéciale chargée d'examiner le projet de loi de nationalisation no. 384, Paris, October 1981.
5 M. Beaud, Le mirage de la croissance, Paris, Syros, 1983 is a sensitive account. Cf. also V. Lauber, The Political Economy of France, New York, Praeger, 1983. On the early strategy see V. Wright (ed.), Continuity and Change in France, London, Allen and Unwin, 1984. A sharp recent analysis is P. Hall, 'Socialism in one country; Mitterrand and the struggle to define a new economic policy' in P. Cerny and M. Schain (eds), Socialism, the State and Public Policy in France, London, Pinter, 1985, pp. 81–107.
6 M. Beaud, op. cit., p. 41.
7 P. Hall, op. cit., p. 84.
8 M. Beaud, op. cit., p. 131.
9 Ibid., p. 153.
10 J. Mandrin, Le Socialisme et la France, Paris, Le Sycomore, 1983.
11 Ibid., p. 119. The main arguments in this section are from pp. 97–192. For statements of alternative policy see 'Une politique économique pour la gauche', Volonté socialiste 15, March 1983 and the summary of Ceres' thirteenth colloquium in ibid., 9–10, June–August 1982.
12 J. Mandrin, op. cit., p. 114.
13 'Congrès de Bourg-en-Bresse: motions nationales d'orientation', Le Poing et la

rose 104, September 1983.

14 Beaud postulates two solutions – a more statist mode of production or an 'alternative' one concentrating on quality of production rather than quantity and attempting to move social relations in a more *autogestionnaire* direction. Ceres has retained little of this approach.

15 J.-P. Chevènement in *En jeu* 5, September 1983, p. 34–41.

16 Cf. the lampoon of the daily *Libération*, a spoof edition of which (baptised *Libation*) was given free to readers of *En jeu* 14, July–August 1984.

17 J. Julliard, 'Mitterrand entre le socialisme et la République', *Interventions* 1, November–December 1982, pp. 87–102.

18 Ibid. 10, August–December 1984.

19 On Ceres' new republicanism see J.-P. Chevènement, 'Pour réussir ensemble', *En jeu* 14, July–August 1984 and more generally his *Apprendre pour réussir*, Paris, Livre de Poche, 1985.

20 *Le Monde* and *Le Figaro* 24 March 1983.

21 P. Hall, op. cit., p. 93.

22 *Le Monde* 24 March 1983.

23 *En jeu* 5, September 1983, p. 38.

24 On socialist foreign policy generally see M.-C. Smouts, 'The external policy of F. Mitterrand', *International Affairs* 59, April 1983. For defence cf. J. Howorth, 'Consensus of silence: the French socialist party and defence policy under F. Mitterrand', ibid. 60, pp. 579–600.

25 J. Howorth, 'Defence Policy under François Mitterrand' in P. Cerny and M. Schain (eds), op. cit., pp. 125–6.

26 Mandrin, op. cit., pp. 193–226. For general Ceres statements on foreign policy see Non 14, July–August 1982, pp. 40–51 (the summary of Ceres' 13th colloquium) and Chevènement's Bourg speech in *Volonté socialiste* 22, November 1983.

27 Mandrin, op. cit., pp. 216–17.

28 The argument developed by Alain Joxe, a PSU member who writes for Ceres, holds that Soviet submarines depend heavily on a few easily targetable ports; thus the Pershings nullify them as a possible second-strike weapon. See *En jeu* 4, July–August 1983, pp. 24–5.

29 Cf. Chevènement's call for France to 'reforge historic links with Russia', *Le Monde* 11 May 1983.

30 We do not mean that Ceres is hostile to Solidarnosc, for declarations of support can be found; it is just that the fraction chooses not to stress them. It is striking that in *Le socialisme et la France* there is, as one reviewer pointed out, not one mention of Solidarnosc (G. Jourdan in *Pour l'autogestion*, June 1983).

31 *Le Monde* 18 December 1984.

32 Y. Poirmeur and C. Pannetier, 'Les Socialistes français, la crise et l'Europe', *Le Monde diplomatique*, April 1984.

33 This reform was somewhat unspecified but included making community preference compulsory and extra measures to favour Mediterranean and small producers. Clearly it is a reform which would appeal to French farmers, especially socialist ones, but hardly to the socialist voters of Northern Europe.

34 Mandrin, op. cit., p. 221.

35 Mandrin claims, apparently seriously (p. 216) that France is the only Western state which can be perceived as acting without neo-colonialist or imperialist motives. A former Ceres Third World specialist told us that, rhetoric apart, the

fraction's preferences lay with Westernising, industrialising regimes, often fairly authoritarian (Sadam Hussein's Iraq being a *locus classicus*). Certainly this fits well with the technocratic thrust of Ceres and helps explain its contempt for thirdworldist socialism, especially of the sentimental variety.

36   P.-L. Séguillon, 'Les cent premiers jours de la diplomatie socialiste', *Non* 9 October 1981, pp. 17–36.

37   Les Gracques, *Pour réussir à gauche*, Paris, Syros, 1983. For a comparison of this with Ceres' position in 1983 see D. Hanley, 'Le changement and its censors', *Journal of Area Studies*, Autumn 1983.

38   F. Bazin, *La Croix*, 28 May 1983; J.-Y. Lhomeau, *Le Monde* 24 September 1983.

39   The lack of realism of this AES is criticised by Paul Fabra in *Le Monde* 1 November 1983.

40   For Ceres' own view of its performance at Bourg see *En jeu* 7, November 1983, pp. 8–9 and *Volonté socialiste* 21 and 22, September and November 1983.

41   *Le Monde* 5 November 1983.

42   *Le Canard enchaîné* 2 November 1983.

43   *Le Figaro* 11 September 1983.

44   P. Avril, 'Le président, le parti et le groupe', *Pouvoirs* 20, 1982, pp. 115–26.

45   For examples of Ceres interventions in the *Comité directeur* in favour of the AES see *Volonté socialiste* 28 and 35, March and July 1984 respectively. Cf. also the bullish comments on the draft budget for 1985 by J.-P. Planchou, deputy for Paris in *Le Monde* 17 October 1984 and the plan for investment-led growth by A. Grjebine in *En jeu* 10 March 1984, which seeks to attract capital by confidence-building fiscal measures.

46   *Le Monde* 22 December 1984. The main bias of the new regulations is towards tighter conditions of financing for private schools while leaving their character intact.

47   *Le Monde* 24 August 1984.

48   *Le Monde* 7 December 1984.

49   *En Jeu* 10, March 1984, pp. 8–9.

CHAPTER 7

Ceres' achievement – appraisal and comparison

Tout grand dessin a besoin pour s'accomplir d'une pépinière d'hommes qui soit d'abord le foyer d'une ambition commune.

J.-P. Chevènement, 1984

7.1 CERES' ACHIEVEMENT – AN APPRAISAL

In Chapter 2 we identified a number of hurdles which a serious left fraction must surmount. Retrospectively it would seem that Ceres performance on this score has been honourable but thus far no more. Programmatically, the fraction has clearly helped instil some of the characteristic PS themes of the seventies – *autogestion*, commitment to left unity, a strategy of economic expansion based on nationalisations, planning and redistributive keynesianism. More particularly it has helped swing the party away from its long-standing Atlanticism and unilateralism towards a more independent line, based on a French deterrent. In terms of intra-party influence, it has registered significant percentages of support, occupied key posts on the national executive and controlled at times considerable numbers of federations. Its members have figured as councillors, mayors, deputies, and latterly as ministers. It has even spawned imitations abroad.[1]

This could not be said to amount to hegemony inside the PS, though it is widely admitted that characteristic Ceres preoccupations are shared well beyond the fraction's juridical limits (as measured by congress scores). Still less does it constitute ascendancy within the wider electorate; but then even few of the PS majority would nowadays believe that the victory of 1981 meant hegemony for their particular view of socialism either. These victories were the expression of a desire for moderate change, and subsequent failure to satisfy this has hit the party as a whole; though it is possible to claim that the majority will in the end suffer worse than Ceres. It is true that while in government the fraction proved unable to stem the tide of economic revisionism (indeed its main, defensive, successes were in the military field and limited at that). It is true also that the general ideological crisis of the PS which has grown apace since its entry into government, has also affected Ceres;[2] concepts like *autogestion* and the voluntarist assumptions about the economy have been found wanting and little has emerged to replace them save vague notions of 'modernisation' and the Republic. This crisis has hit all of the PS, but it is possible that Ceres has some advantages over its rivals here, and we shall discuss them later. Certainly the fraction has not disappeared, as some predicted. Indeed it has laid down a very useful base for the *après-Mitterrand*, which must soon begin. So long as the PS remains a plausible government party (which it will even if it loses office in 1986 or 1988) the fraction will have, we believe, a major role to play.

But let us first explain Ceres' success. Although our study has concentrated on subnational cases, it is still possible to single out some general features. First, organisation itself is a *sine qua non*, whether to take over a moribund federation or to fight a well-entrenched apparatus. This may be a truism, but if anyone was ever tempted to believe that the right ideas will triumph spontaneously by force of attraction, study of our federal examples and indeed of the struggles at national level in congress and CD will show the naïvety of such an idea. In democratic organisations issues are indeed decided by *rapports de force*, but those rapports have to be expressed in the end electorally. This means arguing with people and persuading them to attend meetings, to ensure that the desired policies are carried and, once carried, implemented and not reversed. Ceres knew this and worked at it. Indeed the greatest tribute to its organisation was that it forced its rivals, especially Mauroy and Rocard, to do the same; even the Mitterrandists who simply inherited much of the old SFIO apparatus were forced to organise more so as to beat off this challenge. A crucial level of organisation is the federal one. Although France is a centralised state, this works two ways. On the one hand political structures are vertical and more powers are exercised by the centre; but on the other, the department has become a locus of activity and power and will be more so as the decentralisation laws progress. As local office is also very much a springboard to national (in a much more direct way than in the UK), this puts a premium on local struggles as part of the conquest of influence and also necessitates the emergence of able local élites who must to some extent be autonomous from Paris to succeed. Ceres has responded particularly well to this challenge.

The quality of élites is in fact another key element. Without necessarily endorsing fully the maxim at the head of this chapter, it seems indubitable that able and committed leadership played a crucial role in Ceres' rise, nationally in the sense of creating an ideology and organisational framework, then keeping it visible in the media, and then locally in terms of the alliance strategies pursued. Our case studies have shown the breadth of such strategies and the degree of compromise used in the pursuit of influence. We should perhaps take this opportunity to rebut the suspicion that many Ceres federal operations are simply opportunistic, with local bosses seeking power for its own sake. We believe this to be true only in a minority of cases, and one proof of this is the fact that overwhelmingly local Ceres leaders continue to support the national orientations of the fraction. In many cases it would have been simpler to do a deal with local rivals before congress and thus guarantee one's own position comfortably. But this does not seem to have happened much, with the major departures being principled as in the Pierret split. The fact is that if the party is to be shaped as Ceres wishes, then some degree of power must be won; and the French system is such that this means winning first at local level. Every search for power entails a strategy, though, and it is a tribute to the quality of Ceres élites that they have proved so inventive here.

Organisation and leadership are crucial but alone they will not cement a fraction. Ideology is vital here. We contend that Ceres developed a firmly rooted left ideology, a sort of Sorelian myth of the principled, self-managing socialist party. It was transformative but had none of the bureaucratic undertones which many feared hidden beneath the discourse of the PCF. Too crude to please scientific analysts (but they are rarely political operatives) it proved able to galvanise much of the young talent flooding into the party after 1971. The ideology had its weaknesses and even its contradictions, but also an underlying consistency – not least in its resolve to ally the changing of French society with a distinct world role for a socialist France and its strong emotional commitment to the French national tradition. This is indeed the most striking and durable feature of Ceres ideology. This ideology helped build not just a machine but a real activist community, dedicated to a particular vision of socialism, but compatible with that of the PS as a whole and realisable only through the latter as the key partner in the left government. This community suffered damage – some of it self-inflicted – during the battles of the late seventies but it emerged at the end slimmer, more exclusive perhaps, but no less determined.

Other factors specific to the party also worked in Ceres' favour. One was historical and institutional, namely the fact that the PS has always been (cf. Section 2.2) highly fractionalised and that as a result members have come to see this almost as a way of life. This made it hard for enemies, much as they tried, to present Ceres as foreigners, part of a sinister conspiracy which had settled into the party. Left fractions have always had their place, from Guesde to Zyromski/Pivert to the Mollet of 1946. Thus when the fragments of 1971 were reassembled Ceres could take its place perfectly normally. There was one largely unwritten proviso however – that Ceres (or any other group) know when to set limits to its fractional activity. Ceres has usually known when to call a halt.[3] Excesses like Chevènement's suspension in 1970 for publicly attacking the leadership and the illegal federation at Nancy have been rare. Usually Ceres has taken its critiques to the limit of the tolerable (cf. the 1983 Bourg congress) but always drawn back when further action would have meant either disciplinary reprisals or a weakening of the party's electoral prospects; it is in the (nowadays rare) intervals between elections that the fraction's comments are at their most barbed.[4] Having chosen the reformist party it logically must remain there until it can win hegemony; and the road to hegemony contains many 'couleuvres à avaler'. This is the perennial dilemma of left fractions – how many shortcomings or compromises to be endured now in the name of a hypothetical conquest of hegemony in the future? Coates and others have long ago concluded that the lefts are wasting their time and would be better employed outside the party in openly revolutionary organisations.[5] Only history will say who is right in this particular gamble. For the present we may conclude that having chosen to work within reformism, Ceres has been logical enough to assume the constant compromise with others which this choice necessarily entails.

Ceres adroitness was also linked to the quality and strategies of its opponents. In the early days Ceres was challenged by Poperenism for the position of the left pole. Yet by 1973 the Poperenists had fallen so far back as to be forced to throw in their lot with Mitterrand. To be sure they put a brave face on it, suggesting that the PS was now sufficiently anchored on the left to justify their gambit. But this blitheness conceals a number of questions which only further research will answer. How well did the Poperenites realise the need to wage a federal and local battle to advance their ideas? Why were they unable to convert their initial capital of goodwill into durable support? Are these two questions related? And what were the inadequacies of their leadership in all this? The answers to these questions would shed valuable light on the early years of the PS, still not well understood in general. As it is, we may admire the sheer militant effort put in by Ceres after 1971; but that alone does not explain the eclipse of their rivals which enabled that effort to fructify. As for the Mitterrandists during this time they had enough to do in solidifying their own somewhat heteroclite and largely inherited machinery without worrying over much about a left rival. As for Mollettism, its by now largely discredited remains had largely settled for a place with Mitterrand or in some cases Mauroy. Thus the early inattention or failings of rivals allowed Ceres to rapidly build a sizeable base in a growing party. By the time the majority, reinforced by the arrival of the Rocardians, had got round to attacking the troublesome leftists it was probably too late for a bureaucratic or ideological offensive to succeed. Chevènement's remark about *being able* to create a *rapport de forces* assumes its full flavour here.

There are also factors relevant to the wider political environment – the first of these is the party system. The PCF is crucial here. With France in the 1970s bipolarised into a two-by-two system, with four participants of roughly equal strength, PCF behaviour was vital for the PS as a whole and for Ceres in particular. But there is no simple relationship between these three forces and indeed the problem varies over time. Early on in the full unitary phase when there was much public support still to be had, the party as a whole and Ceres could benefit, while the PCF stagnated. As the latter's resentment grew at a deal which suited only its rival and as its hostility increased, so did the dangers for Ceres. Given its chosen proximity to the PCF it was always likely to lose support so long as public (and increasingly party) opinion wanted a left government, but without PCF strings attached. Rocard over-read this trend in opinion and was too blunt with the PCF in public, whereas Mitterrand, with his unitary rhetoric but refusal to concede much in terms of programme or government participation, seems to have judged the public mood better. Ceres however clung close to the PCF until very late in the day and its Metz score suggests that it probably suffered proportionally.

This question will remain vital to the fraction's future, however, unless the PCF pales into total insignificance (unlikely now, given the impending change to PR for parliamentary elections). Indeed the change in the electoral system will be capital for the future of PCF and Ceres alike. Its first effect will be autonomise the PCF, as its hard-core vote will probably stabilise somewhere between 12 and 15 per cent, with roughly that percentage of deputies. Assuming then that a Mitterrand government after a left defeat in 1986 were to work on the basis of some 'centre–left' arrangement, without PCF support, and assuming it to be no more successful than the present one, there would open up a considerable space for a left opposition – both within the PS (for many members would never countenance a centre–left alliance) and of course beyond it, including the PCF. Much would depend on how the latter behaved – and at present signs of renewal are few – but if ever there were the impulse for a broad-left opposition, Ceres would be well placed to influence it. All this is pure speculation but it does bring out the importance of the electoral system and of the PCF connection in explaining Ceres progress; both will continue to influence it decisively.

A wider factor which aided Ceres was the changing nature of French society. The rise of a salaried middle class with high levels of education, in a polity marked by a tendency to express issues in highly ideological form, created the demand for a political vehicle to express the aspirations of such groups. Pace its workerist language the PS has come nearest to satisfying these demands. For members of this class with a political bent it was a heaven-sent opportunity. The very fragmentation of the PS with its multiplicity of structures, all providing opportunities for activity, and even more so its flexible discourse, which could touch wide-ranging sensibilities, made it a perfect vehicle. Ceres took at least its fair share of this new support. At its height its ideological flexibility was such that it catered simultaneously for sensibilities ranging from thirdworldist catholics to sectarian *laïcard* Guesdists, apostles of a decentralised quality-orientated economy to strident productivists; what held them together was the novelty of Ceres' *autogestionnaire* discourse and mistrust of the *anciens*. But there are limits to how far discourse, even when accompanied by electoral victory, can paper over real cultural differences. It is thus no accident that once electoral progress declined, these differences burst out. Nevertheless the substantive point stands, namely that the new middle classes were very receptive to a radical yet plausible left discourse, which Ceres was able to concoct better than most.

A final cause of Ceres' rise is what we might call the oppositional factor. By 1971 it had been fifteen years since the last period of socialist government, Mollet's, and this had been a coalition; by 1981 the gap had swollen to a quarter of a century. Thus memories of socialist failures were not *immediately* present in people's minds. They were certainly present, for every left fraction and every party trying to renew itself needs some kind of anti-model or bogyman to which it can point as a sort of exorcism; avoid men like this and mistakes will never be made again. This means a representation in the party's folk-memory of an idealised villain ('the party right'), which may actually have been an obstacle to serious reflection about the limits and possibilities of socialist parties and their lefts. Had Mollet's period of office – or *a fortiori* Blum's – been nearer in time, there might have been more reflection not only on the shortcomings of these leaders but also on the inability of the lefts of their day to do anything about it. In other words Ceres' left critiques gained from the fact that the social-democratic bogyman whom they attacked was far away and ill-known. Now that the PS has a recent and visible record in government it will be interesting to see if the left benefits quite so much from criticising this experiment – the more so as it was actually a participant.

To conclude then, Ceres success can be explained generally by a number of macro-considerations, which concern the nature of the electorate, the party and electoral system and the long socialist absence from office. But these only created conditions in which a left pole might succeed; for potential to become reality Ceres needed a resilient organisation and leadership at national and federal levels. These elements could then, using another key factor, an operative ideology, weld something resembling not just a fractional group but an ideological community. These leaders then needed great tactical flexibility and above all awareness of when not to overstep the line. Because most of these conditions were well met and because of failures by rivals, Ceres was able to succeed reasonably well as a left fraction.

7.2 BEYOND THE PS – A COMPARATIVE PERSPECTIVE

If the PS is an interesting case in itself, we are still led to ask what the experiences of Ceres within it can tell us about the phenomenon of left fractions in general. There is still much research to be done on these groups from a comparative perspective and we are aware that there is a long way to go before any durable hypothesis can be evolved. Nevertheless it might be possible to suggest a general schema for the success or failure of left fractions in reformist socialist parties. Clearly the more parties which could be incorporated into the analysis, the more plausible it would be and there is still much work to be done on different national cases. But on the basis of what we have seen hitherto we might just be able to glimpse tentatively an emergent model.

It seems possible to isolate a number of variables which may have relevance for the success or failure of a left pole. If we look first at systemic factors, a key one would seem to be the presence of an alternative radical party, particularly a communist party. Without such a party, meaningful left politics is likely to be confined to the space of the reformist party, making the opportunity for the expansion of its left pole potentially greater. With it, the left socialists will always have to face the problem of relating to it without capitulating or seeming to. There is of course nothing axiomatic about either of these possibilities and we still need to know what happens to left socialists when the communists collapse with relative suddenness, as in Spain.

We also need to consider what happens when there is a plausible centre–left alternative, i.e. when the party is squeezed on its right. The British case is too recent to conclude, but in countries where such forces are viable even if small (the Netherlands perhaps) it is not clear that this necessarily strengthens the hand of the left. In fact such centre–left parties are usually found in multi-party systems, often with some element of PR, where coalitions are the rule. This suggests that the key element in the success or failure of left fractions may have less to do with their parties' rivals on left or right than with the way their party performs in government. We would suggest that loss of office following a period of disappointing rule should be a good opportunity for a left pole,[6] when the experience is repeated twice over (as in the British case) then its chances should be high indeed. But in such cases the left is likely to find itself rising in a party whose overall stock is shrinking; its victory may thus prove Pyrrhic, and the problems of winning hegemony beyond the party will loom larger than ever.

A crucial question is whether the left can identify with any wider, not specifically socialist, culture. We have tried to show how Ceres has used an underlying resentment of Anglo-Saxon hegemony in French culture and attempted to link it to a concept of a Latin and Mediterranean France, seeing France as heir to a progressive tradition of foreign involvement. If such a cultural storehouse can be tapped it may prove a useful adjunct for a voluntarist left; the francophone Belgian PSB has a left which seems to have embarked on this particular task. To some extent this gambit depends upon the saliency of the national question in the country concerned and on its historical legacy; it would be hard for instance for a party such as the Dutch PvdA to find fertile veins to exploit here. But the same is not necessarily true of the Labour party and its left. This now operates in a country in decline, but where myths about the national past still play an extremely potent role. The Labour left might have much to gain by attempting to explain Britain's declining situation in terms of the two-bloc hegemony and exploring the possibility of a specifically British mode of development in conformity with the historical legacy of Britain.

Such subcurrents need careful handling however if they are not to box the left into over-narrow categories of support. A salutary example of this danger is provided by the example of secularism, long one of the most potent allies of continental socialism. We have seen the problems which Ceres experienced over this question. This raises the question of how far left socialists can use elements from non-socialist culture, and how far they are at the mercy of these. Again there is no automatic answer and we must look beyond such general considerations at the working of the parties themselves.

Party traditions are clearly important. If fractionalism was always accepted, as in France and Italy, then the left should have a head start. In countries like the UK, where one united party emerged early and opposition was forced into marginality (as with the ILP), it becomes much harder to organise a serious left opposition. Not only is the party apparatus tougher and better equipped, but unity is likely to be a key element of party culture, so much so that fractionalists are likely to be despised as troublemakers or even interlopers from outside.

But party structure is a more crucial variable than party culture. A party of individual members offers *a priori* a higher chance of organising a successful left fraction; this is even truer if the party uses internal PR as in the PS. Parties with federal-type structures combining individual members with categorial are proportionally harder for the left – first because of the sheer multiplicity of the structure with its different levels of unequal weight, each with their own decision-making process. This makes coordination of a sustained fractional effort difficult. More crucially though, these parties have to satisfy different demands – global transformation of society and satisfaction of much more immediate interest. The higher the pressure of the latter, the harder the left's task, for it is unlikely that the two demands can be demonstrated to coincide very readily.

Whatever the strength of the above determinants there still remains the organisation (in the widest sense) of the left itself. It must have a workable ideology, sound leaders at all levels and ample activists with energy and ability. Even if all the above conditions combine to the favour of the left (a most unlikely assumption) it will still come to nothing unless it combines these organisational features in good measure. Voluntarism may not be able to achieve everything for the left, but without it it will accomplish nothing.

We might conclude then that the best possibility for a left fraction lay in a country with a strong underlying national problematic where the socialist left, alone or in coalition, had performed badly more than once within recent memory, yet where the forces immediately to the left and right of the reformist party were somehow unable to erode its dominant position as the force of change. Ideally this party would need to have known a tradition of internal pluralism, with a leadership unable to stifle dissent by bureaucratic means. Finally it would need to be a party without sectional cleavages, purely devoted to social transformation. Considering the developed states, it seems hard to spy a party that comes anywhere near meeting these conditions; and if there was one, it would still only mean that the left fraction had a good chance. The problems of winning hegemony beyond the party would be as large as ever. Small wonder that the lot of left socialists is a hard one. But it is in their nature to persevere and they will be with us for a long time yet.

7.3 POSTSCRIPT – CERES AND THE FUTURE

What does the future hold for Ceres? It is clearly still a long way from achieving its ambitions, but we cannot say that it has been without effect. Nor should we write off its prospects.

Ceres has existed barely twenty years and its party has had one term of office. This alone should rule out hasty predictions. But there are a number of factors to be considered. First, when Mitterrand's career finally ends, probably at the latest in 1988 with either refusal to stand again or defeat, the problem of his succession will become posed. Secondly, even if the PS loses office by then, its status as the main opposition party to the returning right will remain. Thirdly, then, the party must choose carefully its leader, who will also be its future presidential candidate. Many would back the man who will probably be Mitterrand's choice, Laurent Fabius. If it chooses him the PS will, rhetoric apart, be opting for continuation of the orthodox style of social-democracy which has prevailed since 1982. It must be asked how far this will be able to carry an electoral majority.

The other main candidate, Michel Rocard, is now a less likely winner, not least in that the substance of some of his policy options and indeed some of his discourse has gradually found its way into the practice of the party majority during its conduct of government. Fabius in short has stolen some of Rocard's clothes and if his high opinion poll standing continues, the advantages of a Rocardian leadership might be less apparent to many party élites. The Rocardians may find it harder now to organise their support within the party, since the Mitterrandist majority has for years now devoted much of its efforts to the slow but steady weakening of Rocardian networks within the federations. Rocard's resignation from government in April 1985 when the introduction of PR was announced looked like the first move in a long overdue bid for leadership; but it was probably too late by then.

The party's choice might then in the end lie between Fabius and Chevènement, right and left. Much will depend on the wider environment when the choice is made, particularly the behaviour of the PCF. Ceres and Chevènement will offer blood, sweat and tears – a programme of statist productivism, bolstered by an ethic of Republican civics and solidarity, all of it in the context of defending France's place in the world. What they propose will be seen as distinct from the modernisers in the majority, so the party will have a choice. Logically the right starts as favourite. But if domestic and international circumstances become more sombre and if the PS feels that French people are receptive to a message of 'public safety' (the 1793 slogan which Ceres has been using of late), then Ceres might, thanks to its diligent espousal of the national interest emerge as a more plausible alternative. The long patient overtures towards the patriotic right, towards those Republican sectors of society that take seriously the values of effort and discipline stressed in *La République moderne* might begin to pay off. Certainly the left which a Ceres presidential campaign would incarnate would have moved some way from that of 1970. There would be less participation and more discipline; less criticism, more authority. But the underlying posits would still remain. Ceres is still a left which hates capitalism and seeks to transform it and which has always seen national mobilisation as a key to that transformation.

Whether a Ceres-led PS could win an election and what it would do in office may be left to speculation. For the moment the prospects for Ceres are far from depressing. As the economic crisis deepens and the modernisers' efforts flag, the long odds against the socialist left might shorten. As a celebrated adage from a different struggle has it, social-democracy's danger might yet be Ceres' opportunity.

NOTES TO CHAPTER 7

1 M. Duytschaever, 'Aspiration et stratégie de la gauche du PSB en Flandre', *Socialisme* 127, February 1975, pp. 225–34.

2 P. Perrineau, 'Le PS de l'affirmation à la crise d'identité', *Projet* 187, July–August 1984, pp. 796–801.

3 The most difficult issue in this context has invariably been the distance to be kept from the PCF. The withdrawal of the latter from government in mid-1984 only half solved the problem. If it seemed to presage the end of left unity, it promised by the same stroke to remove one of the more important props of Ceres identity. The fraction's reaction seems to have been to avoid public statements as far as possible and practise *attentisme* (wait and see what the PCF would do). The problem also affects the other fractions besides Ceres, of course.

4 This awareness of the limits which must not be transgressed if unity is to be maintained is something which Ceres shared with Aneurin Bevan, though Ceres' whole approach to fractionalism is quite different.

5 D. Coates, 'Space and Agency in the Transition to Socialism', *New Left Review* 135, September–October 1982, pp. 49–63.

6 Recent examples would be the growth of the left in the Swedish SAP after the 1976 defeat, as evidenced in the growing interest in the Meidner plan, and the developments in the SPD since Schmidt's loss of office.

SELECT BIBLIOGRAPHY

This bibliography lists work of direct relevance to the topic studied and should be read as a supplement to the references given in the notes to each chapter. Unless otherwise stated, English titles are published in London, French ones in Paris.

1 MAJOR WORKS BY CERES AND ITS ACTIVISTS

Le Ceres par lui-même, Bourgois, 1978
L'Enlèvement de l'Europe, Entente, 1979
M. Charzat, Georges Sorel et la révolution au XXe. siècle, Hachette, 1977
— Otto Bauer et l'austromarxisme, Martinsart, 1977
— Le Syndrôme de la gauche, Hachette, 1981
M. Charzat and G. Toutain, Le Ceres – un combat pour le socialisme, Calmann-Levy, 1975
J.-P. Chevènement, Apprendre pour entreprendre, Livre de Poche, 1985
— La droite nationaliste devant l'Allemagne, IEP mémoire, 1960
— Etre socialiste aujourd'hui, Cana, 1980
— Les Socialistes, les communistes et les autres, Aubier-Montaigne, 1977
— Le vieux, la crise, le neuf, Flammarion, 1975
J.-P. Chevènement and P. Messmer, Le Service militaire, Balland, 1977
P. Guidoni, Histoire du nouveau PS, Téma, 1973
— La Cité rouge, Toulouse, Privat, 1978
J. Mandrin (pseudonym of various Ceres leaders), L'Enarchie ou les mandarins de la société bourgeoise, Table Ronde, 1967
— Le Socialisme et la France, Le Sycomore, 1983
— Socialisme ou socialmédiocratie, Le Seuil, 1969
D. Motchane, Clés pour le socialisme, Seghers, 1973
L. Praire and C. Pierre, Plan et autogestion, Flammarion, 1976
Socialisme et multinationales – colloque de la fédération de Paris du PS, Flammarion 1976

2 CERES PRESS, REVIEWS, ETC.

Cahiers du Ceres (original theoretical review) 1967–1972 (11 numbers)
Cahiers socialistes (ad hoc issues on specialised topics) 1974–1977 (7 numbers)
Le Crayon entre les dents (student monthly) 1976–1978 (13 numbers)
Frontières (theoretical monthly) December 1972 – August 1975 (24 numbers) replaced by Repères September 1975 – December 1979 (43 numbers running consecutively to those of Frontières.)
Non! Repères pour le Socialisme (two-monthly review) May 1980 – December 1982 (16 numbers), replaced by En jeu, pour la République et le socialisme (monthly)
Volonté socialiste. Internal bulletin which took over from the roneotyped Bulletin mensuel. Usually in a 4-page format it has had the following frequency: Volonté socialiste, bulletin du Ceres January 1970 – June 1975 (39 numbers); Volonté socialiste, nouvelle série November 1975 – March 1981 (98 numbers); Volonté socialiste, nouvelle formule from March 1981. Currently appearing fortnightly.

3 WORKS ON FRENCH SOCIALISM

Anon., *Le Gauchisme, maladie congénitale du PS*, Libertés, 1977

J. Attali, *La nouvelle Economie française*, Flammarion, 1977

G. Ayache and M. Fantoni, *Les Barons du PS*, Fayolle, 1977

P. Bacot, *Les Dirigeants du Parti Socialiste*, Lyon, Presses Universitaires de Lyon, 1979

D. Baker, 'The Politics of Socialist Protest in France: the Left Wing of the Socialist Party, 1921–39', *Journal of Modern History* XLIII, March 1971, pp. 2–41

M. Beaud, *Le Mirage de la croissance*, Syros, 1984

D. Bell (ed.), *Contemporary French Political Parties*, Croom Helm, 1982

D. Bell and B. Criddle, *The French socialist party*, Oxford University Press, 1984

D. Bell and E. Shaw (eds), *The Left in France*, Nottingham, Spokesman, 1983

D. Bensaid, *L'Anti-Rocard*, La Brèche, 1980

A. Bergounioux, *Force Ouvrière*, Seuil, 1975

M. Berson, P. Ory and G. Delfau, *Les Chemins de d'Unité*, Téma, 1974

J.-M. Bichat, 'Le Socialisme dans le Midi de la France', *Revue Française d'études politiques méditerranéennes* 17, May 1976, pp. 53–69

J.-F. Bizot, L. Mercadet and P. Van Eersel, *Au Parti des socialistes*, Grasset, 1975

D. Bleitrach, J. Lojkine, E. Oary, R. Delacroix and C. Mahieu, *Classe ouvrière et social-démocratie: Lille et Marseille*, Editions Sociales, 1982

D. Blume, R. Bourderon, J. Burles and J. Charles, *Histoire du réformisme*, Editions Sociales, 1976

L. Bodin and J. Touchard, *Front Populaire*, Colin, 1961

J.-M. Borzeix, *Mitterrand lui-même*, Stock, 1973

A. Boublil, *Le Socialisme industriel*, PUF, 1977

B. Brown, *Socialism of a Different Kind*, New York, Greenwood, 1982

C. Bunodière and L. Cohen-Solal, *Les nouveaux Socialistes*, Téma, 1977

R. Cayrol, 'Les militants du PS', *Projet* 88, September–October, 1974, pp. 929–40.

—'Le PS et l'autogestion', *Projet* 98, September 1975

— 'L'univers politique des militants socialistes', *Revue française de science politique* XXV, February 1975, pp. 23–52

— 'PS – enfin les difficultés commencent', *Projet* 118, September 1977, pp. 917–28

— 'Le godillot et le commissaire politique: six contradictions à propos du PS', *Projet* January 1982, pp. 32–41

R. Cayrol and K. Evin, 'Comment contrôler l'union: les relations PC–PS depuis 1971', *Projet* 121, January 1978, pp. 64–74

R. Cayrol and C. Ysmal, 'Les militants du PS – originalité et diversités', *Projet* 165, May 1982, pp. 572–86

P. Cerny and M. Schain (eds), *Socialism, the State and Public Policy in France*, Pinter, 1985

J.-P. Chagnollaud, 'La Fédération socialiste de Meurthe et Moselle', *Annales de l'Est* 1978, pp. 137–66

R. Chapuis, *Les Chrétiens et le socialisme*, Calmann-Lévy, 1976

J. Charlot, 'Le double enchainement de la défaite et de la victoire', *Revue politique et parlementaire*, May–June 1981, pp. 15–28

X. Charvet, *Le Ceres en Savoie, 1968–79*, thèse de doctorat, Grenoble IEP, 1980

G. Codding and W. Safran, *Ideology and Politics – the Socialist Party of France*, Boulder, Colorado, Westview Press, 1979

J. Colton, *Leon Blum, Humanist in Politics*, New York, Knopf, 1966

Y. Craipeau, 'Le Ceres et les problèmes de la transition', *Critique socialiste* 22, March–April 1975, pp. 15–28

M. Dagnaud and D. Mehl, *L'Elite rose*, Ramsay, 1982

J.-M. Donegani, 'Itinéraire politique et cheminement réligieux; l'exemple des catholiques militants du PS', RFSP XXIX, August–October, 1979, pp. 693–738

F.-G. Dreyfus, *Histoire des gauches, 1940–74*, Grasset, 1975

O. Duhamel, *La Gauche et la Cinquième République*, PUF, 1980

A. Duroy and M. Schneider, *Le Roman de la rose*, Seuil, 1982

M. Duverger, *Lettre ouverte aux socialistes*, Albin Michel, 1976

C. Estier, *Journal d'un fédéré*, Fayard, 1970

K. Evin, *Michel Rocard ou l'art du possible*, Simoen, 1979

R. Ferretti, 'Les militants de la fédération du Bas-Rhin du PS', *Nouvelle Revue Socialiste* 14–15, 1975, pp. 8–16

J.-J. Fiechter, *Le Socialisme français de l'affaire Dreyfus à la grande guerre*, Geneva, Droz, 1965

D. Gallie, *In Search of The New Working Class*, Cambridge University Press, 1978

— *Social Inequality and Class Radicalism in France and Britain*, Cambridge University Press, 1983

F. Gardois and A. Boyer, 'La Messe en latin', *Faire*, 39–40, January–February, 1979, pp. 29–33 and 39–47

F.-O. Giesbert, *François Mitterrand*, Seuil, 1977

H. Goldberg, *The Life of Jean Jaurès*, Madison, University of Wisconsin Press, 1962

R. Gombin, *Les Socialistes et la guerre*, Mouton, 1970

C. Goux, *Sortir de la crise*, Flammarion, 1978

Les Gracques, *Pour réussir à gauche*, Syros, 1983

B. Graham, *French Socialism and Tripartism*, Weidenfeld and Nicolson, 1965

N. Greene, *Crisis and Decline – the French Socialist Party in the Popular Front Era*, New York, Cornell University Press, 1969

A. Guédé and G. Fabre-Rosane, 'Sociologie des candidats aux élections législatives de mars 1978', RFSP XXVIII, October 1978, pp. 840–58

A. Guédé and S. Rozenblum, 'Les candidats aux élections de 1978 et 1981', RFSP XXXI, October–December 1981, pp. 982–99

D. Guérin, *Front Populaire, révolution manquée*, Maspéro, 1970

G. Guille, *La Gauche la plus bete*, Table Ronde, 1970

H. Hamon and P. Rotman, *L'Effet Rocard*, Stock, 1980

— *La Deuxième Gauche*, Ramsay, 1982

P. Hardouin, 'Les caractéristiques sociologiques du PS', RFSP XXVIII, April 1978, pp. 220–56

E. Hinterman, *Pour une social-démocratie française*, Albin Michel, 1979

C. Hurtig, *De la SFIO au nouveau parti socialiste*, Colin, 1970

R. W. Johnson, *The Long March of the French Left*, Macmillan, 1981

D. Johnstone, 'How the French Left learned to love the Bomb', *New Left Review*, 146, July 1984, pp. 5–36

J.-P. Joubert, *Révolutionnaires de la SFIO*, FNSP, 1976

P. Joxe, *Parti socialiste*, Epi, 1973

T. Judt, *La Reconstruction du parti socialiste 1921–6*, FNSP, 1976

— *Socialism in Provence, 1871–1914: a Study in the Origins of the Modern French Left*, Cambridge University Press, 1980

J. Julliard, 'La logique partisane – l'exemple du PS', *Esprit* XLVII, 1979, pp. 65–77

— 'Mitterrand entre le Socialisme et la République', *Interventions* I, November–December 1982, pp. 87–102

M. Kesselman, 'Systèmes de pouvoir et cultures politiques au sein des partis politiques français', *Revue francaise de sociologie* XIII 1972, pp. 485–515

J. Kergoat, *Le Parti socialiste*, Le Sycomore, 1983

J. Lacouture, *Léon Blum*, Seuil, 1977

— *Mendès France*, Seuil, 1981

J. Lagroye and H. Machin, *Le factionnalisme dans le PS français*, ECPR Workshop Paper, 1980

L. Laignel, *Les Exclusions du PS depuis 1971*, DES mémoire Paris I, 1976

S. Lash, *The Militant Worker; Class and Radicalism in France and America*, Heinemann, 1984

V. Lauber, *The Political Economy of France from Pompidou to Mitterrand*, New York, Praeger, 1983

B. Lazic, *L'Echec permanent: l'alliance socialiste–communiste*, Laffont, 1978

— 'Le Ceres, ou les singes de Lénine', *Commentaire* I, 1978, pp. 39–52

G. Lefranc, *Le Mouvement socialiste sous la Troisième République*, Payot, 1963

— *Les Gauches en France*, Payot, 1973

— *Histoire du Front Populaire*, Payot, 1974

G. Le Gall, 'Le nouvel ordre electoral', *Revue politique et parlementaire*, July–August 1981, pp. 1–32

— 'Du recul de la droite vers l'hégémonie du PS', *Revue politique et parlementaire*, May–June 1981, pp. 29–41

N. Lieber, 'Ideology and Tactics of the French Socialist party', *Government and Opposition* XII, Autumn 1977, pp. 455–73

D. Ligou, *Histoire du socialisme en France, 1871–1961*, PUF, 1962

D. Lindenberg, *Le Marxisme introuvable*, Calmann-Levy, 1975

D. Loschak, *La Convention des Institutions Républicaines*, PUF, 1971

J. Marcus, *French Socialism in the Crisis Years*, New York, Praeger, 1958

C. Marjolin, *Une fédération du nouveau parti socialiste: étude structurelle de la fédération de Paris, 1969–73*, DES mémoire Paris I, 1973

P. Mauroy, *Héritiers de l'avenir*, Livre de Poche, 1981

F. Mitterrand, *Ma part de vérité*, Fayard, 1969

— *Un Socialisme du possible*, Seuil, 1970

— *La Paille et le grain*, Flammarion, 1975

— *Politique*, Fayard, 1977

— *Ici et maintenant*, Fayard, 1980

J. Mossuz, *Les Clubs et la politique en France*, Colin, 1970

A. Noland, *The Founding of the French Socialist Party*, Cambridge (Mass.), Harvard University Press, 1956

N. Nugent and D. Lowe, *The Left in France*, Macmillan, 1982

J.-L. Parodi and P. Perrineau, 'Les Leaders socialistes devant l'Opinion', *Projet* 134, April 1979, pp. 475–92

Parti Socialiste, *Changer la vie*, Flammarion, 1972

— *Programme commun de gouvernement: propositions socialistes pour l'actualisation*, Flammarion, 1977

— *Pour le socialisme: livre des assises*, Stock, 1974

— *Projet socialiste*, Flammarion, 1980

— *Statuts*, Club socialiste du livre, 1982

P. Pellissier, *L'Idéologie rocardienne, repérage et articulation des concepts fondamentaux*, DES mémoire, Paris, IEP, 1981

P. Perrineau, 'Le PS, de l'affirmation à la crise d'identité', *Projet* July–August, 1984, pp. 796–801

T. Pfister, *Les Socialistes*, Albin Michel, 1977

A. Philip, *Les Socialistes*, Seuil, 1967

M.-A. Poisson, *La Vie Nouvelle et la politique, 1968–71*. DES mémoire Paris IEP, 1972

J. Poperen, *La Gauche française, 1958–65*, Fayard, 1969

— *L'Unité de la gauche, 1965–72*, Fayard, 1975

— *Le nouveau Contrat socialiste*, Ramsay, 1985

H. Portelli, *Le Socialisme français tel qu'il est*, PUF, 1980

— 'Au rendez-vous du PS', *Esprit* XLV, April–May 1977, pp. 178–84

— 'Que se passe-t-il au PS?', *Projet* 121, January 1978, pp. 55–63

— 'Guerre de succession au PS', *Projet* 136, June 1979, pp. 739–42

— 'Nouvelles classes moyennes et nouveau parti socialiste' in G. Lavau, G. Grunberg and N. Mayer, *L'Univers politique des classes moyennes*, FNSP, 1983, pp. 258–73

— 'Les socialistes et l'exercice du pouvoir', *Projet* 168, October 1982, pp. 921–32

— 'L'intégration du PS à la Cinquième République' in O. Duhamel and J.-L. Parodi (eds), *La Constitution de la Cinquième République*, FNSP, 1985, pp. 230–41

G. Pudlowski, *Jean Poperen et l'UGCS*, Saint Germain des Prés, 1975

R. Quilliot, *La SFIO et l'exercice du pouvoir, 1944–58*, Fayard, 1972

J. Rabaut, *Tout est possible: les gauchistes français, 1929–44*, Denoel, 1974

M. Reberioux, *La République radicale*, Seuil, 1975

R. Remond, 'Echec de la gauche: est-ce la faute des catholiques?', *Projet* 126, June 1978, pp. 732–6

P. Renouvin and R. Remond (eds), *Léon Blum, chef de gouvernement*, Colin, 1965

P. Rimbert, 'Le parti socialiste SFIO' in *Partis politiques et classes sociales en France*, Colin, 1955

J.-P. Rioux, *Révolutionnaires du Front Populaire*, UGE, 1973

M. Rocard, *Parler vrai*, Seuil, 1979

— *Questions à l'état socialiste*, Marabout, 1972

M. Rocard and J. Gallus, *L'Inflation au coeur*, Gallimard, 1975

G. Rochu, *Marseille – les années Defferre*, Moreau, 1983

J. Rollet, *Le Parti socialiste et l'autogestion*, thèse de doctorat, Paris, IEP, 1982

P. Rosanvallon, *L'Age de l'autogestion*, Seuil, 1976

P. Rosanvallon and P. Viveret, *Pour une nouvelle culture politique*, Seuil, 1977

Y. Roucaute, *Le Parti socialiste*, Huisman, 1983

M. Sadoun, *Les Socialistes sous l'occupation*, FNSP, 1982

N. Sadoun, *Les courants de gauche au PS*, DES mémoire Paris I, 1973

J. Sagnes, *Le Midi rouge*, Anthropos, 1982

A. Salomon, *PS: la mise à nu*, Laffont, 1980

A. Savary, *Pour le nouveau parti socialiste*, Seuil, 1970

W. Schonfield, 'La stabilité des dirigeants de partis politiques: le personnel des directions du parti socialiste et du mouvement gaulliste', *RFSP* XXX, June 1980, pp. 477–505

— 'La stabilité des dirigeants des partis politiques' *RFSP* XXX, August 1980, pp. 846–86

H. Simmons, *French Socialists in Search of a Role*, Ithaca, NY, Cornell University Press, 1970

J. Touchard, *La Gauche en France depuis 1900*, Seuil, 1977

A. Touraine, *L'Après-socialisme*, Grasset, 1980

G. Toutain, *Le Ceres – tentative de renouveau du PS*, DES mémoire, Paris faculté de droit, 1973

R. Verdier, *PS–PC, une lutte pour l'entente*, Seghers, 1976
— *Bilan d'une scission*, Gallimard, 1981
P. Viveret, 'Le Ceres entre le vieux et le neuf', *Faire* 30, April 1978, pp. 36–40
— 'La gauche piégée dans l'Etat', *Projet* 166, June 1982, pp. 666–74
H. Weber, 'Après le congrès du PS: le Ceres dans l'opposition', *Critique communiste*
April–May 1975, pp. 21–31
C. Willard, *Les Guesdistes*, Colin, 1965
— *Socialisme et communisme français*, Colin, 1967
S. Williams (ed.), *Socialism in France from Jaurès to Mitterrand*, Pinter, 1983
F. Wilson, *The French Democratic Left, 1963–9*, Stanford, Stanford University Press, 1971
M. Wolf and J. Osselin, *Les Ascenseurs de la ZUP*, Maspéro, 1979
V. Wright (ed.), *Continuity and Change in France*, Allen and Unwin, 1984
G. Ziebura, *Léon Blum et le parti socialiste, 1872–1934*, FNSP, 1967
Special numbers (principally or entirely devoted to socialist party)
Faire, *Dossiers pour 1978*, Stock, 1977
Interventions 5–6, August–October, 1983
Pouvoirs 21, 1982
RFSP XXVIII, April 1978

4   GENERAL AND COMPARATIVE WORK ON REFORMIST SOCIALISM

A. Bergounioux and B. Manin, *La Socialdémocratie ou le compromis*, PUF, 1979
A. Bihr and J.-M. Heinrich, *La néo-social-démocratie ou le capitalisme autogéré*, Le Sycomore,
1980
W. Brandt, B. Kreisky and O. Palme, *La Socialdémocratie et l'avenir*, Gallimard, 1976
J. Braunthal, *History of the International*, Nelson, 1966
B. Brown, *Eurocommunism and Eurosocialism*, Cyrco, 1979
C. Buci-Glucksman and G. Therborn, *Le Défi social-démocrate*, Maspéro, 1980
F. Castles, *The Social Democratic Iamge of Society*, Routledge and Kegan Paul, 1978
B. Denitch, *Democratic Socialism*, New York, Allanheld, 1981
— 'The Socialist Left in Europe', *Dissent*, Summer 1977, pp. 261–70
J. Droz, *Histoire général du socialisme*, PUF, 1977
F. Fejtö, *La Socialdémocratie quand-même*, Laffont, 1980
Institut Socialiste d'Etudes et de Recherches, *La Socialdémocratie en questions*, RPP–PUF,
1980
Le Monde, *Les métamorphoses du socialisme*, 9–13 October, 1984
Le Monde Diplomatique, *Social-démocraties européennes*, September 1981
F. Parkin, *Class, Inequality and Political Order*, MacGibbon and Kee, 1971
— *Marxism and Class Theory: A Bourgeois Critique*, Tavistock, 1979
W. Paterson and I. Campbell, *Social Democracy in Postwar Europe*, Macmillan, 1974
W. Paterson and A. Thomas, *Social Democratic Parties in Western Europe*, Croom Helm,
1977
A. Pelinka, *The Social Democratic Parties in Europe*, New York, Praeger, 1983
J. Petras, 'The Rise and Decline of Southern European Socialism', *New Left Review* 146,
July–August 1984, pp. 37–52
H. Portelli (ed.), *L'Internationale Socialiste*, Editions Ouvrières, 1982
A. Przeworski, 'Social Democracy as a Historical Phenomenon', *New Left Review* 122,
July–August 1980, pp. 27–58
M. Rocard et al., *Qu'est-ce que la Socialdémocratie?*, Seuil, 1979

J. Ross (ed.), *Profils de la Socialdémocratie européenne*, La Brèche, 1982

R. Scase, *Social Democracy in Capitalist Society*, Croom Helm, 1977

A. Wolfe, 'Has Social Democracy a Future?', *Comparative Politics* 11, 1978, pp. 100–25

INDEX

achievements, Ceres 254–65
activist, Ceres, profile of 177–97
Anderson, P. 105
anti-Mitterrandism 77–8
Auroux, J. 214–15
Autain, François 167, 221–5, 234, 243
autogestion 65–9, 111, 146, 190
Avice, E. 167, 234

Bacot, P. 180
Badet, L. J. 214–15
Baker, D. 34–5
Barre, Raymond 63, 66, 239
Bataille Socialiste 34–6
Beaud, Michel 128, 136, 236–7
Belfort 131, 154, 163, 177, 201–7, 226, 228
Beller, D. 4
Belloni, F. 4
Benn, Tony 2
Bergeron, André 171–2
Bizot, J.-F. 135
Blum, Léon 29, 34–9, 82, 260
Bockel, J.-M. 234
Bondoux, Thierry 135, 235
Bonnet, S. 207–8
Brown, B. 64, 68

Carassus, Pierre 169, 248
Carraz, Roland 166, 234
Cayrol, Roland 5, 10–11, 155, 180–9, 221
Ceres: achievements 254–65; activist, profile of 177–97; electoral position 165–8; and federal politics 201–29, 255–9; functioning of 131–50; in government 232–51; history 5, 52–3, 122–30; ideology 60–115, 256–7; international links

176–7, 262; press and publications 125–6, 139, 141–2; resources 139–41; strengths 150–77; structures 122–97; and unions 168–76
Chagnollaud, J.-P. 210, 212–13
Charvet, X. 163, 229
Charzat, Michel 87, 108, 123–7, 132–3, 156, 167, 235, 248
Chevènement, Jean-Pierre 6, 60, 65, 68, 71, 80–3, 90–2, 100–1, 122–32, 138, 143, 146, 167, 176, 193, 202–10, 218–19, 232–5, 239–43, 250, 254, 257, 265
Cheysson, C. 244–7
Chirac, Jacques 129, 193
Coates, D. 257
Coffineau, Michel 135, 216, 219
comité directeur (CD) 39–42, 138, 147–8
commission administrative permanente (CAP) 30–1, 37
communism 78–90; *see also* PCF
Confédération Française Démocratique du Travail (CFDT) 28, 134, 171–3, 186–7, 217
conseil national (CN) 30, 37, 39
Cot, J.-P. 163, 229, 246
courants 5, 148, 194
coverage 7–9
Crick, Michael 81, 141
Cureau, Gérard 208–13

Déat, Marcel 37
defence policy 90–103, 243–5
Defferre, Gaston 43, 45, 129, 208, 227, 233; Defferrism 51, 124
de Gaulle, Charles 39, 95–6, 102; Gaullism 38, 44–5, 62, 66, 208
Delors, Jacques 130, 237–9, 245
Derville, J. 227
discipline: Ceres 142–6; PS 146–50